MW00387747

THE DAY DIXIE DIED

Southern Occupation, 1865–1866

Thomas and Debra
Goodrich

STACKPOLE
BOOKS

Published by
STACKPOLE BOOKS
5067 Ritter Road
Mechanicsburg, PA 17055
www.stackpolebooks.com

Printed in the United States of America

10 9 8 7 6 5 4 3 2 1

FIRST EDITION

Library of Congress Cataloging-in-Publication Data

Goodrich, Th.
The day Dixie died: Southern occupation, 1865-1866 / Thomas Goodrich and Debra Goodrich.
p. cm.
Includes bibliographical references and index.
ISBN: 0-8117-0487-4
1. Reconstruction—Southern States. 2. Southern States—Social conditions—1865–1945. I. Goodrich, Debra. II. Title.

F216.G66 2001
973.8'1—dc21

2001020868

To William C. "Jack" Davis,
for all that he has given

ACKNOWLEDGMENTS

THANKS GO OUT TO THESE DEDICATED ARCHIVISTS, THE UNSUNG HEROES of the historical world:

Mark Palmer and Willie Maryland, Alabama Department of Archives and History, Montgomery; Tom Wing, Fort Smith National Historic Site, Fort Smith, Arkansas; Ron Wilson, Appomattox National Historic Site; Bettie Spratt and Sheila Heflin, Owensboro/Daviess County Public Library, Owensboro, Kentucky; Pat Hodges, Kentucky Museum, Bowling Green; Karen Moran, Lincoln Heritage Public Library, Dale, Indiana; John Selch, Indiana State Library, Indianapolis; Ron Bryant, Kentucky Historical Society, Frankfort; Marc Wellman and Charlene Bonnette, Louisiana State Library, Baton Rouge, Louisiana; Karen Kaiser, Sherman, Texas, Public Library; John Reynolds, the Reynolds Homestead, Critz, Virginia; John and Ruth Ann Coski, Museum of the Confederacy, Richmond; Randy Hackenburg, United States Army Military History Institute, Carlisle, Pennsylvania; Daniel Rolph, Historical Society of Pennsylvania, Philadelphia; and Fred Bauman, Manuscripts Division, Library of Congress. Thanks also to the staffs of the Virginia State Library, the Arkansas State History Commission, the Kansas State Historical Society, the Anderson, South Carolina, Public Library, the Tennessee State Library and Archives, the Illinois State Historical Society Library, and to those willing to share personal collections: Roger Norton, Hubert Dye, James Enos, Ronald Leonard, Rod Beemer, Jim James, and Randy Leonard.

A special thanks to Leigh Ann Berry, editor, for many things, but mostly, her patience. Finally the authors sincerely wish to thank Charles and Scarlet Coalson, and Denise Coalson for their support throughout this project.

CONTENTS

Part One

I intend . . . to restore the Union, so as to make it . . . a Union of hearts and hands as well as of states.

Abraham Lincoln

PROLOGUE

The Better Angel

Asa: Miss Mary, I wish you'd leave off those everlasting dairy fixings, and come and take a hand of that along with me.
Mary: What, and leave my work? Why, when you first came here, you thought I could not be too industrious.
Asa: Well, I think so yet, Miss Mary, but I've got a heap to say to you, and I never can talk while you're moving about so spry among them pans, pails and cheeses. First you raise one hand and then the other, and well, it takes the gumption right out of me.

IT WAS THE THIRD ACT OF A MARGINAL PLAY; LIGHT COMEDY AT BEST. FOR years, *Our American Cousin* had been a staple among American theatergoers. It was well past its prime now, however, and many in the audience this night knew the words by heart. And yet, as mediocre as the fare on stage was, an air of energy and electricity permeated the theater. Stale and familiar as the lines were, each witty jest and repartee was received with rounds of undeserved shouts and laughter.[1]

Although the thoughts of some in the theater might have been focused on the actors as they performed their well-worn roles, the hearts of all were directed elsewhere—up to the flag-draped box above the stage on the right; up to the four figures seated within; up to the bearded man in black who sat in a red rocking chair; up to the man who was smiling; up to the American president.

It had been a week of unparalleled, uninterrupted jubilation. Across its length and breadth, the Federal Union celebrated like it had never celebrated before. Millions of flags, great and small, were hoisted; hundreds of miles of bunting were draped or hung; cannons roared, rockets soared; men and women danced and sang, kissed and cried. After four bloody years of fear, pain, and frustration, the inevitable yet somehow startling words struck the country "like a thunderbolt."

"RICHMOND IS OURS," blared the headlines. "*The Old Flag Floats over the Rebel Capital* . . . VICTORY! THE UNION *WILL* BE PRESERVED!!"

"The news sped through the country . . . on the wings of lightning," exulted the *Chicago Tribune,* "and lighted up the nation with a blaze of glory."[2]

As if from a single mind, one impulse seized all, and within minutes of hearing the news, the streets of Northern cities and towns were filled with celebrating citizens. In Philadelphia, a spontaneous parade by the city's fire department, "with bells ringing and steam whistles screaming," was all but drowned out by the "nearly mad" cheering of citizens lining Chestnut Street.[3] At Des Moines in far-flung Iowa, "the capital city is wild with excitement," telegraphed a correspondent, "flags and streamers fill the streets, bells are ringing, cannon firing, and the stores all closed, while yells and huzzas, tell the joy that fills the people."[4] When the same news reached San Francisco soon after, said a reporter, it "created an almost instantaneous burst of the wildest enthusiasm. The city was literally swathed in the Stars and Stripes."[5] On the streets of New York, "the people fairly danced," wrote a witness.

> To state that they howled would sound harshly and flat, but it would nevertheless be a simple truth. . . . Down in Wall Street a chorus . . . almost made the ancient piles of stone and brick tremble in sympathy. More than ten thousand human beings chanted, as with once voice, the now favorite national hymn of "Glory Hallelujah," with an accompaniment of shouting and jumping and stamping beyond all description.[6]

George Templeton Strong was in the New York crowd that day:

> Never before did I hear cheering that came straight from the heart. . . . All the cheers I ever listened to were tame in comparison. . . . I walked about on the outskirts of the crowd, shaking hands with everybody, congratulating and being congratulated by scores of men I hardly know even by sight. Men embraced and hugged each other, *kissed* each other, retreated into doorways to dry their eyes and came out again to flourish their hats and hurrah.[7]

Whether they shouted and sang on the stately, lamp-lined streets of Boston, Bridgeport, Providence, or Portsmouth, or danced and drank in the muddy backwaters of Keokuk, Kokomo, Saginaw, or Topeka, the "Glorious Jubilation" varied only in numbers, not intensity. As explosive as the demonstrations were throughout the victorious North, nowhere was the celebration more heartfelt than in the nation's capital.

When the startling news first reached Washington, from the various government offices, clerks, supervisors, and military staff ran out the doors "as though school was dismissed for vacation."[8] At the Interior Department, wrote a spectator, "the clerks almost ran crazy and all rushed into the long corridors that run around the building raising a cheer that roused that section of the town." At the War Department, "the crowd sang 'Rally Around the Flag,' and cheered until they were hoarse."[9] "All who did not drink were intoxicated," wrote one reveler, "and those who did, were drunk."[10]

At night, "tens of thousands of rockets were constantly mounting heavenward . . . and falling again like a rain of jewels."[11] On the Hill, the Capitol burned like a beacon from thousands of lamps. On one section of the building, a huge transparency glowed from its gaslights: "This is the Lord's doing; it is marvelous in our eyes."[12]

One week later, when news arrived that the heretofore indomitable Rebel chieftain Robert E. Lee had been compelled to surrender at Appomattox by Lt. Gen. Ulysses Grant, those in the Union who imagined they had no energy left to celebrate found out otherwise. "Glory to God, the End of bloodshed has come at last," hurrahed one excited man in Washington.[13] "Yes," agreed the *New York Times* perceptively: "The great struggle is over. . . . The history of blood—the four years of war, are brought to a close. The fratricidal slaughter is all over. The gigantic battles have all been fought. The last man, we trust, has been slain. The last shot has been fired."[14]

And of all those souls in America, none had longed more to hear that last shot fired than the tired, gaunt-looking man in the flag-draped box at Ford's Theater. For more years now than he cared to count, Abraham Lincoln had carried the weight of that ghastly bloodshed on his shoulders. "It seems to me that I have been dreaming a horrid nightmare for four years," confided the president, "and now the nightmare is over."[15]

Few who had seen Lincoln's care-worn face and stooped figure over the past months could doubt that indeed, it had been a terrible, traumatic nightmare. On this the night of April 14, 1865, however, those in the theater noticed a new look lighting up the president's face. Although the stage

Abraham Lincoln
LIBRARY OF CONGRESS

had been Lincoln's great passion, for the past four years it had been more a refuge from the defeats and disappointments of the battlefield and an escape from the squabbles and petty feuds of Washington than a source of enjoyment. Tonight, though, was different. As one, audience, actors, and president joined together to savor the moment; as one, audience, actors, and president united to celebrate the victorious conclusion of the Great National Undertaking.

"The acting was excellent . . . ," remembered one of those in the crowd, "and the President and Mrs. Lincoln seemed to enjoy it highly. . . . I could detect a broad smile on Uncle Abraham's face very often."[16]

"Never was [he] more happy . . . ," added another viewer. "Many pleasant allusions were made to him in the play, to which the audience gave deafening responses, while Mr. Lincoln laughed heartily and bowed frequently to the gratified people."[17]

"'Father Abraham' is there," mused a young woman who, although she could not see the president in his box, felt his presence nonetheless. "Like a father watching what interests his children, for their pleasure rather than his own. . . . They laugh and shout at every clowning witticism."[18]

> **Asa:** Oh! he was a fine old hoss, as game as a bison bull, and as gray as a coon in the fall. . . .
> **Mary:** Tell me, Mr. Trenchard, did he never receive any letters from his daughter?
> **Asa:** Oh yes, lots of them, but the old cuss never read them, though, he chucked them in the fire, as soon as he made out who they come from.
> **Mary [Aside]:** My poor mother.
> **Asa:** You see, as nigh as we could reckon it up, she had gone and got married again his will, and that made him mad, and well, he was a queer kind of a rusty, fusty old coon, and it appeared that he got older, and rustier, and fustier, and fustier an coonier every fall.

Festive and infectious as the atmosphere in Ford's Theater was this night, those who occasionally glanced up at the flag-draped box unwittingly caught glimpses of the future. "At . . . times," noted a viewer, "he rested his face in both his hands, bending forward, and seemingly buried in deep thought."[19]

Although the war had been won, a peace yet remained to be settled. Terrible as the fighting had been, reconstruction of the defeated Southern states would now occupy the president's time and demand, no doubt, even greater efforts of statesmanship. Already, dark and savage warnings were echoing in the halls of the U.S. Congress and across much of the North—warnings that a cruel, crushing vengeance should and must be visited on the defeated and prostrate South. Some leading radicals were in favor of treating the conquered states as vassals or colonies, their wealth leached from them in the coming years with little or nothing in return. Imprisonment and mass executions of Southern political and military leaders were demanded by others. Only the week before, when a crowd began chanting, "Hang him, hang him," after the name of Jefferson Davis, fugitive president of the Confederacy, was mentioned, Lincoln's own vice president, Andrew Johnson, led the chorus. Had he the power, Johnson growled, he would hang Davis "twenty times higher than Haman."[20]

But Andrew Johnson did not have the power. And, as the vice president certainly knew, neither he nor any similar group of men could successfully oppose the wishes of the most popular American leader since Washington. Although the president's approach to the defeated South might shift by degrees as time passed, of one thing Johnson and his radical Republican fellow travelers could be certain: So long as Abraham Lincoln led, there would never be a place in his heart for revenge.[21]

"He was particularly desirous to avoid the shedding of blood, or any vindictiveness," recalled one who had spoken with the president earlier that day. "He gave plain notice . . . that he would have none of it. 'No one need expect he would take any part in hanging or killing these men, even the worst of them. . . . Enough lives had been sacrificed; we must extinguish our resentments if we expect harmony and union.'"[22]

"With malice toward none; with charity for all . . . let us strive on . . . to bind up the nation's wounds . . . to do all which may achieve and cherish a just and lasting peace." With such words were revealed the soul of Abraham Lincoln. When others, with hearts brimming full of malice, would have allowed their hatred free rein and greedily devoured a fallen foe, this great, good man, despite all the pain, vilification, and cruel insults of the past four years, yet trusted that the "better angels of our nature" would prevail if only allowed to do so. "He was more devoid of anger, clamor, evil-speaking and uncharity than any human being I ever knew or heard of," wrote friend and newsman Noah Brooks.[23] It was this quality of Lincoln, this innate magnanimity, that separated the man from those around him; and it was this feature, more than anything else, that the people recognized and loved in him. So long as "Father Abraham" led, the people would, like trusting children, faithfully follow.

But tonight, for a few merciful moments, at least, the president's mind was not on war, politics, or reconstruction.

"He sat looking on the stage his back to us and out of our sight behind the flags except occasionally when he would lean forward," recounted Helen DuBarry. "Mrs. Lincoln was in front of him. . . . We saw her smile & turn towards him several times."[24]

> **Mrs. Mountchessington:** I am aware, Mr. Trenchard, you are not used to the manners of good society, and that, alone, will excuse the impertinence of which you have been guilty.
> **Asa:** Don't know the manners of good society, eh? Well, I guess I know enough to turn you inside out, old gal—you sockdologizing old man trap!

It was then, amid the ensuing waves of laughter that swept the theater, that a shot rang out. Like everyone else in the crowd, Helen DuBarry was startled:

> [We] look up at the President's Box merely because that was the direction of the sound and supposing it to be a part of the performance. . . . We all looked again on the stage—when a man

The assassination of Abraham Lincoln KANSAS STATE HISTORICAL SOCIETY, TOPEKA

> suddenly vaulted over the railing [of the box]—turned back & then leaped to the stage—striking on his heels & falling backward but recovered himself in an instant.[25]

"With singular audacity . . . [he] stood there long enough to photograph himself forever in the minds of those in the throng who had never seen him before," said a stunned witness. "They saw a slim, tall, graceful figure, elegantly clad, waving a dagger with a gesture which none but a tragedian by profession would have made; a classic face, pale as marble, lighted up by two gleaming eyes."[26]

"*Sic Semper Tyrannis* . . . The South Is Avenged!" shouted the handsome, dark-haired man, who then stalked dramatically from the stage.

Waiting for his cue to go on, Edwin Emerson was standing in the wings as the man passed by him:

> Even after he flashed by, there was quiet for a few moments among the actors and the stage hands. No one knew what had happened. Then the fearful cry, springing from nowhere it seemed, ran like wildfire behind the scenes: "The President's shot!"
>
> Everyone began to swirl hither and thither in hysterical aimlessness. Still the curtain had not been rung down—for no one seemed to have retained a scintilla of self-possession—and the actors on the stage were left standing there as though paralyzed. Then someone dropped the curtain and pandemonium commenced.[27]

"Though the audience left their feet, they seemed bereft not only of all power of action, but even all power of thought," one of those in the crowd remembered. "A vacant, doubting look was stamped upon each face."[28] When what had just occurred finally dawned on the audience, an explosion of emotions was let loose.

"There will never be anything like it on earth," wrote witness Helen Truman. "The shouts, groans, curses, smashing of seats, screams of women, shuffling of feet and cries of terror created a pandemonium that . . . through all the ages will stand out in my memory as the hell of hells."[29]

Amid cries of "Kill him!" "Lynch him!" "Shoot him!" a confused onlooker watched as "part of the audience stampeded towards the entrance and some to the stage."[30] "They swayed back and forth, indignation and menace succeeding to irresolution," another of the crowd wrote. "All spoke, but no one said anything."[31] "Strong men wept, and cursed, and tore the seats in the impotence of their anger," recalled Edwin Bates.[32]

Overcome by shock, pain, fear, and confusion, Helen DuBarry was led away by her husband. "I could not control myself & sobbed aloud," the young woman admitted.[33]

When police and soldiers finally arrived, the hall was soon cleared, and eventually, after the dying president was carried across the street, a heavy silence settled over the building once more. But already, the echoing ring of the pistol report was spreading far beyond the theater and city to every corner of the land. And with the sound came the grim realization to many that not only had a man been killed, but the "better angel of our nature" had been slain as well.

CHAPTER 1

The Bright Dream

THE GRIEF WAS AS OPPRESSIVE AS THE UNENDING RAIN. PEOPLE NORMALLY looked for comfort in their religion, but the services this day only gave vent to their sorrow and suffering. In one humble church, the minister's words failed to assuage the pain; the wounds were too deep, too raw, too recent. He then called for a hymn, a familiar, soothing tune: "When Gathering Clouds Around I View." There was no organ. A single voice bravely began the song, but after a few notes, the words trailed, then finally faltered. A second worshiper picked up the tune, but soon she too fell into sobs. A lone woman then arose in her pew. With trembling voice, she began the hymn, then continued, but none joined in. Around her, only the weeping of the congregation was heard.[1]

If there was any ray of light in the oppressed hearts of these mourners, it lay just outside, beyond the doors. Despite their great distress and awful agony, to the quiet surprise and relief of most citizens, Federal occupation of Richmond was nothing like they had imagined. Union troops who entered and occupied the former capital of the Confederacy were generally civil, sometimes considerate, and on numerous occasions even chivalrous. And yet, understandably, the women of Richmond in their deep pain had been visibly cold to the victors, determined to give no offense but also determined to ignore them in every possible way.

"For two days after their entrance," Thomas DeLeon wrote, "the Union army might have supposed they had captured a city of the dead. . . . Clad almost invariably in deep mourning—with heavy veils invariably hiding their faces—the broken-hearted daughters of the Capital moved like shadows of the past."[2]

"There was no intentional slight or rudeness on our part," explained one of those black-clad ladies. "We did not draw back our skirts in passing federal soldiers, as was charged in Northern papers; if a few thoughtless

Ruins of Richmond LIBRARY OF CONGRESS

girls or women did this they were not representative. We tried not to give offense; we were heart-broken; we stayed to ourselves."[3]

There were moments that proved nearly unbearable. One of the most agonizing incidents came with President Lincoln's arrival in Richmond, underscored by the absence of Confederate president Jefferson Davis. Even worse was the lowering of the Stars and Bars and the raising of the Stars and Stripes. Weeping was heard behind closed windows on street after street.

To their great credit, Federal officers for the most part respected the distress they felt all about them and did not flaunt their victory. Had it not been for the efforts of these soldiers, the fire that had raged in Richmond upon their entry would have left many homeless. To say that the citizens were grateful would be exaggerating, but they at least recognized the humanity on the part of the victors.

One of those occupying soldiers described the demeanor of the Richmonders: "[They were] amazed at our magnanimity and lack of enmity toward them; content to receive us, if not with open arms (who could expect it!) at least with trustful and respectful welcome; [they] decided already in their hearts to work cordially with us in smoothing over the furrows of the past."[4]

This young soldier's perceptions, well-meaning as they were, nevertheless were a tribute to Richmonders' ability to hide their true feelings. In his youthful optimism, the soldier failed to sense the depth of grief and humiliation that he had helped cause. As a young Jewish woman in the city later related, Yankees who desired some sort of social normalcy simply did not understand that their mere presence was painful to those whose homes had chairs made vacant by Federal bullets. Wrote Phoebe Yates Pember:

> There were few men in the city at this time; but the women of the South still fought their battle for them; fought it resentfully, calmly, but silently! Clad in their mourning garments, overcome but hardly subdued, they sat within their desolate homes, or if compelled to leave that shelter went on their errands to church or hospital with veiled faces and swift steps.[5]

If there was any consolation at all to those of vanquished Richmond, it was the knowledge that surviving loved ones were coming home. Although the news of Lee's surrender "sank like lead into the already broken hearts of the citizens," the lone bright thought chasing away at least some of the gloom was the warm knowledge that their soldiers would at last return.[6] Windows that had been sealed shut to the bleak, burned landscape were now thrown wide open to watch for familiar figures and faces.

Agonizing days passed, however, before the first gray uniforms began to appear. They came on starving mounts, mostly, or barefoot and barely clad. One morning, a small group of horsemen appeared across from Richmond at the pontoon bridge just over the James. According to a witness:

> By some strange intuition, it was known that General Lee was among them, and a crowd collected all along the route he would take, silent and bareheaded. There was no excitement, no hurrahing; but, as the great chief passed, a deep, loving murmur, greater than these, rose from the very hearts of the crowd. Taking off his hat and simply bowing his head, the man great in adversity passed silently to his own door; it closed upon him, and his people had seen him for the last time in his battle harness.[7]

The arrival of Robert E. Lee, revered even by many in the North, only heightened the sense of magnanimity among the conquerors. Recalled George Bruce, with whose family Lee's wife was staying: "The Northern soldiers were bivouacked on the lawn and street in front of our house. Learning that General Lee was there, they kept up a constant clamor, calling for an appearance. When he went out on the balcony they cheered him. It was all very strange."[8]

If ever the hearts of these women would be softened, it would be accomplished by scenes such as these and the stories their husbands and brothers told of Appomattox. Humiliated and humbled by surrender, the men were astonished at the kind treatment they received.

"I must confess," wrote one Virginia soldier who surrendered with Lee, "that before I went to sleep that night, because of the soldierly sympathy of the Union soldiers . . . coupled with the generous terms of our surrender, and the rations so kindly furnished us, I began to regard my future with very different eyes from those through which I viewed it in the afternoon."[9]

"The conduct of the victors was beyond all praise," a comrade added. "They sent our starving men provisions, and not a shout of exultation nor the music of a band was heard during all the time we were at Appomattox."[10]

Rapprochement was in the air, due "in great part," proclaimed a Washington newspaper, "to the heroic valor and generous fortitude of the Army of Virginia . . . and to the spotless virtues of its unrivaled chief. . . . We are too full of joy in our belief that we have detected the dawnings of a generous and magnanimous policy on the part of our rulers. . . . The bright dream of a re-united country comes over us."[11]

Lee himself had acknowledged the generous terms of the surrender when he commented that his men had laid down their arms as much to Abraham Lincoln's charity and good will as to Ulysses Grant's artillery.[12]

Although the wounds of many, North and South, would remain deep for years to come, perhaps a true healing for others had already begun.

As the *Arago* lay at anchor off Charleston Harbor on the morning of April 14, 1865, a dispatch boat sailed swiftly in her direction. Circling the ship, the excited crew of the smaller craft waved, then, as they drew closer, shouted the incredible words to those on deck: "Lee has surrendered!"

"To describe the scene that followed . . . is impossible. . . ," said a jubilant man on board. "The emotion among our passengers found vent in the wildest demonstrations of joy." Although first word had reached New York only hours after they set sail south, everyone aboard the *Arago* would concur: Late though it may have been, never was the timing of such startling news more appropriate, or more enthusiastically received, than at this very moment. "It was," the witness concluded, "the . . . crowning perfection to the glad national ceremony assigned today."[13]

Fort Sumter, April 14, 1865 LIBRARY OF CONGRESS

Too large to cross the bar in the shipping channel, the *Arago* was forced to transfer her joyous passengers to a smaller steamer, the *Delaware.* The weather was warm but breezy, and the smaller ship was "tossed like an eggshell" against the hull of the *Arago.* Nevertheless, with her illustrious cargo aboard, the *Delaware* finally shoved off. Soon the excited party lining the rail saw sights and landmarks on the coastline easily identified, "all bearing names familiar to readers of war dispatches in those eventful four years past," said a viewer. "Morris Island, James Island, Sullivan's Island, Folly Island, Forts Wagner and Shaw and Moultrie and Gregg and Ripley and Pinckney, and in the midst of all . . . Fort Sumter."[14]

Everywhere in the city of Charleston—on every flagstaff, at every fort, over every outpost—the bright national banner proudly flew . . . everywhere, that is, save Sumter itself. There, only a naked staff stood against the blue sky. As the *Delaware* approached, the bare pole rising from the blasted heap that was once a fort could be plainly seen by the prominent spectators leaning from the deck: Henry Ward Beecher, Gen. John Dix and Gen.

Abner Doubleday, William Lloyd Garrison, and the most famous man of all on this day, Robert Anderson. With arms folded securely around his prize, the major general was now returning to its rightful home the same flag he had lowered from that bare pole exactly four years before.

To anyone just awakening from a dream, the spectacle in the harbor must have looked like yet another siege of Charleston. "A brilliant gathering of boats, ships, and steamers of every sort had assembled around the battered ruin of the fort," recalled President Lincoln's private secretary, an awe-inspired John Nicolay. "The whole bay seemed covered with the vast flotilla, planted with a forest of masts, whose foliage was the triumphant banners of the nation."[15]

Excursionists came from as far away as New England. Naval stations along the coast from Florida to Fort Monroe sent delegations. A steamer delivered thousands of emancipated slaves to add significant symbolism to the event.[16] When the boats had finally docked at the fort and the crowd was finally seated, Robert Anderson at last stepped up to the stage.

After the audience had quieted, and with tears in his eyes, Anderson began to speak. "I thank God I have lived to see this day. . . ," the general said simply. "May all the world proclaim glory to God in the highest, on earth peace and good will toward men."[17]

"Precisely as the bells of the ships struck the hour of noon," noted Nicolay, "General Anderson, with his own hands seizing the halyards, hoisted to its place the flag."[18]

Among the thousands assembled, a cheer rose up that lasted a full fifteen minutes. "It was a scene never to be forgotten . . . ," recorded Esther Hill Hawk. "The glorious old flag floats once more over the spot where it was for the first time humbled."[19]

After the singing of the "Star Spangled Banner," the renowned theologian Henry Ward Beecher then took the podium and delivered the much anticipated keynote address. Grasping his hat and notes in the high wind, Beecher honored the Chief Magistrate. "We offer to the President of the United States our solemn congratulations that God has sustained his life. . . ." But much of his oration targeted the traitors, not the heroes. Although the minister urged the throng to hold no grudge against the majority of Southerners who had merely been followers—"For the multitude drafted and driven into this civil war, let not a trace of animosity remain"—Beecher was virulent in his attacks on the leaders of the rebellion, the "instigators" of the war. Voicing the vengeful spirit in many Northern hearts, the orator turned his sights on the swift-approaching Day of Judgment:

> Every orphan that their bloody game has made, and every widow that sits sorrowing, and every maimed and wounded sufferer . . . will rise up and come before the Lord to lay upon these chief culprits . . . their awful witness . . . and from a thousand battle fields shall rise up armies of airy witnesses . . . every pale and starved prisoner shall raise his skinny hand in judgment. Blood shall call out for vengeance.[20]

The lengthy oration was interrupted many times by cheers and applause. Perhaps the most dramatic moment came when Beecher pointed overhead to the banner. "The surging crowds that rolled up their frenzied shouts as the flag came down are dead, or scattered, or silent, and their habitations are desolate. . . . The soil has drunk blood and is glutted; millions mourn for millions slain, or, envying the dead, pray for oblivion; towns and villages have been turned back into wilderness."[21]

Neither Beecher nor anyone else needed remind the people of Charleston—that element most conspicuously absent from this celebration—of the painful truth of the words just uttered. Charleston, wrote a Boston correspondent, was "a city of ruins, of desolation, of vacant houses . . . of rotting wharves, of deserted warehouses, of weed-wild gardens, of miles of grass-grown streets, of acres of pitiful and voiceful barrenness."[22] Much of the citizenry was exiled, widowed, orphaned, crippled, or dead.

That evening, as a fitting reminder of their vanquished condition, the people of Charleston, like ghosts behind drawn curtains, watched as the victorious visitors retired to the city following the day's events. Once there, many proceeded to gala balls at the Middleton Mansion, Charleston Hotel, and other prominent landmarks, from whose verandas secessionist beauties had watched the bombardment of Fort Sumter in 1861. The beauties on the verandas this night were the wives and daughters of Unionists.

At dinner, Robert Anderson stood and proposed a toast. Normally shy and retiring, the handsome, silver-haired general nevertheless raised a glass to his commander in chief, who was, at that moment, on his way to Ford's Theater:

> Join me in drinking the health . . . of the man who, when elected President of the United States, was compelled to reach the seat of government without an escort, but a man who now could travel all over our country with millions of hands and hearts to sustain him. I give you the good, the great, the honest man, Abraham Lincoln.[23]

Although the festivities continued far into the following day, where the mere mention of Lincoln's name "elicit[ed] the wildest and noisiest enthusiasm [with] hats and 'kerchiefs, swung to the wildest cheers," for Robert Anderson, the slate was finally clean.[24] The pain and humiliation of the worst day in his life had at long last been erased forever by the glory and pageantry of the greatest day in his life. It was with such pleasant memories as this that the general set sail from Charleston for duty again in the North.

Once back in New York, Anderson sent his official report of the Fort Sumter affair to Secretary of War Edwin Stanton: "The duty assigned me by you has been performed. The flag lowered at Fort Sumter, April 14, 1861, was by God's blessing restored to its standard April 14, 1865. Would to God you could have been present to have witnessed the ceremony. [But] Great God! What saddening, crushing news meets us."[25]

The "saddening, crushing news" that Anderson spoke of would so dominate the press that it would be days before Northern papers had the space for accounts of Fort Sumter's symbolic celebration.

CHAPTER 2

Outrage

TERRIBLE NEWS

President Lincoln Assassinated
at Ford's Theater.

A REBEL DESPERADO SHOOTS HIM THROUGH THE HEAD AND ESCAPES!

Secretary Seward and Major Fred Seward
Stabbed by Another Desperado!

IN ONE BLINDING FLASH, AN ENTIRE NATION OF TWENTY MILLION SOULS had plunged from the mountaintop of light and hope and happiness to the abyss of darkness and despair. From cheers, toasts, songs, and laughter, the Federal Union was transformed in the briefest of moments into a land of sobbing men, women, and children surrounded by the black of mourning.

"Old men are weeping on the streets," wrote a witness from Council Bluffs, Iowa.[1] "Almost everyone looks as though they had lost a dear friend," said a man in Delaware.[2] "In hearts once joyous with the brightening beams of peace, there is now unutterable grief," an old friend and neighbor of the slain president, Rev. Francis Springer, sadly recorded. "Eyes but lately aglow with the dawn of a lovely future are dimmed with tears. Silent but absorbing sorrow oppresses every soul."[3]

The shock of the act and its cruel timing left all stunned, speechless, incredulous. That this humble, homely man who had risen to greatness by labor and merit alone, this selfless captain who had successfully guided the ship of state through the storm of swirling black water ringed by dark and dangerous breakers, should now be struck down the instant he entered port seemed to many not the inscrutable act of a just God, but the work of his satanic counterpart. Lincoln, the "Great Emancipator"; Lincoln, "Honest Abe"; Lincoln, "Father Abraham"; Lincoln, "the better angel of our souls"; Lincoln . . . now dead, slain by the very evil he had sought to know, understand, and love.

"That is the news," announced the *New York Herald,* "which has swept away from the public mind every sentiment of leniency or conciliation towards the conquered brigands of the South."[4]

"People who pitied our misguided brethren yesterday, and thought they had been punished enough already . . . talk approvingly of vindictive justice and favor the introduction of judges, juries, gaolers, and hangmen," George Templeton Strong noted astutely.[5]

As the above make clear, when shock and sadness waned among the people, hatred and anger rushed to fill the void. "The excitement here is terrific . . . ," reported Edwin Bates from Washington on the day Lincoln died. "The street corners & hotels are crowded with people swearing deep & deadly vengeance to all rebels & the whole south."[6]

One man in the capital, a man who could not contain his happiness, was overheard expressing joy in the assassination. "The words hardly left his mouth," wrote a witness, "before the bullet from the pistol of a union soldier went crashing through his brain."[7] In the same city, on the same night Lincoln was shot, thousands of snarling rioters tried to storm the Old Capitol Prison where Confederate prisoners were jailed. "Come out & see the rebels burn," shouted the mob to any and all along the way. Only a cordon of police and troops prevented a wholesale massacre.[8]

In New York, one man was clubbed by a policeman and sentenced to six months in jail for exclaiming, "Old Abe, that son of a bitch, is dead, and he ought to have been killed long ago." Another foolhardy man in the same city was flung headfirst from the Brooklyn ferry for "disloyal language."[9] For the same offense, several men were reportedly murdered in Boston.[10] At Indianapolis, five Federal soldiers who clapped and announced they would "have a hoe-down" on Lincoln's grave were quickly arrested. Dragging the men outside, comrades hung the culprits by their necks so that only their toes touched. Finally, after the faces of all had turned black, the five were cut down.[11] Following a like comment, another soldier was yanked from his sickbed in a Delaware hospital and fettered with a ball and chain.[12] At Terre Haute, Indiana, an Irishman was shot dead in his tracks for shouting that he was "glad . . . Lincoln was dead and in hell." In neighboring Illinois, a man in Cairo was riddled by fifteen balls for a similar statement.[13] Even in the slain president's hometown of Springfield, a bookkeeper was mobbed for impetuously celebrating the "damned good news."[14]

In the blinding fury of the moment, scores throughout the Union who uttered similar sentiments were shot, stabbed, hung, or beaten to death.[15] When the supply of vocal victims ran low, Democrats, "Copperheads," or anyone with a history of opposition to the Republican administration were next.

In Cincinnati, rioters reportedly murdered several men, then rampaged through the streets, smashing and burning property of anyone suspected of disloyalty. The office of the *Westminster Democrat* in Maryland was destroyed and its editor slain. In far-off California, gangs of Unionists ransacked Democrat newspapers, then lynched any bold enough to protest. At the same time, scores of "rebel fiends" were swooped up in neighboring Nevada and flung into Fort Alcatraz.[16] Neither age nor gender shielded victims from the wrath of the mob.

"There are women among us," declared the editor of an Indiana newspaper, "who wept for sorrow when Richmond was taken—who lamented when Lee surrendered—who rejoiced when Lincoln was assassinated. There are women in the North who, to-day say those things for which men have been imprisoned, shot and hung."[17]

At the village of Indianola in Iowa, a rumor spread that an old widow—known for her anti-Republican sentiments—had rejoiced over the news from Ford's Theater. According to the Des Moines *Statesman:*

> Without giving the subject the least investigation . . . a number of women, among them the wife of the presiding elder of the Methodist church, visited the house of Mrs. Patterson, and compelled her, an invalid, to leave her house and carry an emblem of mourning, which . . . was a flag, and march around the town. She protested that she had not uttered a word of exultation at the death of the President and implored them to confront her with [the] witness; but her protestations were answered by the insulting reply that she was lying. She assured them that she was unable to walk the distance required, and if forced to perform the humiliating service they must carry her. Her protestations of innocence, her demand for the proof, her widowhood, and even the precarious condition of her health, had no power to move their pity. Go she must and they forced her out of the house and dragged her around the streets to be scoffed and jeered at, tearing her dress nearly off.
>
> Not content with inflicting this gross indignity upon the sick woman, they attempted to compel her little daughter, thirteen years of age, to perform the same service, and because she

> had spirit enough to resist the outrage, she was beaten and bruised until blood streamed from her nose and her arms were black and blue.[18]

Elsewhere, other women were treated similarly.[19] Nor was high station a safe haven from the mob's madness. When citizens in Buffalo noticed that the residence of ex-President Millard Fillmore displayed no symbols of mourning, a crowd of several hundred gathered and, in a "spirit of incendiary violence," splashed gallons of black ink over the home.[20] Likewise, a gang of "patriotic young men" stormed the Staten Island home of ex-President John Tyler, terrorized his widow, then snatched from the parlor a "fancy tri-color" banner thought to be a Rebel flag.[21]

Social deviants and outcasts also found themselves handy targets. Drug addicts, alcoholics, and common drunks were beaten or arrested on the simple theory that they were celebrating the news of Lincoln's death. Similarly, four men in the Washington suburb of Georgetown were hurled into jail cells because they were found garbed in female attire.[22]

Not everyone in the North joined the mob. Indeed, better hearts and minds recoiled in horror at the terror sweeping America.

"Every act of mob violence is a national calamity and shame," raged one of the few voices of reason, Horace Greeley of the *New York Tribune.*[23] "What lower depth of degradation can we reach . . . ," echoed an Iowa editor. "Such an exhibition . . . we venture to say has not occurred since the mobs of Paris which originated the bloody and disgraceful French Revolution of 1798. Have our people gone stark mad?"[24]

In areas of the South already occupied by Union troops, elation at Lincoln's death was a virtual death sentence for men and imprisonment for women.[25] In Nashville, a man on Church Street was heard to mutter that he was "glad the damned abolition son of a bitch was dead; he ought to have died long ago!"

"Before the words had fairly left his lips," said a bystander, "a soldier shot him through the heart, and plunging his bayonet into the falling body, pinned him to the ground!" That night, a "vigilance committee" of shouting soldiers scoured Nashville, ensuring that U.S. flags flew from every Rebel home in town.[26]

In New Orleans, where five men were murdered for displaying mere "indifference" to the assassination, Sarah Morgan noted the incongruity of the Crescent City in mourning:[27]

> Men who have hated Lincoln with all their souls, under terror of confiscation and imprisonment which they *understand* is the

> alternative, tie black crape from every practicable knob and point, to save their homes. . . . The more thankful they are for Lincoln's death, the more profusely the houses are decked with the emblems of woe.[28]

At another occupied city, the wife of a Federal officer who, together with her husband, boarded with a Southern widow described what happened when news from Ford's Theater arrived:

> Every house was ordered to be draped in black, and where the rebel inmates refused, it was done for them. . . . A squad of Northern boys organized themselves into an inspection committee and went from street to street to see that no house was left undraped. When I suggested to Mrs. Stuart that she had better hang out something black and save trouble, she turned upon me and exclaimed passionately: "I'd rather die first. . . ."
>
> The committee . . . came down the street upon which Mrs. Stuart lived, and seeing the house undraped, halted before it. There was a dead silence for a few moments that was more ominous than curses would have been. Then hoarse cries of "rebel sympathizer" broke from the crowd. The ringleader . . . stalked forward and pushed open the door without ceremony and demanded to know why the house was not draped. I sprang forward and stood between him and Mrs. Stuart and tried to explain to him that my husband had gone down the street to get us some black, and that as soon as it came I would hang it out. "Yes; but she must hang it up," he cried, pointing threateningly at Mrs. Stuart. "Every damned rebel must this day kiss the dust for this dastardly act. She must do it herself. . . . It must be something of her own, too."
>
> "What, I show a sign of mourning for Abraham Lincoln—I, who but for him would not be husbandless and childless today!" came from Mrs. Stuart's lips.
>
> "Well, now, we'll see about that," he replied. "Come, boys," he called to the squad without, "some of you hold this she-devil while the rest of us search her house for something black." The front room, dining hall and kitchen downstairs and my bedroom upstairs yielded nothing, but when they entered Mrs. Stuart's private room, just back of mine, I knew from the shouts of triumph that they had found something; but I was hardly prepared for the sight when a few minutes later they

came rushing down the stairs waving with frantic gesticulations Mrs. Stuart's long crape veil; the veil that she had worn as a widow for her husband . . . and . . . her son. . . .

"Here, madame, we have found just the thing," cried the leader, "and you yourself must hang it up, right in front, too, where all may see it, or, by George, your life won't be worth a candle. . . !" She stared at them for a few seconds with eyes in which hate, horror and revenge strove for mastery. Then, with a mighty effort, she shook herself free from her captors and in a strangely calm voice said: "Give it to me, I will hang it up where you wish. Only leave the room, leave the premises; go across the street; you can see me from there; and you, madame," she said, turning to me, "you go with them. . . ."

We all crossed the street and looked anxiously at Mrs. Stuart's front door. . . . Just then she came out on the veranda. I noticed she had changed her dress since we had come away. She was all in black—her best black; her mourning weeds. She carried a chair in one hand, while the crape veil was thrown over her shoulder and wound once about her neck. We all watched her intently. Her movements were slow and deliberate. She mounted the chair and . . . then she took the veil . . . and threw it through the opening, while at the same time she put something else through. What it was we could not tell at that distance, and then . . . she gave her chair a vigorous push with her foot and her body hung suspended in midair. Several seconds elapsed, in which we all stood as if frozen to the spot, staring at that dangling body across the street. Then, with a cry of horror . . . we rushed over. . . . [But] it was too late.

Under the crape veil . . . with a strong cord firmly knotted about her neck, hung all that was mortal of that once proud southern woman.[29]

CHAPTER 3

The Damning Spot

> We come into the house of God this morning, under a cloud so dense, so dark, so appalling, that, like children in the night, we know not which way to turn. A week ago, and these walls rang with jubilant strains of praise for the victories we had won. . . . In the very hour of our triumph, a blow as terrible as it was unforeseen comes with stunning force to remind us that the brightest morning may widen into the darkest day. . . . Our good and wise President, the Father of his people . . . has fallen by the hand of a cowardly assassin, and millions are orphaned by the stroke. . . . The boasted chivalry, the scum and refuse of humanity, will gloat large-eyed and eager-eared, over the details of the dying President. . . . Their brutal shouts, borne on the far Southern winds . . . will mingle with your tolling bells, and the sad sounds of your grief.[1]

SO WENT THE SERMON OF A PREACHER IN SALEM, MASSACHUSETTS, ON THE Sunday following the assassination. Similar words that day sounded ten thousand times over from pulpits across the Union. Few in the North, high or low, felt that the assassin of Abraham Lincoln had actually acted alone. Coming as it did at the very moment when the Confederacy teetered on the brink, many saw the murder as a last-ditch attempt to avert the inevitable. In their blinding rage and sorrow, Unionists such as this minister viewed the killer as a mere symbol or embodiment of an entire people.

"The murderer was not alone. His accomplices were legion . . . ," Lincoln's old friend, Springer, said knowingly. "It was not done on private or individual responsibility. The awful deed involves the character and responsibility of the whole rebel fraternity."[2]

The editor of the *Chicago Tribune* agreed:

> His is not an isolated case. There were hundreds and thousands of men in the Southern States who possessed his principles . . . who would have perpetrated the same crimes had they had the same nerve as he. He has shown us the rebellion in all its enormity, slavery in all its hideous shapes, and has impressed upon the American people a more deeply seated loathing and hatred for the leaders of this rebellion and the accursed institution which has goaded them on. . . . He accepted as truth the constant assertions of Jeff. Davis that Mr. Lincoln was a tyrant. . . . He is the embodied result of the teachings of Jeff. Davis and his followers.[3]

In their heedless, headlong attempt to retrieve the irretrievable, continued the *Tribune,* Southerners had unwittingly sealed their doom.

> The foolish rebels have killed their best friend. The man who stood between them and retribution, who alone had the will and power to shield them from the punishment their crimes deserve, is slain by them. . . . No man but Abraham Lincoln could restrain the American people from visiting righteous wrath upon the heads of the wicked leaders of the accursed rebellion. No living man possessed the confidence and affection of the people and army as he.[4]

"But he is slain," echoed an Ohio editor, "slain by slavery. That fiend incarnate did the deed. Beaten in battle, the leaders sought to save slavery by assassination. Their madness presaged their destruction. Abraham Lincoln was the personification of Mercy. Andrew Johnson is the personification of Justice. They have murdered Mercy, and Justice rules alone."[5]

On the day of Lincoln's death, Andrew Johnson was sworn in as the seventeenth president of the United States. The former tailor was a staunch, unremitting Unionist from East Tennessee, and his hatred of Southern aristocracy and secession was widely known. Despite an embarrassing drunken display during Lincoln's second inaugural, in Andrew Johnson the radical wing of the Republican Party felt that they now had, at long last, a man who measured up to their standards. In fact, many radicals—eager to grind the last vestige of Southern pride and culture into the dust—greeted Lincoln's death with barely concealed joy.

Reveals a leading radical, George Washington Julian of Indiana:

> While everybody was shocked and grieved at Lincoln's murder, the feeling was nearly universal that the accession of Johnson to the presidency would prove a godsend to the country. Aside from Mr. Lincoln's known policy of tenderness to the rebels . . . his well-known view on the subject of reconstruction was as distasteful as possible to the radical Republicans.[6]

"Johnson, we have faith in you!" exclaimed Sen. Benjamin Wade of Ohio. "By the Gods, it will be no trouble now running the Government!"[7]

And even those of lesser pretensions, those who had no personal or political axes to grind, those who suddenly and passionately felt embittered by Lincoln's death, even those believed much as John Downing did:

> While I mourn the national loss as deeply as anyone, I yet think that we should rejoice that now the Rebel Chiefs will receive justice instead of mercy. The South will find to its cost that the wrong man has been killed, and will rue the day that Abraham Lincoln died. . . . The Southern people have jumped out of the frying pan into the fire.[8]

The first challenge facing the new president was running down the murderer. As to his identity, there was absolutely no doubt. The handsome face of John Wilkes Booth, who came from the famous family of Shakespeareans, was one of the more familiar in America. Many of those in the crowd at Ford's that night recognized the dark, dapper figure as he stalked dramatically from the stage. Ironically, even Lincoln himself had witnessed a Booth performance . . . a performance at none other than Ford's Theater. Although the president had "applauded him rapturously" and even wished to meet him backstage, the thespian contemptuously spurned the gesture, stating afterward that he would "sooner have applause from a negro."[9]

Even though the manhunt was focused on Virginia and Maryland, in the hysteria following the murder, any winning young man with dark hair, who drank too much, was in the minds of many, potentially the presidential assassin.[10] From Maine to Minnesota, Booth was reportedly spotted by hundreds of breathless "eyewitnesses."[11] Some of the accused were collared and arrested. One shabbily dressed young man who resembled the assassin was roughly examined on a riverboat in Kansas simply because he had a "suspicious look" and "seemed anxious to avoid everyone who came on board."[12] Another startled young stranger in Erie, Pennsylvania, narrowly avoided the hangman's knot. Moments after being let down, the shaken

Edwin Booth

U.S. MILITARY HISTORY INSTITUTE, CARLISLE BARRACKS

victim wondered aloud "if every good-looking man is to be in constant danger of swinging from a lamp post because Booth is reported to be a handsome fellow?"[13]

Because of their brother's deed, the Booth family was already paying a terrible price. "The tongue of every man and woman was free to revile and insult us . . . ," revealed the assassin's sister, Asia. "If we had friends they condoled with us in secret; none ventured near."[14] Scheduled to appear at Pike's Opera House in Cincinnati on April 16, Junius Brutus Booth was "compelled" to flee the city for his life when a mob of over five hundred surrounded his hotel. Another brother, Edwin, canceled his upcoming performances in Boston and vowed never to step onto a stage again.[15] It was just as well, advised an angry Philadelphia editor, since "no man bearing the name of the criminal shall, within our lifetime, be permitted to appear before an American audience."[16] The twenty-four hours following Lincoln's death were, wrote the shattered Edwin to a friend, "the most distressing day of my life. . . . While mourning, in common with all other loyal hearts, the death of the President, I am oppressed by a private woe not to be expressed in words."[17]

Ironically, earlier in the war, Edwin and others were scurrying to catch a train as it left a New Jersey station. In the crush, a young Union officer nearby had slipped from the platform and was about to fall under the moving wheels, when Booth instinctively jerked him up and away to safety. The grateful young man proved to be none other than Robert Todd Lincoln, son of the American president.[18]

That John Wilkes Booth was merely the tip of a greater conspiracy, few at the time doubted. Already, many friends, associates, and mere acquaintances of the murderer were being swooped up and brutally interrogated.[19] But among outraged Unionists, the feeling was general that the conspiracy reached right up to the highest levels of the Rebel government. Many Northern readers readily recalled the reprinted ads from Southern newspapers:

> ONE MILLION DOLLARS WANTED TO HAVE PEACE BY THE 1ST OF MARCH. If the citizens of the Southern Confederacy will furnish me with the cash, or good securities for the sum of one million dollars, I will cause the lives of Abraham Lincoln, William H. Seward and Andrew Johnson to be taken by the first of March next. This will give peace, and satisfy the world that cruel tyrants can not live in a land of liberty. If this is not accomplished, nothing will be claimed beyond the sum of fifty thousand dollars, in advance, which is supposed to be necessary to reach and slaughter the three villains. I will give one thousand dollars towards this patriotic purpose. Everyone wishing to contribute will address box X, Cahaba, Alabama, December 1st, 1864.[20]

Also, but a few weeks previous to the assassination, Rebel newspapers had promised their despondent readers that a great blow would soon be struck—a blow, they said, "that would astonish the world." To many, the dreadful irony of the words now seemed perfectly clear.[21]

Although his initial task was the capture of Booth, Andrew Johnson set his sights higher. Unlike Lincoln, who had been quite content to let his defeated adversary escape to live out his life in exile, the new president wanted to capture Jefferson Davis in the worst way.[22]

"Treason," Johnson growled, "is the highest crime in the calendar, and the full penalty for its commission should be visited upon the leaders of the Rebellion. Treason should be made odious." In addition to "odious" treason and secession, Andrew Johnson now added murder to the hated Rebel leader's list of capital crimes.[23]

"Be it never forgotten," goaded the *Chicago Tribune,* "that all this had the approval of the arch-fiend Davis, that it was done after consultation with him, and under his directions. The damning spot of the pirate flag is on his brow; it cannot be washed out, not even in his own vile blood."[24]

In the red rage and fury following the assassination, after words such as the above were read and reread hundreds of times, the North was nearly unanimous in its verdict. For his crimes—for treason, for secession, for assassination—Jefferson Davis should suffer "the most disgraceful death known to our civilization," demanded the *New York Times,* "death on the gallows."[25]

During the winter of 1860–61, when the secession crisis was rending the nation in twain, Johnson and Davis had squared off in the chamber of the U.S. Senate. Shaking an angry fist in the face of the wealthy Mississippi slave owner, the tailor from Tennessee declared, "Sir, if I possessed the authority, I would hang you by the neck until you were dead, if you attempt to commit treason against the Government of the United States."[26]

Andrew Johnson now had the "authority" . . . and Andrew Johnson was determined to use it. "They shall suffer for this," vowed the new American president, "they shall suffer for this."[27]

CHAPTER 4

The Fugitive

FROM HEAD OF STATE OF ONE OF THE LARGEST AND MOST POWERFUL nations on earth, Jefferson Davis had become a flying fugitive in a fast-fading domain where old friends and admirers were deserting him "like rats from a ship." In all his long and painful route through North Carolina, rare was the homeowner willing to shelter the Confederate president and risk Yankee retaliation. Nevertheless, on April 19, as he stood on the porch of Lewis Bates—the only man in Charlotte bold enough to open his doors—Davis refused to give up hope. With his dream of a separate and sovereign nation crashing down all about him, the president was determined to fight "to the last ditch."

After the fall of Richmond and his escape from the burning capital, Davis had persisted in his efforts to rally the people to their cause. Announced the Southern leader on April 5:

> We have now entered upon a new phase of the struggle. Relieved from the necessity of guarding particular points, our army will be free to move from point to point to strike the enemy. . . . Let us but will it, and we are free. . . .
>
> I will never consent to abandon to the enemy one foot of the soil of any of the states of the Confederacy. . . . Let us not despond then, my countrymen; but, relying on God, meet the foe with fresh defiance and . . . unconquerable hearts.[1]

Several days later, when sketchy reports reached him and his cabinet at Danville, Virginia, that Lee had surrendered at Appomattox, the news was greeted by Davis with "a silence," said one present, "more eloquent of great disaster than words could have been."[2] When the surrender became official at Greensboro, North Carolina, a short time later, the Confederate president momentarily lost control and silently shed "bitter tears."

"He seemed quite broken at the moment by this tangible evidence of the loss of his army and the misfortunes of its General," a witness wrote. "All of us, respecting his great grief, withdrew."[3]

As crippling to Davis as this last blow was, nothing proved more devastating to his will than the loss of faith among those around him. During a conference with his cabinet and top generals on April 13, the president insisted that independence might still be won if only all did their duty. "I think that we can whip the enemy yet . . . ," he argued, "[but] we haven't any time to lose." When only cold silence greeted his comments, the Southern leader asked Joseph Johnston his opinion.

"My views are, sir, that our people are tired of the war, feel themselves whipped, and will not fight," the lieutenant general pronounced. "Our country is overrun, its military resources greatly diminished. . . . My small force is melting away like snow before the sun and I am hopeless of recruiting it. We may, perhaps, obtain terms which we ought to accept."[4]

Asked their thoughts, four of five cabinet members concurred with Johnston. Given the loss of support among his highest-ranking officials, Davis realized only too well that he could not hope to prolong the struggle east of the Mississippi River for long. When it was mentioned that Abraham Lincoln was willing to help him flee the country, even offering a navy warship to do so, the proud president quickly recovered: "I will do nothing to place myself under obligation to the Federal government. . . . I have no idea whatever of leaving Confederate soil so long as there are men in uniform ready to fight."[5]

With the morale to fight on in the East obviously crushed, Davis looked west to the Trans-Mississippi. There, in that vast and largely forgotten domain, a stand might yet be made. Indeed, the sheer extent of the region, which still comprised parts of Arkansas, Louisiana, and above all, Texas, with its abundant and largely untapped natural resources, ensured that a prolonged struggle was at least possible. But more importantly, the fire to fight on was seemingly still aglow in the West. Although many troops in the Trans-Mississippi were naturally shattered by news from the East, especially after Lee's surrender, others had steeled their nerves, determined that come what may, they would "see the thing through."

"When I say they are not discouraged . . . ," wrote a Louisiana soldier, "I speak but the truth. . . . So far from it having a demoralizing effect upon the troops of this Brigade . . . it nerves them with an unalterable and unconquerable purpose to retrieve these losses. . . . [We] will never reconstruct or submit."[6]

Jefferson Davis
NATIONAL ARCHIVES

"Oh horrors!" echoed another young Louisianan, Lt. Jared Sanders. "Can any man with warm southern blood coursing through his veins think for one moment of submission to such ignominy! No! We cannot, will not yield! . . . We finally must succeed if we fight it to the last."[7]

And from Texas, that most indomitable of men, Gen. Jo Shelby, vowed he would, if necessary, "fight the enemy step by step to the Rio Grande. . . . If Johnston follow Lee and . . . if the Cis-Mississippi Department surrender its arms and quit the contest, let us never surrender . . . ," the Missourian urged his men. "Let us . . . resolve with the deep, eternal, irrevocable resolution of freemen, that we will never surrender!"[8]

With the cause all but lost in the East, Davis set his sights on reaching far-off Texas. Once there, the contest might be continued, and if all else failed, exile in Maximilian's Mexico and even French intervention on the side of Confederate independence were still possibilities. It was with these thoughts that Davis and his refugee Rebel government moved south through North Carolina.

As the wagons and carriages composing the presidential party rolled out from Greensboro, escorted by a motley array of soldiers, sailors, and civilians, signs of national chaos and dissolution were met at every turn. Painful as this was to behold, paramount on Davis's mind were the whereabouts and safety of his wife, Varina, and their four small children. Though they too were escaping south, they were doing so without a large escort, over roads infested with Yankee cavalry, Unionist bushwhackers, and gangs of highway robbers. And yet, as distracted as the president undoubtedly was, he nevertheless maintained his composure in all situations. During conferences with those in his entourage, he was dignified but polite; in his exchanges with civilians he encountered along the way, he was charitable and compassionate. When the terrified daughter of a host in Salisbury interrupted breakfast one morning, sobbing, "Oh, Papa. Old Lincoln's coming and going to kill us all," Davis gently quieted the child.

"Oh, no, little lady," he said softly, "Mr. Lincoln isn't such a bad man, he doesn't want to kill anybody and certainly not a little girl like you."[9]

Soon after Davis reached Charlotte and the home of Lewis Bates, a cheering body of Confederate cavalry rode up to greet their commander in chief. At almost the same time, the president was handed a telegram. After reading the startling words for a silent moment or two, he handed the note to others nearby.

"It is sad news . . . ," Davis said upon learning of Lincoln's death. "I am sorry. We have lost our best friend in the court of the enemy."[10]

When the message was read to the cavalrymen, and some began to cheer, Davis raised his hand for silence.[11] Although Lincoln had been a remorseless foe of secession and slavery, Jefferson Davis understood better than most that the slain U.S. president harbored no hatred or animosity for the South. Not so his successor. Andrew Johnson's well-publicized hatred of planter aristocracy left no doubt in anyone's mind that his approach to the conquered land would be infinitely worse than his predecessor's.

There was something else that Jefferson Davis now clearly understood. Whereas Lincoln was satisfied merely to see his adversary escape the country, Andrew Johnson would exert all his energies to capture his ancient foe and parade the proud aristocrat through the streets of the North like a caged beast. The flight of Jefferson Davis now gained greater impetus.

Before leaving Charlotte, Davis beseeched General Johnston one last time to slip away from the army facing him, under Gen. William T. Sherman, and join the government on the trek to Texas.

"Such a force could march away from Sherman and be strong enough to encounter anything between us and the Southwest," the president explained to Johnston. "If this course be possible carry it out and telegraph your intended route."[12]

Unfortunately for Davis's plans, the only road Joseph Johnston planned to travel was the road to capitulation. Believing the war was irretrievably lost, Johnston had no intention of prolonging the death and destruction simply to escort to Texas Jefferson Davis, his old personal and political rival. On April 17, Johnston and Sherman met at Durham Station, not far from the North Carolina capital, Raleigh, to discuss surrender terms. Only a short time before, Sherman had received an urgent message, and it was this note that the general now handed to Johnston.

"The perspiration came out in large drops on his forehead," remembered Sherman, "and he did not attempt to conceal his distress."[13]

It was, remarked a shaken Johnston, the "greatest possible calamity" for the South. Although Sherman was perfectly aware that neither Johnston nor any of his men had taken part in Lincoln's death, the Union general nevertheless took the precaution of withholding word from his own troops until he had placed a strong guard around Raleigh.

When the horrible news was later revealed, Sherman's soldiers, like their civilian counterparts in the North, were initially stunned to silence. And, as with their civilian counterparts, when the shock of the soldiers began to wear away, a murderous rage swiftly took control.

"Awful was the excitement," recorded one Yankee soldier. "The boys are raving about it. Revenge is uttered from most every lip."[14]

"May the Lord have mercy upon the Country we pass through and the Rebels we catch . . . ," warned another Federal soldier. "Few men will stop from committing any outrage or crime they may wish to. . . . I hope Andrew Johnson will put down the screws tight [and] by thunder the army will sustain him if it hangs every man & burns every house in the whole South."[15]

Despite Sherman's precautions, thousands of his men marched on Raleigh that night, determined to burn the capital to the ground. Only the muzzles of cannons and Sherman's tireless efforts prevented a wholesale massacre.[16]

While Sherman kept a sharp check on his men's passions in North Carolina, the Jacobin mood in the North was given free rein. In a climate fully as frenzied and vicious as that on the day Lincoln was shot, many in the North demanded victims in partial payment for the death of their beloved leader. While Davis, Vice President Alexander Stephens, cabinet members, and other high Confederate leaders were demanded, even the magnanimous and internationally respected Robert E. Lee was not overlooked.

"He is one of the guiltiest of all rebel fiends," railed the *Chicago Tribune,* "and could we do it lawfully, without a breach of our own national honor, we would hang him with patriotic pleasure."[17]

When others joined the howl for Lee's arrest and death, an outraged General Grant stepped in and vowed that he would resign rather than see the man who had surrendered to him in good faith harmed. "People who talk now of further retalliation [*sic*] and punishment . . . ," Grant wrote his wife, "do not conceive of the suffering endured already or they are heartless and unfeeling and wish to stay at home, out of danger, whilst the punishment is being inflicted."[18]

Although national esteem for Grant largely ended the hue and cry for Lee's blood, the savage demand for revenge on Southerners, high and low, only grew louder. Surprisingly, much of the focus of this anger, those yet rebellious souls in the fast-fading Confederacy, knew little or nothing of the murderous mood sweeping the North. Had they so known, it might have given many due cause to pause and reconsider their future.

CHAPTER 5

Grapevine Batteries

"I HATE THE REAR WITH ITS LONG-FACED CITIZENS WHO CROAK, CROAK, croak . . . ," complained Lizzie Hardin. "One might as well be in the midst of a frog pond."[1]

"We . . . are bewildered, groping in impenetrable darkness and mystery," added Floride Clemson.[2]

As Lizzie intimated, and as Floride spelled out, every other person in what remained of the Confederacy were by turns sickened and heartened, elated and saddened, jubilant and depressed. And finally, Southerners were utterly spent and worn by the barrage of rumors battering their land.

With their nation's infrastructure all but smashed, goods and services were extremely scarce. The scarcest commodity of all, however, was factual news.

"There is no longer a mail, no R.R. or other conveyances for passengers or commodities, no newspaper except those printed by Yankees . . . of which one rarely reaches us by chance," Edmund Ruffin jotted in his diary at his home in Amelia County, Virginia.[3]

It took days, sometimes weeks, for accurate accounts of even the greatest events to reach some areas. Occupied port cities had the most reliable communications. As news items traveled inland, however, they were embellished with every mile until only a shred of truth remained. When these bits of information arrived, the emotional tide rose with hope or plummeted with despair. Often, bad news was repeated so many times that it had the ring of "wolf" about it. Such was the response of John Dooley upon hearing of the fall of Richmond:

> Of course that's all nonsense! Can't fool me like that. I've heard of Richmond being taken too often to believe any such rumor as that! But suppose there should be truth in the rumor? Just

Emma LeConte
THE SOUTH CAROLINIANA LIBRARY, UNIVERSITY OF SOUTH CAROLINA, COLUMBIA

> supposing now Richmond has been captured; what on the face of the earth am I to do? Cut off from home; no money; no clothes; the very thought is distracting; no, no, it cannot be so.[4]

Happiness, livelihood, survival—all were suddenly dependent on the winds of rumor. "If we are poor in everything else we are at least rich in rumors," one woman sarcastically wrote from Georgia.[5] At times, the emotional upheaval was so unbearable that they would have preferred no news. "We have not yet heard the particulars, indeed, I hardly want to know them," the woman confided in her diary after yet another Confederate defeat. "I think sometimes that we may almost congratulate ourselves that the Yankees by tearing up our railroad have reduced our mails from two a day to two a week."[6]

"I will never believe another . . . rumor that means hope to this unhappy land," penned a depressed Emma LeConte. "The only question now is not 'What hope?', but 'What new bitterness?'"[7]

"The whole country seems to be steeped in a fatal lethargy," observed John Dooley, "unwilling or unable to resist or forward anything. Every one is content to permit approaching events to take an unimpeded course no matter what results may follow. Groups stand around the street corners listening to the news and rumors, but no one asks what's to be done?"[8]

For most, it must have seemed as if the earth were shifting beneath them. "It is difficult to comprehend and impossible to describe, the state of uncertainty in which we lived at the time," George Cary Eggleston reminisced.[9] "Ten thousand rumors were afloat," said another more succinctly. "People knew nothing and suspected everything."[10]

Dispatches became so outlandish that even hoped-for words could not be believed. Throughout the war, but especially toward the end, Southerners prayed for foreign intervention, knowing it could well reverse even the worst situations. Some, like Lizzie Hardin, felt that if the South could not be independent in its own right, it would be far better to become a province of France, England, Mexico, "or anything," rather than rejoining the detested Union.[11] But the reports of foreign aid were so preposterous in the final days that most Southerners realized they could not possibly be true:

> *The French fleet has defeated the Yankee fleet and taken New Orleans.*
>
> *The British have blockaded the port of New Orleans with ironclads.*
>
> *The French have opened the port of Galveston.*
>
> *The British have landed one hundred thousand men in Canada.*

Even if these rumors of aid from Europe had been true, one lady aptly observed, coming on the heels of Richmond's fall and Lee's surrender as they did, what difference would it make? "It's no good if the surgeon arrives after your throat's been cut," she bitterly noted.[12]

"Too late," another said simply, "too late, if true."[13]

No better example of the consternation sweeping the South existed than that created by General Lee's surrender of the Army of Northern Virginia. After so many victories, against such odds, this news seemed so outrageous that many refused to believe it, deeming it a rumor. Writing from Texas, Kate Stone admitted that the loss of Southern cities like Charleston, Wilmington, Mobile, and especially Richmond was a terrible blow, but "all that is nothing compared to the awful report from the Yankee papers that Gen. Lee, our strong arm of defense, has capitulated. All this is too dreadful to believe. . . . All refuse to believe such disaster . . . [yet] over every pleasure sweeps the shadow of evil news. It may be true. It may be true."[14]

A group of soldiers in Georgia, when told the rumor, dismissed it with a shout of derision, exclaiming that "they would not believe it if they were standing by to see it with their own eyes."[15]

Nevertheless, and as desperately as they wanted to go on believing in the invincibility of Lee and their new nation, skeptical journalists gave little credence to the reports which stated that the general had gained "two immense victories" and that Grant had lost over one hundred thousand men and was suing for peace. "We are inclined to question the statement that Lee's army, in retreat has been enabled to gain 'two immense victories,'" wrote one incredulous editor, who angrily referred to the rumor mills as "grapevine batteries."[16]

No matter how many reports came of the surrender at Appomattox, Southerners turned their heads in stony disbelief. Eventually, though, there was nowhere to turn. A Confederate girl recorded that fateful day:

> There came along a soldier in gray. He was dirty, and ragged, and barefooted, and he looked on the ground sadly as he moved upon his way, walking slowly, as if he had come from afar and felt footsore and weary. Mr. C—— ran out upon the roadside and accosted him. Was there any news?
>
> The man answered, "News? Wall, yes; I reckon there is! Ain't yer heared it?"
>
> "No, indeed. We have heard nothing. What is it?"
>
> There was a ghastly silence. This piece of news seemed to be an unutterable thing for the soldier in gray.
>
> "Do speak! For God's sake, what is it?"
>
> Then the man in gray lifted his bowed head slowly, and replied, "Lee has surrendered!"
>
> "It is not true! It cannot be true!"
>
> But it was true.
>
> "Wasn't I there?" asked the soldier, whose voice sounded as if his heart were broken. "Wasn't I there?"[17]

An eyewitness recounted another such incident:

> I am listening to an escaped officer who asserts that he was with the army when Sheridan's cavalry rode in and dispersed their ranks. He says he saw whole regiments scattered and mingled in inextricable confusion along the roads, looking in vain for food and a commander. He describes how the Yankee cavalry rode

> them down without mercy, and how this and that general fled in dismay. Concluding that this talker is a gasbag, I leave him and go elsewhere for information.[18]

After soon encountering great numbers of soldiers from Lee's shattered army, the man above was forced at last to concede the cold, hard truth. "Worse than the loss of our capital," he sadly muttered, "that the noble and invincible army of Lee should be hewn and hacked to pieces by a vile host of Yankee hirelings."[19]

"If the heavens had fallen there could have scarcely have been greater consternation and grief in our midst," recorded Virginian Lucy Buck of that fateful day.[20]

"Almost everyone in the room burst into tears," noted Lizzie Hardin when rumor became grim truth. "Not a word was spoken except when someone sobbed out, 'we are not whipped yet! We will fight in the Trans-Mississippi,' or, 'I hope we will fight till there is not a man left!'"[21]

While many, like Lizzie's friend, searched for silver linings, remaining optimistic was nearly impossible. "We tried to keep up our spirits by singing some of the favorite war songs," remembered Eliza Andrews, "but they seemed more like dirges now."[22] With the fall of each city chipping away at their dreams of independence, Southerners struggled to put the news, or the bits and pieces of news they received, into a context that afforded them a small grain of hope. Upon learning that Montgomery had been evacuated without a fight, one Alabama editor strained to find cheer by pointing out that the town's defenders had not been "wantonly or unnecessarily sacrificed" and were now free to fight another day. "There is no danger of our subjugation," soothed the journalist confidently.[23]

"EVERY ONE bears the LATEST and most RELIABLE news," wrote Sgt. William Heartsill facetiously from Texas after hearing the latest rash of rumors:

> First; Andy Johnson and Secty Stanton have been assasinated [*sic*]. Second, Genl Joe Johnston and Genl Sherman have agreen upon terms of peace. . . . Third; England and France have CERTAINLY recognized the Confederate States. Fourth; The Emperor Napoleon has landed a large Army on the Texas coast. 5th, Joe Johnston has surrendered with ONE HUNDRED AND THIRTY THOUSAND men (the other THREE HUNDRED AND FIFTY THOUSAND I suppose were drowned in TAR river NC) Sixth. . . . Lincoln has "Gone up the spout."[24]

At least one rumor in the six was soon confirmed, however—Lincoln's murder.

"I remember how one poor woman took the news," said Myrta Lockett Avary. "She was half-crazed by her losses and troubles; one son had been killed in battle, another had died in prison, of another she could not hear if he were living or dead; her house had been burned; her young daughter, turned out with her in the night, had died of fright and exposure. She ran in crying: 'Lincoln has been killed! Thank God!' Next day she came, still and pale: 'I have prayed it all out of my heart,' she said, 'that is, I'm not glad. But, somehow, *I can't* be sorry. I believe it was the vengeance of the Lord.'"[25]

"We thought we had been delivered from our worst enemy," wrote one woman. Others felt it was only a fitting end for someone who had inaugurated the war and sent so many to their graves. "What torrents of blood Lincoln has caused to flow," lamented another Southerner.[26]

"Hurrah! Old Abe has been assassinated!" wrote a joyous Emma Le Conte from Columbia, South Carolina. "This blow to our enemies comes like a gleam of light. We have suffered till we feel savage. The first feeling I had when I heard the news were announced was simply gratified revenge. The man we hated has met his proper fate."[27]

On board a train in Georgia, Eliza Andrews arrived at the depot as another locomotive pulled in from Augusta. "Somebody thrust his head in at the window and shouted: 'Lincoln's been assassinated . . . !' Somebody laughed and asked if the people . . . didn't know that April Fools' Day was past; a voice behind us remarked that Balaam's ass wasn't dead yet, and was answered by a cry of 'Here's your mule!' But the truth of the report was soon confirmed. Some fools laughed and applauded, but wise people looked grave and held their peace."[28]

As Eliza noted, when their euphoria had quieted, many Southerners took a sober second look at the assassination and its implications for their defeated homeland.

"Our sorrows and misfortunes are never to cease," lamented Frances Fearn:

> I can only see dark, terrible days ahead of us. . . . Coming at this time it is the greatest misfortune, and will be more disastrous in its effect upon the South than anything that could have happened. What a madman Booth was not to realize this! and it is terrible to think of the many innocent people that are going to be made to suffer in consequence of his mad and unjustifiable

Frances Fearn
UNIVERSITY OF NORTH CAROLINA
LIBRARY AT CHAPEL HILL

> act. This awful crime cannot be wiped out by the hanging of Booth only. I fear others will be made to pay very dearly for it; if not with their lives, it will be in other ways of suffering and humiliation.[29]

"It is a terrible blow to the South," added Eliza Andrews, "for it places that vulgar renegade, Andy Johnson, in power."[30]

The joy resulting from Lincoln's death was dealt a bittersweet blow by the terrifying knowledge that the vindictive and radical Andrew Johnson would now reign in Washington. "His name stunk like carrion in the nostrils of the Southern people," Ella Thomas of Georgia penned in her diary.[31]

"Already there had been talk of trying our officers for treason, of executing them, of exiling them," recalled another Southern woman, "and in this talk Andrew Johnson had been loudest."

Horrified by the news, searching desperately for any straw that might translate into the triumph of their cause, frantic Southerners constructed fantastic yet—given the overall uncertainty of the times—plausible scenarios.

"Andrew Johnson, in terror of the consequences and the vengeance of the infuriated North, has fled the country," John Dooley jotted in his journal. "The whole North is in confusion, anarchy. The Peace party are fighting the Republicans, Grant's army is disbanded."[32]

"Now they say Andy Johnson is killed, & two of his cabinet, & that Grant will be dictator, then that Lee is to be president, & Grant vice president," wrote Floride Clemson from South Carolina.[33]

The rumors came so fast and furious in the Shenandoah Valley of Virginia that Joseph Waddell could hardly enter them in his diary fast enough:

> Among them that Andrew Johnson had been killed, and that Washington, Philadelphia and New York were in flames. Also, reported by some one who came up the valley that Grant had been killed, and that fighting was going on in Washington City. . . . Trouble, suspense, anxiety.[34]

Such illusions soon were shattered by reality, however. When the smoke of rumor had finally cleared only the "righteous retribution upon Lincoln" was left for Southerners to savor. "One sweet drop among so much that is painful . . . ," Caroline Jones told a friend. "He at least cannot raise his howl of diabolical triumph over us."[35]

Nothing would deny many in the South their moment of supreme satisfaction.

"We could not be expected to grieve . . . for Mr. Lincoln," confessed Myrta Lockett Avary, "whom we had seen only in the position of an implacable foe at the head of a power invading and devastating our land."[36]

Newspapers remaining in Confederate hands deemed the act evidence of God's vengeance.[37] Declared the *Chattanooga Daily Rebel,* published in Selma, Alabama:

> Abe Lincoln . . . the political mountebank and professional joker, whom nature intended for the ring of the circus, but whom a strange streak of popular delusion elevated to the Presidency . . . has fallen. His career was as short as it was bloody and infamous. He has gone to answer before God for the innocent blood which he has permitted to be shed, and his efforts to enslave a free and heroic people.[38]

At Matamoras, Texas, hundreds of Rebel soldiers held an impromptu celebration in front of the hotel to cheer Lincoln's death. While beer, wine and champagne flowed, a pile of sand was fashioned in the shape of a grave and on top of it a headboard was stuck: "To the memory of the damned Ape Lincoln."[39]

And as for the assassin himself, far from feeling he was a madman and a murderer, many considered him a "modern Brutus":

> All honor to J. Wilkes Booth, who has rid the world of a tyrant and made himself famous for generations. Surratt [*sic*] has also won the love and applause of all Southerners by his daring attack on Seward. . . . How earnestly we hope our two avengers may escape to the South where they will meet with a warm welcome.[40]

CHAPTER 6

Every Man's Hand

Chicago Tribune, April 17, 1865:

> The escape of . . . Booth, and his confederates can only be for a few days or hours. Millions of eyes are in vigilant search of them, and soon they will be in the hands of justice. . . . They will be followed . . . in hot pursuit, and woe to him who attempts to screen them. No place on this side of perdition can shelter them.[1]

DESPITE THE *TRIBUNE*'S ASSURANCES, AND DESPITE THE GREATEST MAN-hunt in American history, the murderer of President Lincoln remained at large. After nearly a fortnight of investigation, interrogation, and search, John Wilkes Booth continued a free, if much sought-after, man. From throughout the North, hundreds of well-meaning but overly zealous individuals reported spotting Booth in barrooms, hotels, and train stations. Although unintended, photography studios around the country aided the search when they sold thousands of images of the assassin to the wildly curious public. In a similar vein, the Indiana State Museum announced that it was preparing an "exact" likeness of the murderer in wax, "as people are all anxious to see what such a demon is like."[2]

Additionally, numerous "biographies" of the actor appeared in newspapers and pamphlets, many designed not so much to inform the public of the assassin's life as to reveal his innate depravity. "Bastard son," an "inveterate drunkard," an actor whose only great roles were those of villains. "It was in him . . . ," ran one capsule biography, "and in portraying Richard, Iago and Shylock, he was portraying himself. . . . Only a man possessing the worst passions could so closely represent them."[3]

John Wilkes Booth
NATIONAL ARCHIVES

Because many believed that the assassination conspiracy reached to the highest levels, more than a few Americans felt that Booth's escape had been expedited by the Confederate government and that the murderer had no doubt reached safety in the Deep South, Canada, or abroad. As the days passed, and as the likelihood of catching him diminished, their suspicions seemed confirmed. And yet, as Lt. Luther Baker and his file of hard-riding cavalrymen were soon to discover, after the space of nearly two weeks, Booth had gone little more than fifty miles from Ford's Theater.

Acting on a sequence of tips, in the dark, early-morning hours of April 26, 1865, Baker and his men quickly surrounded a tobacco barn near Port Royal, Virginia. Inside, John Wilkes Booth and his friend David Herold lay on the hay asleep. Since the night of the assassination and his escape from the capital into the Maryland countryside, Booth had been preoccupied with public reaction to his deed. Believing himself a patriot and hero for killing a tyrant, the actor was troubled, then depressed by what he heard from others and read in the newspapers. The words of a New York reporter were typical:

> The blow of an assassin—fool as well as villain—has extinguished, in the blood of Mr. Lincoln, the main hope on which the conservatives have been resting for the checking of the extreme policy of the radicals. If there was a political motive in the act, it was the act of an idiot. He has ennobled the victim of his rage, as a martyr for all history.[4]

"God only knows what incentive impelled this devil to the commission of this horrible and damning crime . . . ," said the St. Louis *Republican*. "But one thing is certain—no man has ever been so effectually damned to everlasting fame as J. Wilkes Booth, the perpetrator of this cowardly, dastardly crime."[5]

Such a reaction might well have been expected in the North. But even in his beloved South, although many praised him in secret and now carried his photograph, others reviled him in public. "Our expressions of disgust for the dastardly wretch who could have conceived and executed such a diabolical deed can scarcely be uttered," former South Carolina governor William Aiken announced before a large crowd in Charleston.[6]

"No one but a maniac would be guilty of such a crime . . . ," remarked a man attending another such meeting of citizens in neighboring Georgia. "I trust there is not a drop of Southern blood in the assassin. If so, I would feel we were disgraced in the sight of God and man."[7]

It was with this tormenting thought that all his efforts had been for naught that Booth and his companion were startled from their sleep.

"You must give up your arms and surrender," Lieutenant Baker shouted to the two men inside. "We have come to take you prisoner. . . . We will give you five minutes to surrender or will burn the barn."

Scrambling to his feet, hobbling on a crutch used since breaking his leg during the escape, Booth was startled by the voice.

"Who are you and what do you want?" he nervously asked, trying desperately to clear his thoughts. "We want you, we intend to take you prisoner," answered Baker.

After a brief pause to consider his situation, the actor hurled back a defiant response. "Give me a chance for my life," he shouted. "I am a cripple with one leg. Withdraw your men 100 yards from the barn and I will come out and fight you. . . . I will never surrender; I will never be taken alive."

"If you don't do so immediately," threatened Baker, "we will set fire to the barn."

The silence from the barn was soon broken. "Here is a man who wants to come out," announced Booth.

When young David Herold, wide-eyed and frightened, appeared at the barn door, he was quickly jerked clear. Realizing that further talk was futile, the Federals then set fire to the building.[8]

"Within a few minutes the blazing hay lighted up the inside of the barn," wrote a witness at the scene. "Booth was discovered leaning on a crutch which he threw aside, and with a carbine in his hands came towards the side where the fire had been kindled, paused, [then] looked at the fire a moment."[9]

"The flames appeared to confuse him, and he made a spring toward the door, as if to attempt to force his way out," recalled Sgt. Boston Corbett as he peered through a crack.

> I was not over eight or ten yards distant from him. . . . I was afraid that if I did not wound him he would kill some of our men. . . . As he passed by one of the crevices in the barn I fired at him. I aimed at his body. . . . I took deliberate aim at his shoulder, but my aim was too high. The ball struck him in the head, just below the right ear, and passing through came out about an inch above the left ear. I think he stooped to pick up something just as I fired. . . .
>
> After he was wounded I went into the barn. Booth was lying in a recumbent position on the floor. I asked him where are you wounded? He replied in a feeble voice, his eyeballs glaring with brilliancy, "In the head, you have finished me." He was then carried out of the burning building into the open air.[10]

Among the items found on Booth was a diary. Ran the entry for April 21:

> After being hunted like a dog through swamps, woods, and . . . chased by gun boats till I was forced to return wet[,] cold and starving, with every mans hand against me, I am here in despair. And why; For doing what Brutus was honored for, what made Tell a Hero. And yet I for striking down a greater tyrant than they ever knew am looked upon as a common cutthroat. . . . I hoped for no gain. I knew no private wrong. I struck for my country and that alone. . . . I do not repent the blow I struck. I may before my God but not to man.[11]

While a doctor was sent for, Booth was dragged away insensible from the burning barn to the porch of a nearby home. Regaining consciousness, he clung to life throughout the dark morning hours.

"About an hour before he breathed his last," continued Corbett, "he prayed us to shoot him through the heart and thus end his misery. His sufferings appeared to be intense."[12]

A correspondent for the *New York World* described his final moments:

> Booth had asked to have his hands raised and shown him. They were so paralyzed that he did not know their location. When they were displayed he muttered, with a sad lethargy, "Useless, useless." These were the last words he ever uttered. As he began to die the sun rose and threw beams into all the tree-tops. . . . The struggle of death twitched and fingered in the fallen bravado's face.—His jaw drew spasmodically and obliquely downward; his eyeballs rolled toward his feet, and began to swell; lividness, like a horrible shadow, fastened upon him, and with a sort of gurgle and sudden check, he stretched his feet and threw his head back and gave up the ghost.[13]

Tossing Booth's body into a wagon, and with a rope fastened around David Herold's neck as he trudged along, Lieutenant Baker and his joyous men returned to Washington with their prize.

Although the actual assassin was dead, the swirling hunt for accomplices intensified. At almost the exact moment that Booth expired, his brother Junius was arrested in Philadelphia and led away to Old Capitol Prison in Washington. Also jailed was John Ford, owner of the now infamous theater, and several cast members of *Our American Cousin.*[14]

Determined to leave no stone unturned, investigators went to almost any lengths to uncover the conspiracy. In Louisville, the death of a man who purportedly "confessed" to killing Lincoln drew national attention and official inquiry, as did the suicide of a passenger aboard an Atlantic steamer who felt himself somehow implicated in the plot.[15] Another suicide victim in Baltimore was dug up, embalmed, then shipped to Washington to be examined by government surgeons. Other than his having been "depressed and melancholy," there appeared no connection between the corpse and the assassin.[16]

As to the body of Booth, it too was examined. After a photograph was taken of the remains, the shattered vertebra was then removed and given to the Army Medical Museum. Once there, the curious, the morbid, or the simply sadistic could see for themselves "the intense agony in which Booth must have passed his long hours of lingering death."[17]

Less than forty-eight hours after that "lingering death," amid great secrecy and security, the earthly remains of John Wilkes Booth were hauled to the Arsenal on the banks of the Potomac River. There, in the dead of night, beneath a floor of the Old Penitentiary building, the corpse was silently buried.[18]

"They carried the body off into the darkness, and out of the darkness it will never return," said the *New York World*. "In the darkness, like his great crime, may it remain forever, impalpable, invisible, nondescript, condemned to that worse than damnation, annihilation."[19]

While most in the North were elated that the assassin had finally been brought down low, others felt cheated. In expiation for his great crime, many believed only a trial and public execution were sufficient. More than a few would have favored torture. One "well-known English poet," Dr. C. Mackay, suggested that "preparatory to the hanging of the monster . . . a vigorous daily application of the whip on his hacked carcass, on the night and morning of every day" would have been fitting.[20] Others recommended that Booth's body be dismembered and placed on public display, a spectacle many no doubt would have savored.[21]

After reading and hearing accounts such as the above, some were understandably aghast at the savagery displayed. When it was mildly suggested by one New York editor that "even the devil deserved his due," that even Booth, though his crime be enormous, had nonetheless displayed more than a little daring and bravery, the journalist was silenced by his outraged peers.

"His whole history is a history of libertinism, baseness, and dishonor," lectured the *Baltimore American:*

> Any attempt to illumine a lifetime of shame and misconduct is a wretched sham. If he had any redeeming qualities, he has swamped them all by a crime whose magnitude is not paralleled in the annals of human events. . . . He has left a name infamous beyond expression. "Dowered with the hate of hate, the scorn of scorn," and any apology for his damning misdeed should be crushed forever. Let him take his place where he belongs; let the evil he has done live after him; and let not those whom he has so foully wronged, the good and true and loyal men of the whole nation, be sickened with pitiful attempts to make a martyr of a villain, to array in the garb of a hero a monster of crime, and to surround with fragrant flowers and rainbow colors the exit of one who died like a dog.[22]

Meanwhile, as Booth's body was being hurried to perdition and everlasting infamy, the remains of his victim were moving steadily toward martyrdom. Following a stately and unprecedented funeral service in the capital, the cold form of Abraham Lincoln was placed aboard a special train for the long journey back to his home in Illinois. That all Americans might have the opportunity to pay respects and say a final farewell, a grand funeral procession was organized, the likes of which the world had never seen.

Following stops in Baltimore and Harrisburg, the somber but elegant cars reached Philadelphia. There, the casket was carried inside Independence Hall and opened. Even before the doors were unlocked at 6 A.M. for public viewing, the streets just beyond, said a spectator, were crammed with "one living mass of humanity . . . [that] swayed backward and forward like a surging ocean." One estimate placed the line of those waiting to enter at seven miles long.[23]

The train, again bearing the coffin, continued on to New York City where the crowds were even larger. "Washington, the Father; Lincoln, the Savior of His Country," read a huge sign as the casket was borne down Broadway. Lining the street, a "dense human hedge twelve or fifteen feet deep" watched in silent awe, while overhead, others who had paid as much as a hundred dollars for a window peered down.[24]

"The hue is rather bloodless and leaden . . . ," a reporter observed as he gazed on the body at City Hall. "The dark eyebrows seem abruptly arched; the beard, which will grow no more is shaven close. . . . The mouth is shut, like that of one who had put his foot down firm, and so are the eyes, which look as calm as slumber."[25]

From New York City, where hundreds of thousands had viewed the body, the funeral train traveled up the Hudson Valley to Albany, then west toward Buffalo. And with nearly every mile of the route, day and night, fair weather or foul, the track was lined with silent, bareheaded men, weeping women, and confused children. As the train rattled westward, crowds grew larger. Tiny whistle stops with normal populations of a few hundred souls now swelled to thousands. At Syracuse, thirty thousand mourners defied a midnight storm merely to view the passing cars.[26]

It was at Cleveland, though, one week after the train had departed Washington, that Americans first began to appreciate the degree of love they felt for Lincoln and his place in history. Despite a torrential downpour, virtually the entire population turned out, with over ten thousand viewers per hour, for fifteen hours, passing the coffin. Upon witnessing the sorrow-stricken crowds, one of those on the train wrote that the city was "unexampled in the depth of emotion."[27]

Even so, as the funeral train continued its journey, another passenger noted that the "deep sorrow . . . seems, if possible, to deepen, as we move Westward."[28]

"Truly," wrote one reporter, "a nation mourns."[29]

Tremendous and heartfelt as the outpouring of grief and sorrow was, as the train wended westward, and as millions of Americans made what now amounted to a holy pilgrimage, outrage was directed once again at the authors of so much misery and woe. In a way that Lincoln never would have wished, his death kept alive the raging fires of hatred.

CHAPTER 7

God's Curse

> With heart-sickening anxiety, with forebodings too dreadful to be whispered, we listened for tidings from our beloved, our unhappy and fugitive President.[1]

THUS WROTE SALLIE ANN PUTNAM OF RICHMOND, EXPRESSING THE thoughts of thousands throughout the South. For most, the whereabouts of Jefferson Davis was the greatest of mysteries. Sallie herself heard reports of his safe passage over the Mississippi River, then of his escape to, and warm welcome in, Mexico.[2] In reality, however, Davis was far from the Mississippi and nowhere near Mexico. Instead, he was painfully winding his way south and west through Georgia, hoping against hope with each weary mile that a miracle might yet occur.

The president's passage proved slow and erratic. To avoid Yankee patrols, which now threatened his route at every turn, Davis was often forced to double back east when his destination was west, veer north when escape lay to the south.[3] Unlike the shameful treatment he had received in much of North Carolina, many of those he passed in South Carolina and Georgia greeted their leader warmly, even reverently. Despite the very real threats of reprisal, diehards would not deny their president.

"Crowds of people flocked to see him, and nearly all were melted to tears," Eliza Andrews wrote from Washington, Georgia, on May 4. "Gen. Elzey pretended to have dust in his eyes and Mrs. Elzey blubbered outright, exclaiming all the while, in her impulsive way: 'Oh, I am such a fool to be crying, but I can't help it!'"[4]

For these people and others on his route, and despite every heart-wrenching reverse they had suffered, Jefferson Davis, "calm and dignified" still, was positive, if pathetic, proof that the end had not yet come; that the cause, even at this late date, was not entirely lost. As long as he and his fugitive government lived, hope lived.

"I would crawl from here to Canada on my knees to save them," the young Kentucky refugee Lizzie Hardin wrote in her diary at Eatonton, Georgia. She continued:

> I know that some persons would laugh to hear me say that in spite of all our misfortunes, of all our grief, my faith in our ultimate independence is not shaken. But it is the truth. From the first gun that was fired to this moment I have been animated by a hope—not weak, not wavering—but strong, steady and confident, founded upon the justice and mercy of God, and even though the events of the past two weeks have been like the crash of worlds, I cannot give it up. God will not let such a nation as the Yankees triumph finally. We shall at last be free.[5]

"Every man is a traitor & coward who doesn't go with him, & fight to the death to keep us from this disgraceful reunion," twenty-year-old Pauline De Caradeuc of Aiken, South Carolina, commented in her journal.[6]

When all else was lost, the hope of a nation now rested on their president's westward escape to the Trans-Mississippi, where an army might yet be rallied for a last stand. There, Davis announced confidently, "we can carry on the war forever."[7]

"Texas alone, can prolong the conflict at will," wrote the editor of an Austin newspaper.[8]

"Smaller parties than we now have," asserted one Louisiana soldier, "bold & daring men, carrying on a partizan warfare, as did Sumter & Marion, can protract this war indefinitely."[9]

Although many in the West were understandably depressed by news from the East, and even at that moment were deserting the Southern flag, others, in Texas and elsewhere, were determined to fight on, or "at least," vowed Trans-Mississippi commander Edmund Kirby Smith, to hold out "until President Davis reaches this department."[10]

Unknown to Smith and others waiting in the Trans-Mississippi for their leader, it would have taken a minor miracle for President Davis to have traversed the Yankee-occupied South and reached Texas before late April. And after that time, it became virtually impossible.

$100,000
REWARD IN GOLD
HEADQUARTERS CAVALRY CORPS,
MIL. DIV. MISSISSIPPI
MACON, GA., April 28, 1865

> One Hundred thousand dollars' reward will be paid to any person or persons who apprehend and deliver Jefferson Davis to any of the military authorities of the United States. Several million dollars of specie reported to be with him will become the property of the captors.
>
> J. H. Wilson, Major-General[11]

Not only was Davis being pursued as the "head devil" of the late rebellion and the chief conspirator in the Lincoln assassination, but now, as the posters made clear, the Rebel leader was also being hunted as a common thief who was fleeing with the Confederate treasury, estimated by some to be as much as thirteen million dollars.[12] Hence, the apprehension of Jefferson Davis was now not only patriotic, but also profitable beyond anyone's wildest dreams.

"[This] will sharpen the senses of hundreds of his late victims," assured the *New York Times.* "They will be on his heels like so many ruthless avengers."[13]

As if further incentives were needed, top officials repeatedly spurred their men to greater efforts. "Spare no exertion to stop Davis and his plunder," Secretary of War Edwin Stanton urged his generals in the South.[14] "Follow him to the ends of the earth," demanded an officer to his men in the field.[15]

Neither Jefferson Davis nor his wife, Varina, who had finally joined her husband, knew anything of this. The couple's first clue came at dawn on May 10, near Irwinville, Georgia, when members of the Presidential bivouac were awakened by gunshots nearby.

"We were taken by surprise," recounted one of those in the camp, "and not one of us exchanged a shot with the enemy."[16]

Davis himself decribed it thus:

> I stepped out of my wife's tent and saw horsemen, whom I immediately recognized as cavalry, deploying around the encampment. . . . [My wife] implored me to leave at once. I hesitated from unwillingness to do so, and lost a few precious

> moments before yielding to her importunity. . . . As it was quite dark in the tent, I picked up what was supposed to be my "raglan," a waterproof, light overcoat, without sleeves; it was subsequently found to be my wife's, so very like my own as to be mistaken for it; as I started my wife thoughtfully threw over my head and shoulders a shawl.[17]

After fleeing only a short distance, however, the two were quickly surrounded. "At that," a Federal trooper recalled, "Davis threw off the shawl and waterproof that he had been wearing and Mrs. Davis put her arms around his neck and said: 'Please don't shoot him,' and Davis said: 'Let him shoot, I may as well die here as anywhere.'"[18]

While some soldiers looted the camp and laid claim to everything from the children's toys to the Confederate Treasury—not the millions rumored, but a mere twenty-six thousand dollars—others stood gaping and laughing at their grand prize. According to one of the captives, former Texas governor Francis Lubbock:

> The man who a few days before was at the head of a government was treated by his captors with uncalled for indignity. To cite one instance is sufficient: A private stepped up to him rudely and said: "Well, Jeffy, how do you feel now?" I was so exasperated that I threatened to kill the fellow, and called upon the officers to protect their prisoner from insult. The conduct of the captors throughout was marked by anything but soldierly bearing. . . . They showed the smallness of their souls all the way from overbearing conduct down to the pilfering of small articles.[19]

Throughout the humiliating ordeal, Varina Davis maintained her composure. "Her bearing toward them," observed Governor Lubbock, "was such as was to be expected from so elegant, high-souled, and refined a Southern woman. The children . . . hovered about her like a covey of young, frightened partridges."[20]

The travail of Jefferson Davis had just begun. Soon after leaving with his captors, the Confederate president first learned of the reward on his head for Lincoln's murder.

"This is worse than death itself," said the prisoner, "to be accused of such a crime."[21]

When he spotted Andrew Johnson's signature on the reward handbills, Davis was outraged. "The miserable scoundrel . . . knows it is false. Of

Jefferson Davis as a Prisoner, Macon, Georgia LIBRARY OF CONGRESS

course, the accusation will fail—but now these people will be willing to assassinate me."[22]

Those surrounding Davis were stunned by the charge. To be accused of such a crime, declared Francis Lubbock, was "so preposterous to those of us who knew him that we were at a loss to account for its having been made until we became more fully acquainted with the blind rage that possessed the Northern people."[23]

Along the road to his imprisonment, Davis and his family were greeted by whoops, jokes, and laughter from passing Yankee soldiers.[24] Remembered Varina:

> Within a short distance of Macon, we were halted and the soldiers drawn up in line on either side of the road. Our children crept close to their father, especially little Maggie, who put her arms about him and held him tightly, while from time to time he comforted her with tender words. . . . It is needless to say that as the men stood at ease, they expressed in words unfit for women's ears, all that malice could suggest.[25]

"God's curse rest on all such as he," one Union soldier glared. "How easy it would have been for me to have shot him dead with my pistol as he sat on his horse not forty feet from me."[26]

Worse, by far, however—worse than the cold, murderous eyes of the enemy that watched his every move—were the derisive comments aimed at Davis by his own countrymen.

"Hey, boys," yelled Yankees to surrendered Rebel soldiers they passed, "we've got your old boss back here in the ambulance—we've got old Jeff Davis. . . ."

"Hang him! Shoot him!" some cried. "We've got no use for him."[27]

"Got any of that gold with you, Jeff?" yelled other ex-Confederates. "We want our pay!"[28]

At Augusta, Davis was joined by several other prisoners including the frail vice president of the Confederacy, Alexander Stephens, "slim as a skeleton . . . [and] so feeble as to be hardly able to move about."[29] After passing through streets lined by a jeering, hooting mob, the captives boarded a steamboat to Savannah. From there, the party set sail north up the Atlantic coast, to imprisonment and an uncertain fate.

Just as the fall of Richmond had signaled the end to some Southerners, just as Lee's surrender had seemed the last blow to others, the capture of Jefferson Davis now sounded for many the final and fitting death knell of the Confederacy.

"I was studying my German when father came in and told me," said Emma LeConte. "I laid my head on the table without a word. I did not cry—the days of weeping are past."[30]

"When Gen. Lee surrendered we bitterly mourned it. But when he who stood at the helm of our ship of State went under then did the waters overwhelm us all," reflected Anna Maria Green of Georgia.[31]

"Our Confederacy," observed a heartbroken Sarah Morgan, "has gone with one crash—the report of the pistol fired at Lincoln."[32]

While thousands throughout the South held private ceremonies over the death of their nation, Northerners were saying their own sad farewell. On the morning of May 3, 1865, the whistle sounded for the last stop of the Lincoln funeral train. The following day, under hot, humid skies, all of Springfield and much of Illinois rode or walked the three miles to the ground where they would lay their friend and neighbor to rest. Said one of the speakers that day: "He made all men feel a sense of himself—a recognition of individuality—a self-relying power. They saw in him a man who they believed would do what is right, regardless of all consequences. It was this moral feeling that gave him the greatest hold on the people."[33]

After hymns were sung by the crowd and the gates to the tomb were shut, a final closing word was spoken.

"As the speaker uttered the last words," said one in attendance, "peals of thunder broke through the black clouds which had been gathering overhead, and heavy raindrops spattered upon the ground as if the very clouds were weeping. The cortege resumed its order of march and alone in the last sleep we left all that was mortal of this great and good man, the pure patriot, the immortal martyr, ABRAHAM LINCOLN."[34]

In twelve days, from Washington to Springfield, perhaps as many as ten million people, or half the population of the North, viewed the body, the coffin, or the train and thus were direct, active participants in Lincoln's funeral.[35] For many of these individuals, the man and his ideals had become real and personal.

CHAPTER 8

In Durance Vile

ON THE AFTERNOON OF MAY 22, A SMALL TUGBOAT DOCKED AT THE wharf of Fort Monroe, Virginia. Although several important officials and a large body of troops were on hand to greet the craft, curious spectators were noticeably absent.[1] Under pain of death, no one was allowed within five hundred yards of the dock.[2] Stepping from the boat was Nelson A. Miles. Beside him, and firmly gripped by the major general, was a tall, thin man who looked "much wasted and very haggard," dressed entirely in gray. Without fanfare or delay, Miles led the man from the landing and up to the fort. Once inside the massive walls, the party proceeded to Casemate No. 2.[3]

"They entered," said a witness, "the heavy doors clanged behind them and in that clang was rung the final knell of the terrible, but now extinct rebellion."[4]

Thus did Jefferson Davis, former president of the Confederate States of America, begin his first moments of imprisonment. That the Federal government spared no effort to secure their celebrated charge was made abundantly clear by Assistant Secretary of War Charles Dana:

> The window is heavily barred. A sentry stands within before each of the doors leading into the outer room. . . . Two other sentries stand outside of these doors. An officer is also constantly on duty in the outer room, whose duty is to see his prisoner every fifteen minutes. . . . A strong line of sentries cuts off all access to the vicinity of the casemates. Another line is stationed on the top of the parapet overhead, and a third is posted across the moats on the counterscarp opposite the places of confinement.[5]

Said another witness, post physician John J. Craven:

> Being ushered into his inner cell by Gen. Miles, and the two doors leading thereinto from the guardhouse being fastened, Mr. Davis, after surveying the premises for some moments, and looking out through the embrasure . . . suddenly seated himself in a chair, placing both hands upon his knees, and asked one of the soldiers pacing up and down within his cell this significant question: "Which way does the embrasure face?"
>
> The soldier was silent. Mr. Davis, raising his voice a little, repeated the inquiry. But again dead silence, or only the measured footfalls of the two pacing sentries within, and the fainter echoes of the four without. Addressing the other soldier, as if the first had been deaf, and had not heard him, the prisoner again repeated his inquiry. But the second soldier remained silent as the first, a slight twitching of the eyes only intimating that he had heard the question, but was forbidden to speak.
>
> "Well," said Mr. Davis, throwing his hands up and breaking into a bitter laugh. "I wish my men could have been taught your discipline!" And then, rising from his chair, he commenced pacing back and forth before the embrasure, now looking at the silent sentry across the moat, and anon at the two silently pacing soldiers who were his companions in the casement.[6]

As Davis quickly discovered, although a light was kept burning continually in his all but barren cell and he was closely watched night and day, no one was permitted to speak to him. As painful as this was to a man who lived for conversation, more humiliating by far were the eyes that scrutinized his every move, including visits to the water closet.[7] Not only that, but "neither knife or fork is permitted the prisoner . . . ," an observer noted. "He is forced to manipulate his food in a most primitive manner."[8]

"His only food the ordinary rations of bread and beef served out to the soldiers of the garrison. . . . His sole reading matter, a Bible and a prayer book, his only companions those two silent guards . . . ," wrote Dr. Craven. "Thus passed the first day and night of the ex-President's confinement."[9]

"How changed the scene!" one Northerner rejoiced. "Lincoln enshrined forever in the hearts of a grateful people, canonized throughout the world as the noblest martyr to liberty that ever fell! Davis, in a felon's cell, to be tried, convicted, and (God grant it) *hung,* and his memory a stench in the nostrils of the nations throughout the ages of all time."[10]

Across the Union, an electric thrill raced through millions with word that Jefferson Davis had finally been caught, caged, and cast into a "living tomb." After a four-year buildup of anger and hatred for the man "most responsible" in igniting the Great Rebellion, many were in favor of hanging the Southern leader as swiftly as possible.

"We hope soon," exclaimed one man, "to see . . . [his corpse] dangling and blackening in the wind and rain."[11]

According to the *New York Times,* a trial was hardly warranted, as the list of Davis's crimes was almost limitless:

> [A] murderer, a cruel slave owner whose servants all ran away, a liar, a boaster, a fanatic, a confessed failure, a hater, a political adventurer, a supporter of outcasts and outlaws, a drunkard, an atrocious misrepresenter, an assassin, an incendiary, a criminal who was gratified by the assassination of Lincoln, a henpecked husband . . . a supporter of murder plots, an insubordinate soldier, an unwholesome sleeper, and a malingerer.[12]

Well aware that Davis was to many the most visible symbol of the Lost Cause, the Northern press tried to humiliate him at every turn. Writing to the *New York Herald,* a man claimed that he had talked with Davis's father-in-law:

"How do you feel toward Jeff. Davis, your son-in-law?"

"I want the damned traitor hung, and the sooner the better."

Although few readers were probably aware of the fact, Varina's father had died in Montgomery, Alabama, two years earlier.[13]

"Poets" also joined the sport:

> O may the cussed traitor dwell
> In darkest pits of deepest hell,
> And gnash his teeth and groan and yell.
>
> In burning brimstone may he be,
> While the little devils dance in glee,
> Then lock the door and lose the key.[14]

One of the most shameless attacks directed at the ex-president sprang from Varina's attempt to cover her husband's head with the shawl during the excitement of his capture. From a simple gesture of a frantic woman trying to protect her spouse from the elements, the story was embellished

The Flight of Jefferson Davis: A Northern View

U.S. MILITARY HISTORY INSTITUTE, CARLISLE BARRACKS

with each telling until soon the Northern press was gleefully printing accounts of Davis fleeing his pursuers fully rigged out in ladies' attire.[15]

"Jeff Davis Captured in Hoop Skirts," ran the headlines. "Jeff in Petticoats!" "He is Caught in His Wife's Clothes."[16]

An article appearing in a New York newspaper, "fully confirming the official accounts already published," was typical:

> When the guard went to the tent they were met by Mrs. Davis in dishabille, with "Please, gentlemen, don't disturb the privacy of ladies before they have time to dress."
>
> "All right, madam," said the corporal, "we will wait till you have on your duds."
>
> Presently there came to the tent door an ostensible old lady with a bucket on her arm, escorted by Mrs. Davis and her sister.
>
> "Please let my old mother go to the spring for some water to wash in," said Mrs. Davis in a pleading tone.
>
> "It strikes me your mother wears very big boots," said the guard as he hoisted the old lady's dresses with his sabre, and discovered number thirteen calf skins; "and whiskers, too," said the sergeant, as he pulled the hood from her face; and lo, Jeff. Davis in all his littleness stood before him![17]

A few righteous souls, outraged by the frenzy to unjustly denigrate Davis, stepped forward. "I am no admirer of Jeff. Davis," wrote one Downeaster. "I am a Yankee . . . full of Yankee prejudices; but I think it wicked to lie even about him, or, for the matter, about the devil." The man from Maine continued:

> I was with the party that captured Jeff. Davis; saw the whole transaction from the beginning. I now say . . . that Jeff. Davis did not have on at the time he was taken any such garment as is worn by women. . . . I defy any person to find a single officer or soldier who was present at the capture of Jefferson Davis who will say, upon honor, that he was disguised in women's clothes. . . . I go for trying him for his crimes, and if he is found guilty, punishing him. But I would not lie about him . . . when the truth will certainly make it bad enough.[18]

Nevertheless, in the rush to revile and ridicule their former enemy, few were interested in sober words of truth. "The great head & President of the proud southern Confederacy was caught one morning with his wife's dress on."[19] "Jefferson Davis, in female attire, [was] running through the woods of Georgia."[20] "Jeff. Davis, whilst fleeing in petticoats, had a concealed pillow upon his stomach to excite the sympathy of his pursuers by making them think that he was in an interesting way."[21] And so the stories went. . . .

While the famous showman P. T. Barnum bid five hundred dollars for the "sack" Davis was supposedly captured in, three wealthy Iowans offered the Federal government three hundred thousand dollars for the right to exhibit the Confederate president throughout the country wearing a dress. "Cork minstrels" performed skits on Davis in his "hoops." Chattering newsboys sold copies of their papers while rattling off rhymes of "Jefficoats."[22]

"What a fool," said one lady, "of course the men would all run after him if he was dressed as a woman, and he was sure to be caught."[23]

On the morning following Davis's arrival, Capt. Jerome Titlow entered the prisoner's cell, followed by a blacksmith and his assistant. In the hands of the latter were iron shackles.

"As they entered," wrote Dr. Craven, "Mr. Davis was reclining on his bed, feverish and weary after a sleepless night, the food placed near to him the preceding day still lying untouched on its tin plate near his bedside."

> "Well!" said Mr. Davis as they entered, slightly raising his head.
>
> "I have an unpleasant duty to perform, sir," said Captain Titlow; and as he spoke the senior blacksmith took the shackles from his assistant.
>
> Davis leaped instantly from his recumbent attitude, a flush passing over his face for a moment, and then his countenance growing livid and rigid as death. He gasped for breath, clutching his throat with the thin fingers of his right hand, and then recovering himself slowly, while his wasted figure towered up to its full height—now appearing to swell with indignation and then to shrink with terror, as he glanced from the Captain's face to the shackles—he said slowly and with a laboring chest: "My God! You cannot have been sent to iron me?"
>
> "Such are my orders, sir," replied the officer, beckoning the blacksmith to approach, who stepped forward, unlocking the padlock and preparing the fetters to do their office. . . .
>
> "This is too monstrous," groaned the prisoner, glaring hurriedly round the room, as if for some weapon, or means of self-destruction. "I demand, Captain, that you let me see the commanding officer. Can he pretend that such shackles are required to secure the safe custody of a weak old man, so guarded and in such a fort as this?"
>
> "It could serve no purpose," replied Captain Titlow; "his orders are from Washington, as mine are from him."
>
> "But he can telegraph," insisted Mr. Davis, "there must be

> some mistake. No such outrage as you threaten me with is on record in the history of nations. Beg him to telegraph, and delay until he answers."
>
> "My orders are peremptory," said the officer, "and admit of no delay. For your own sake, let me advise you to submit with patience. As a soldier, Mr. Davis, you know I must execute orders."
>
> "These are not orders for a soldier," shouted the prisoner, losing all control of himself. "They are orders for a jailor—for a hangman. . . . I plead against this degradation. Kill me! Kill me!" he cried passionately, throwing his arms wide open and exposing his breast, "rather than inflict on me, and on my people through me this insult worse than death."
>
> "Do your duty, blacksmith," said the officer, walking towards the embrasure as if not caring to witness the performance. . . .
>
> At these words the blacksmith advanced with the shackles . . . but, as if with the vehemence and strength which frenzy can impart, even to the weakest invalid, Mr. Davis suddenly seized his assistant and hurled him half way across the room. . . .
>
> "I am a prisoner of war," fiercely retorted Davis. "I have been a soldier in the armies of America, and know how to die—Only kill me, and my last breath shall be a blessing on your head. But while I have life and strength to resist for myself and for my people, this thing shall not be done."[24]

When Captain Titlow yelled for assistance, a file of soldiers soon appeared. The struggle was brief but fierce. "It required six men to accomplish it, he the while struggling like a maniac," recalled a witness to the scene.[25] "Mr. Davis was thrown on his back on the cot . . . ," said another present, "and the blacksmith welded the irons on his wrists and ankles."[26]

Dr. Craven concluded:

> This done, Mr. Davis lay for a moment as if in a stupor. Then slowly raising himself and turning round, he dropped his shackled feet to the floor. The harsh clank of the striking chain seems first to have recalled him to his situation, and dropping his face into his hands, he burst into a passionate flood of sobbing, rocking to and fro, and muttering at brief intervals: "Oh, the shame, the shame!"[27]

"There was not a man in that detail," admitted one of the soldiers present, "who would not have gladly given his life to save Mr. Davis from the great indignity to which he had been subjected."[28]

While many, perhaps most, in the North felt the chaining of Davis only fit and proper for so great a criminal, a few, like the men above, were appalled by the treatment. Wrote the editor of the *New York Daily News:*

> For four years he has carried on an open and honorable war . . . against all the power of this nation; and during all these four years—so long as he had the *power* of retaliation, our government never pretended to treat as felons the thousands of prisoners who fell into its hands. . . . Now is it right, that the moment these armies . . . lay down their arms and submit to superior forces, expecting to be treated as defeated but honorable enemies . . . that we should turn upon our gallant foes of yesterday and say to them "Now you are not defeated soldiers—you are captured thieves and murderers: you have not only lost your cause . . . but you have forfeited your lives and lands and goods, as highwaymen brought to justice."[29]

Throughout the South, those who learned of his capture felt helpless to spare their former leader the degradation they knew was to come. "Wish to God, I could die," wept one woman, "to save him from sorrow, and the humiliation which are to be heaped upon his great soul."[30]

But even while the embodiment of the recent rebellion was undergoing humiliation and torture, others of lesser note were also paying the price for losing the war. Indeed, throughout the South, a purge was in progress that was often swift and violent.

CHAPTER 9

Infamous

> Let Davis and [others] . . . meet the fate of Haman. Hang them up on Mason's and Dixon's line, that traitors of both sections may be warned. Let them hang until vultures shall eat the rotten flesh from their bones; let them hang until the crows shall build their filthy nests in their skeletons; let them hang until the rope rots, and let their dismembered bones fall so deep into the earth that God Almighty can't find them in the day of Resurrection.[1]

THUS WROTE A NORTHERN "MAN OF GOD," NOT IN APRIL 1865, BUT early in 1861. With flaming screeds of retribution such as this prevalent so early in the war, Southerners could well imagine the climate in the North now. Thus, in the fury following Lincoln's murder, in the red rage and hatred that swept the Union for all things Southern, those in the crumbling Confederacy who had the ability and means to get out did.

After parting with President Davis during his flight, Judah P. Benjamin quietly slipped into Florida. "Everything satisfied me of the savage cruelty with which the hostile government would treat any Confederate leader who might happen to fall into their hands . . . ," the secretary of state later wrote. "I preferred death . . . to such captivity as awaited me, if I became their prisoner." After a perilous epic journey through swamps and forests, in which a number of disguises were used, Benjamin eventually made his way to England.[2]

Although he, too, might have effected an escape, Florida governor John Milton chose suicide over exile or arrest.[3]

Though relatively few Southerners sought escape in suicide, many refugees found haven in South America, Cuba, Canada, and the Bahamas.

"The men are all talking about going to Mexico and Brazil," noted Eliza Andrews from Georgia.[4] "If we could *only* leave . . . ," said Emma LeConte. "We dream of this and make plans to emigrate—but the means are lacking now. We will have to wait."[5]

Unfortunately for Eliza, Emma, and thousands more living inland, the collapse of Confederate currency and the shattered transportation system in the South left no option but to stay put and await the inevitable. For officials who held high posts in state and national governments, the wait usually was not long.

Recalled young Benjamin Hill, Jr., whose father was a Confederate state senator from Georgia:

> We had all retired, and about midnight were aroused by a loud knocking at the front door. I at once, and without dressing, rushed down to my father's bedroom. I found him already awake. A search was made for a match but there was none in the house, and I went outside to the servant's house. . . . What was my consternation on opening the rear door to find the house surrounded by soldiers, who stood with muskets and on guard. Securing the light I returned at once, but in the mean time the officer at the front door had secured an entrance and with a dozen men was in the bedroom. The officer in command gave him just ten minutes to get ready. He did not leave him for a second, and there was no opportunity for any private leavetaking from wife and children. . . . My father was placed in front of the soldiers and the order given to march.[6]

In addition to President Davis, Vice President Stephens, Navy secretary Stephen Mallory, and other national figures, scores of governors, politicians, and editors from the Southern states were arrested and jailed. Former Texas governor Francis Lubbock found himself tossed into a dark prison cell without benefit of bed or blanket, "just the floor, ceiling, and four walls. Two guards watched at my door, and at times during the night they would come and thrust their lanterns into my face, for what purpose I know not."[7]

Those already jailed, like Lubbock, may have been the fortunate few. In Tennessee, the former Rebel editor of the *Memphis Appeal* "accidentally" fell several stories to his death. Others "committed suicide" by falling under trains or tumbling from bridges.[8] And in Nashville, an ailing Joseph Wheeler also discovered that despite peace and his release from prison, hatred died hard. Wrote the former Confederate general:

Joseph Wheeler
LIBRARY OF CONGRESS

About 4 o'clock p.m. . . . while I was lying on my bed in my room at the City Hotel . . . someone knocked at my door. After partially dressing myself I unlocked my door, when two officers, partially dressed in U.S. uniform, entered, one of whom stated that he at one time had been a prisoner in my hands, and that he had come to thank me for kindness received at the time. The other said he knew me and had called to make his personal respects. After a few moments of polite conversation they arose and bade me good-by. . . . About five minutes after their departure I heard another knock at my door, which I again unbolted as soon as possible, when two other officers dressed in U.S. uniform, neither of whom I had ever seen before, entered. One of them advanced and extended his hand, which I took. While in the act of shaking hands, he remarked, "Is this General Wheeler?" And upon my answering in the affirmative he stated that he was Colonel [J. H.] Blackburn. The other officer immediately seized me by both arms, when Colonel Blackburn . . . struck me violently twice upon my head with a club of consid-

> erable dimensions. I struggled away from the man who held me, and as I left the room both the assailants followed me, the other officer holding a pistol in a threatening manner. I am confident I only prevented him from shooting me by keeping Colonel Blackburn between him and myself. Colonel Blackburn continued his attempts to strike me, but I succeeded in warding off his blows with my arms. Finally a gentleman caught hold of the other officer, when Colonel Blackburn hastily ran back and ran down the stairs. I am satisfied that the attempt was one upon my life, and that the pistol would have been fired at me but from the fact of Colonel Blackburn being between myself and the officer holding it.[9]

While personal purges were in progress, in the halls of the U.S. Congress the cry to punish those already caught in the roundup grew louder with each passing day.

"As for Jeff Davis, I would indict him, I would convict him and hang him in the name of God," declared Congressman George Washington Julian. "As for Robert E. Lee, unmolested in Virginia, hang him too. And stop there? Not at all. I would hang liberally while I had my hand in."[10]

Moreover, efforts to punish secession and expunge the last trace of treason became so intense that some Radicals implied—and some perhaps even hoped—that Southern parents who had named their children for Davis, Lee, and other Confederate heroes might soon pay the penalty.[11]

"Grind down the traitors," U.S. representative Thaddeus Stevens of Pennsylvania urged. "Grind the traitors in the dust."[12]

Although powerless to stop the radical headhunt, many, North and South, considered the purge cowardly, unmanly, and hypocritical. While Union soldiers, those who actually fought the war, were willing to forgive and forget and get on with their lives, "pestiferous statesmen" and others who were "invisible in war and invincible in peace" were now the most hate-filled and bloodthirsty of all.[13] According to the Lynchburg, Virginia, *Republican:*

> It is . . . civilians at the North who "snuffed the scent of battle from afar," who now, that the war is over, and the Southern people powerless for resistance, seek to wreak their vengeance upon the defenseless. Verily, where the lion ceases to prey, the wolf prowls most ferociously. While the brave and magnanimous have already buried the hatchet, the cowardly and pusil-

> lanimous are in favor of directing the keen edge of the axe towards hundreds of thousands of those whom they dared not assist to overcome.[14]

After himself facing the wrath of radicals for his lenient terms of surrender to Joseph Johnston, no less of a man than William T. Sherman was also disgusted by "the howlings of a set of sneaks who were hid away as long as danger was rampant, but now shriek with very courage."[15]

"Surely, if we of the army, if we who have fought these rebels, can forgive them and treat them as brothers again," added a crippled Gen. Daniel Sickles, "the civilians and stay-at-home politicians ought not to be vindictive or implacable."[16]

On June 30, the trial of those accused in the murder of Lincoln and the attempt on Secretary of State William Seward's life came to an end. Although the deep involvement of several conspirators was patent, the role of others was less clear. Nevertheless, to many observers the entire proceeding was a sham.

"If justice ever sat with unbandaged, blood-shot eyes, she did on this occasion . . . ," said former Confederate officer Henry Kyd Douglas. "Although the Court was organized to convict, the trial need not have been such a shameless farce."[17]

Many court procedures were questionable with presentation of evidence and witness testimony tainted or stacked heavily against the defense. Much of the "evidence" heard was circumstantial; much more were mere diatribes designed to inflame an already furious public against the Confederacy and, by association, the defendants. The military panel, noted one observer, was "ordered to try, and organized to convict." And convict it did. Of the eight defendants, half were given prison sentences, and half, including Mary Surratt, received the death penalty.[18]

Coinciding with the greater conspiracy trial was that of George Gayle of Alabama, whose ad in the *Selma Dispatch* had tendered the deaths of Lincoln, Seward, and Johnson in exchange for one million dollars.[19]

Additionally, investigators suddenly uncovered all manner of sinister plots supposedly sanctioned by the Confederate government. From diabolical schemes to burn Chicago and Philadelphia to the ground and to poison New York's water supply, to a satanic attempt by a mysterious doctor to introduce smallpox, yellow fever, and other deadly diseases into the North, the list of reported Southern atrocities seemed limitless.[20]

Of all those individuals arrested, however, none stirred more interest or aroused greater hatred than the commanders of Southern prison camps.

Enraged by years of hair-raising reports on the treatment of Union soldiers—some true, some not—in the wake of Lincoln's death, rare indeed was that Northerner willing to weigh the evidence soberly and impartially.

After the liberation of the camp in Salisbury, North Carolina, prison commander Maj. John Gee was tracked down in Florida, then sent in chains to Washington to await trial for war crimes.[21] In another case, the hated "turnkey" of Richmond's notorious Libby Prison, Dick Turner, was arrested and hurled into "the most dismal, subterranean dungeon of that place of torture." Those who viewed Turner in his cell, "pacing like a caged hyena," savored the scene: "[He was] pale as leprosy, his beard whitening, his deficient teeth ajar, and his eyes full of terror. He is now as mean and cringing in his behavior as, in power, he was insolent and cruel. . . . [H]is pleadings for mercy are presented to all who come near him; but he pleads to hearts of stone."[22]

No single camp or commander struck more horror in Northern hearts, however, than Andersonville and Maj. Henry Wirz. The grim reality of the prison—officially dubbed Camp Sumter—is horrible enough: Over thirty thousand Union soldiers crammed onto a barren bit of land designed for ten thousand, dying by the score daily of disease, malnutrition, neglect, and in some cases, outright murder. An estimated thirteen thousand perished in little over a year of operation. When the prison was finally opened and photographs of living skeletons were broadcast across the North, the cry for Wirz's blood was overwhelming.

In the murderous mood sweeping the North, few paused to consider the climate in which the Swiss-born soldier was forced to work. Stationed at the prison only because he had been severely wounded earlier in the war, the physician was ill equipped to deal with the task before him. With the Georgia infrastructure smashed by Sherman's march to the sea and other Federal raids, supplies of food, clothing, and medicine to Andersonville were a mere trickle of that needed. Wirz's own men were reduced to half rations. Confederate authorities would have been hard pressed to adequately care for the original ten thousand the camp was designed for; when three times that number eventually arrived, the officer was helpless. Greatly exacerbating the situation was Washington's sudden refusal to exchange prisoners. Whereas the North could replace with ease men lost to capture, the South could not. In theory, the move was designed to assure victory and shorten the war. In practice, it guaranteed the slow, agonizing death of thousands.[23]

As an English observer of the American Civil War, Arthur Freemantle had ample opportunity to witness conditions in the South. Wrote the lieutenant colonel to the *London Times:*

> As I traveled throughout the entire Southern States during the height of the war, I had many opportunities of seeing Northern prisoners under a variety of circumstances. I always observed they were treated with generosity and humanity, and not with barbarity. I can quite believe that they must have suffered dreadfully, and been often almost starved at Andersonville—hardships which they had to endure in common with Confederate soldiers, women and children in many parts of the South. . . .
>
> The cruelty of keeping vast numbers of men confined in places where they could only be fed with much difficulty must remain with Mr. Lincoln and not with Davis; for it is notorious that all objections to exchange prisoners came from the North, not from the South.[24]

Though there may have been extenuating circumstances for the hideous conditions suffered by Northerners in Southern prison camps, none such existed for Southerners in Northern camps. Amid a veritable cornucopia of food, clothing, and medicine—a bounty unimaginable in the crumbling Confederacy—Rebel soldiers died by the thousands. Although 9 percent of the inmates died of various causes in Southern camps, of those held in Federal prisons, roughly 13 percent perished.[25]

"The rations continued to fall off . . . ," said a starving Rebel at Rock Island in Illinois, a camp whose mortality rate was perhaps the worst in the North. "Finally [we] were limited to one meal a day, and the prisoners were hungry all the time, and grew gaunt and hollow eyed."[26]

"We were given just enough to eat to make us hungry . . . ," Ben Aker wrote from Camp Chase in Ohio. "I've been told that Camp Chase was the best of the Northern Prisons; if that be true, I want to say that in the South hogs fare better than we did in the Norths best Prison."[27]

Conditions were little better at Point Lookout on the Maryland coast. Recalled a Virginia private: "On one occasion when the tide on the bay was high it brought ashore an old sea gull which had been dead a month or more. It was picked up by a hungry rebel and devoured with a gusto."[28]

"For supper," wrote a Confederate confined in another death pen, "we were allowed all the air we could inhale. . . . It is no wonder that rats were eaten, a dog or two clandestinely butchered, or a cat roasted."[29]

"We can buy from prisoners rats, 25 cents each, killed and dressed," a soldier imprisoned at Elmira in New York revealed.[30]

"The guards would throw down apple cores and peelings and enjoy seeing our starving boys scuffle for them," Mississippian Milton Ryan remembered of Camp Chase. Ryan also recalled how his comrades, "like hungry dogs," would line the banks of a drainage ditch, searching the stinking, gray runoff for scraps of food, with "garbage and excrement all clumped in the same ditch together."[31]

Had starvation been the only trial Rebel prisoners faced, it would have been dire enough. There were other hazards, however.

"We were guarded by a heartless set of wretches," said Milton Ryan. "They had never been to the front, and baptized in battle; therefore they were cruel and mean in the extreme, often shooting unsuspecting prisoners without the least provocation."[32]

Wrote a South Carolina soldier of Rock Island:

> Men were shot on the street without warning and at night the barracks and tents would be shot into, just for pure meanness. The 108th negro regiment was bad enough, but when the 192nd Illinois hundred day men came it was worse. We could find an excuse for the negro, but there was no excuse for these civilized white men.[33]

"If we tried to have a little fun among ourselves, the Yankees would shoot in among us," noted Ben Aker of Camp Chase. "If any of us would throw out a little water, they considered it a sufficient excuse to shoot us."[34]

At Camp Douglas in Illinois, William Henry Blackburn recalled that he was was "treated worse than a dog. [I] have seen men shot down for gnawing on a bone, when they were starving."[35]

And at numerous other Yankee prisons, inmates were shot, starved, and allowed to perish from disease and neglect. Regardless, the victors preferred to focus on the crimes of the vanquished and the "incredible and infamous treatment which Northern captured soldiers received in Southern prisons."[36]

CHAPTER 10

Death of the Dream

EVEN WHILE THE PURGE OF SOUTHERN LEADERS WAS PROGRESSING IN THE East, the last act of the Confederacy was being played out in the West.

"Great disasters have overtaken us . . . ," acknowledged Kirby Smith in an address to his Trans-Mississippi army.

> With you rests the hopes of our nation, and upon your action depends the fate of our people. . . . Prove to the world that your hearts have not failed in the hour of disaster. . . . Stand by your colors—maintain your discipline. The great resources of this department, its vast extent, the numbers, the discipline, and the efficiency of the army, will secure to our country terms that a proud people can with honor accept, and may, under the Providence of God, be the means of checking the triumph of our enemy and of securing the final success of our cause.[1]

Whatever Smith's hope, his words were greeted by a majority of his men with utter amazement.

"The effect of this order upon the troops was marked in the extreme," reported a Federal spy at Shreveport. "The men instantly became dejected. Mutiny and wholesale desertion was openly talked of. This soon gave way to a general apathy and indifference, but through all could be seen by a close observer that the Army of the Trans-Mississippi was in spirit crushed."[2]

"The soldiers are disheartened & disgusted and determined not to sacrifice their lives," confirmed one of those men in Shreveport.[3]

After the fall of Richmond, after Lee's surrender, after Davis's capture, after a myriad of other debacles, rare was that western soldier who felt as Kirby Smith did, that victory might yet be won.

"I think that it is going to be a hard matter for him to get them to believe it," wrote Americus Nelms to his wife in Texas. "The most of the men in this part of the army are whiped. They say there is [no] use in holding out any longer, and that it would be foly [*sic*] in us to fight on this side of the river now. There is a good many that thinks the war is about over and that we will all be home in a few months."[4]

And even for those stalwart few, like Nelms, who were determined to stand by the colors to the bitter end, the pressure to desert at this late date was almost overwhelming. Replied Nelms's wife, Minerva, from the Indian-threatened Texas frontier:

> There is a right smart confusion about so many Indians coming in hear. . . . We are agetting in a pretty fix. My Dear it appears to me like that I would give this hold world to see you now. . . . Men are deserting all the time every wher that I can hear of. . . . I think the jig is about over but I believe that we are going to see sights with the indians. I am looking for them ever day Just swarming like bees and if they do [come] I dont believe that we can raise forses enough to stop them.[5]

Despite Smith's desperate plea, the sixty thousand men in his army melted away "like snow in a thaw."[6] By the hundreds, by the thousands, the men of the Trans-Mississippi simply disbanded. Although most headed home quietly, many others felt that after years of privation, a final accounting was in order.

"I lived four years on goobers, parched corn and rotten meat," one Rebel soldier complained, "and I saw nothing wrong with taking blankets & such from the commissary as they would have been confiscated anyhow by the Yankees when they arrived."[7]

Reported Maj. John Newman Edwards:

> Anarchy reigned supreme in Texas. Government stores, warehouses, manufactories, and treasury offices were sacked, destroyed, or fired. . . . Arsenals were entered and their precious contents scattered wantonly over the country or fired off to celebrate drunken and infernal orgies. A mania for plunder and pillage seized upon the minds of all classes, and the women attended in crowds to urge on the robbers and quarrel among themselves about the spoils.[8]

From Tyler, Texas, twenty-five-year-old Louisiana refugee Kate Stone also watched as the remnants of her once proud Confederacy came crashing down:

> Anarchy and confusion reign all over. Jayhawking is the order of the day. The soldiers are . . . seizing Government property wherever they can find it. . . . At Shreveport the demoralization is worse even than here. The officers are scattering to the four winds, and Jayhawkers and private soldiers are stopping and robbing them whenever found.[9]

"Soldiers!" an angry Kirby Smith addressed his men from Houston:

> I am left a commander without an army—a General without troops. You have made your choice. It was unwise and unpatriotic, but it is final. I pray you may not live to regret it. The enemy will now possess your country, and dictate his own laws. You have voluntarily destroyed our organizations, and thrown away all means of resistance. Your present duty is plain. Return to your families. Resume the occupations of peace. Yield obedience to the laws. Labor to restore order. . . . And may God in his mercy direct you aright, and heal the wounds of our distracted country.[10]

"Humiliated by the acts of a people I was striving to benefit," Kirby Smith had no alternative. On June 2, the Confederate general handed over his command to Federal authorities, effectively ending all organized resistance throughout the South.[11]

Although he had surrendered his department, Smith had no intention of surrendering his person. Well aware of the imprisonment and humiliation of President Davis, stunned by the indictment for treason pending against Robert E. Lee and the radical cries to hang even him, Kirby Smith, in company with other generals and governors from the Trans-Mississippi states, turned west toward Mexico.[12]

Alexandria *Louisiana Democrat,* June 14, 1865

PEACE

> The surrender of the army of the Trans-Mississippi put an end to all resistance to the authority of the government of the United States, and drove the last nail into the coffin of the

> Southern Confederacy. Peace reigns from the St. Johns to the Rio Grande, from the lakes to the gulf, and the flag of the Union waves over the length and breadth of what was so recently a divided country. The armies of the Union now "hold, possess and occupy" every foot of land ever claimed as the property of the Federal government.

> For years back I have had nothing left to make me desire to have my life extended another day, except the hope of witnessing the final defeat of our vile enemies, & the establishment of the freedom & independence of the southern confederacy. Since that hope has given way to utter despair, I have earnestly desired, & prayed, that, from my next succeeding sleep, I might never awake in this life.[13]

So wrote seventy-one-year-old Edmund Ruffin in his diary. Perhaps no man in the South so strongly gloried in the rise of the Confederate States of America, and perhaps no man so strongly mourned its fall than the fiery, white-maned Virginian. Not only had Ruffin been a more than willing witness at the 1859 execution of the abolitionist John Brown after his failed attempt at slave revolt at Harpers Ferry, but so passionate was the old man for separation from the hated Yankees of the North that he reportedly pulled the lanyard that delivered the first cannon shot directed at Fort Sumter in 1861. With the shattering of the Southern dream, however, Ruffin's spirit had plummeted dramatically, and now he viewed death as his only deliverance. Although he was determined not to survive the South's final fall, the avid diarist was eternally curious.

Following the capture of Richmond, Ruffin, like most other Southerners, had pinned his hopes on Robert E. Lee, feeling that this now legendary figure, like George Washington of old, would yet lead his country to victory and independence. When the impossible happened and Lee surrendered, the old man sank into deep despair. But then, in keeping with his character, the Virginian thought he saw a glimmer of hope in the death—the "deserved fate"—of Lincoln. Ruffin's grim satisfaction over this last act was short-lived, however, for filling Lincoln's place came the even more hated Southern renegade and Radical, the "low & vulgar & shameless drunken demagogue" Andrew Johnson.[14] As bitter as this last blow was, Ruffin sat at his desk, scribbling away in his diary. Like a theatergoer who had seated himself when the curtain rose, the inquisitive old man was

Edmund Ruffin
LIBRARY OF CONGRESS

determined to know how the last act of the drama played out before the final curtain fell.

After the surrender of Joseph Johnston's army and the capture of Jefferson Davis, the last ember of hope seemed to have finally been doused. And yet, when Ruffin looked once more to the map, he saw, with his eternal optimism, the West and the army of the Trans-Mississippi and wrote in his diary: "I have confidence that the cause of independence may still be effectively sustained in Texas, & other territory west of the Mississippi. I think there is no doubt that our cause may be maintained successfully there, & . . . may hereafter operate to recover & free the east also. . . . If I was young & able enough to bear a musket, I would very soon attempt to join our forces in Texas."[15]

But when even this hope vanished in smoke with the riots, anarchy, and mass desertions that swept the Trans-Mississippi, Ruffin knew that the Confederacy's end, as well as his own, had finally arrived. On June 17, the old man one last time put pen to paper:

> I here declare my unmitigated hatred to Yankee rule. . . . Would that I could impress these sentiments, in their full force,

> on every living southerner, & bequeath them to every one yet to be born! May such sentiments be held universally in the outraged & down-trodden South. . . .
>
> And now, with my latest writing & utterance, & with what will be near to my latest breath, I here repeat, & would willingly proclaim, my . . . hatred to Yankee rule—to all political, social, & business connection with Yankees, & to the perfidious, malignant, & vile Yankee race.[16]

Arising from his chair, the old man picked up a musket, then sat again. Using a forked stick to press against the trigger, Edmund Ruffin placed the barrel of the gun in his mouth and blew his brains out.[17]

Three weeks later, a much more public ceremony took place in the nation's capital. At 1:15 P.M. on July 7, the four individuals convicted in the conspiracy to kill Lincoln and other government leaders were led out into the yard at the Old Arsenal Prison in Washington. Within the high-walled enclosure, hundreds of soldiers and ticket-holding spectators were also on hand. Thousands more—many willing to pay hundreds of dollars—were turned away.[18]

The heat in the yard was horrific. With virtually no breeze behind the walls, the temperature approached 100 degrees. Many of those present were "almost prostrated" by the conditions.[19] Nevertheless, when George Atzerodt, David Herold, Lewis Powell (alias Payne), and Mary Surratt walked from the dark prison into the searing sun, all attention quickly focused on them. When their eyes had finally adjusted to the glaring light, the first sight that greeted the condemned was the great, grim gallows looming just ahead; the second was the freshly turned earth of their graves nearby.

A correspondent for the *Chicago Times* described the scene:

> Each prisoner was manacled, and Mrs. Surratt headed the procession. She was so physically prostrated that she had to be lifted on the steps leading to the scaffold. In addition to this her limbs were so heavily manacled that her steps were impeded. . . . Once on the platform, she was . . . seated in a chair. She seemed in a fainting condition, leaning on her left arm, and looking sorrowfully upward. A soldier held an umbrella to protect her from the sun. She was attired in a plain black dress and black bonnet. Before the noose was adjusted one of the Catholic priests

> administered the dying service of that church as Mrs. Surratt held the cross to her lips.
>
> Payne was placed next to Mrs. Surratt, and seated on the same drop. His eyes were reddened from weeping, but his face had much color. He seemed very much collected. He was clad in shirt and pantaloons blue, and wore a sailor's straw hat. Harrold [*sic*] and Atzerot [*sic*] were seated next. Harrold looked slovenly. His hair was uncombed, his clothes soiled, and he appeared in his stocking feet. . . . Atzerot was also in his stocking feet, and dressed in coarse gray. He was undemonstrative at first, but soon showed fear. Payne looked at the spectators, kept his head erect, and maintained a half defiant air.
>
> Thus arranged, the death warrants were read. . . .[20]

Of the four victims, the case against Mary Surratt seemed weakest. Throughout the trial, and even during her last sleepless night on earth, the forty-two-year-old widow and mother protested her innocence again and again. Although her boardinghouse had been used as a rendezvous for Booth and the other conspirators, the innkeeper claimed to have been unaware of any plot to kill the president, a statement vouched for in writing by one of the defendants, Lewis Powell. And even had the evidence been overwhelming against her, many recoiled at the thought of hanging a woman and a mother. Winfield Scott Hancock was one. As the officer in charge of the executions, Hancock had no stomach for the duty he was now ordered to perform.

"I have been in many a battle and have seen death, and mixed with it in disaster and in victory," muttered the major general and Gettysburg hero. "I've been in a living hell of fire, and shell and grapeshot, and, by God, I'd sooner be there ten thousand times over than to give the order this day for the execution of that poor woman."[21]

So distraught was he over the grisly task ahead that Hancock had stationed relays of soldiers from the prison to the White House in hopes of a last-minute reprieve. When no such word arrived, the general reluctantly moved ahead with the execution.

"My God, not the woman too?" protested an aide.

"Yes," the grim-faced officer replied, "the woman too!"[22]

Again, from the *Chicago Times:*

> The solemn services being over, all of the prisoners then stepped up and were bound. Atzerot was first bound at the wrists with

> his arms behind him, and his knees and ankles. Mrs. Surratt and the others were bound in the same way. Owing to her dress it took several moments to bind Mrs. Surratt who was held up during the operation. . . . The fatal nooses were opened to admit the heads of the criminals, and the knots, as usual, were adjusted exactly under the left ear. Payne worked his neck in the noose as if dissatisfied with the adjustment, and the noose was widened a little to suit his ample neck. Mrs. Surratt seemed to find some difficulty, and said to those near her "please don't let me fall. . . ." Atzerot, who seemed to grow excited as his moments approached, just before the white cap was placed over his head, attempted, in a gasping manner, to address the spectators. His parched lips would not obey, and it was distressing to see him convulsively endeavoring to make himself intelligible. At last he managed to get out the words: "Gentlemen . . . take warning." The white cap was drawn over his head, as was done with the others, and it was supposed no more would be heard from the prisoners, but just before the drop, Atzerot's voice was again heard in muffled accents, saying: "Good-by, gentlemen, who are before me now; may we all meet in the other world. God help me now. Oh! Oh! Oh!"[23]

Clapping his hands three times as a signal, General Hancock motioned to the executioners. At 1:26 P.M., the trapdoors came down with a "heavy slam," and the bodies fell with a thud. While the victims struggled against death in a futile attempt to break their fetters, the stunned crowd watched in "breathless silence." After thirty minutes, the bodies were pronounced dead, cut down, placed in coffins, then quickly buried.[24]

"As God lives," said the widow's Catholic confessor a short time later, "Mrs. Surratt was innocent of the murder of President Lincoln or of any intent or conspiracy to murder him."[25]

Ironically, the only man in America who could have, and undoubtedly would have, spared Mary Surratt's life had been murdered at Ford's Theater nearly three months earlier.

Several days before the executions, an emotionally drained but grateful Northern populace had celebrated the reuniting of the nation on the eighty-ninth anniversary of its birth. That same day, in a remote corner of the country, a small band of men held a ceremony of their own; a ceremony to commemorate not the birth or rebirth of a nation, but the death of one.

With uncertain exile from their beloved homeland rising just over on the southern shore, Joseph Shelby and the troopers of his hard-fighting "Iron Brigade" paused on July 4 in midstream of the Rio Grande. One last time, "with bared, bowed heads," the Missourians gathered around their flag, then held it aloft for a moment or two so that all might see. Then, lowering it once more, the banner was taken from its staff and weighted with rocks.

"The sun shone out broad and good upon the upturned faces of those engaged in silent prayer . . . ," recalled Major Edwards. "At last, with not a dry eye among all those five hundred stern soldiers, the battle flag . . . was lowered slowly and sadly beneath the water."[26]

Part Two

They have killed him, the forgiver—
The Avenger takes his place. . . .

Herman Melville, "The Martyr"

CHAPTER 11

Silence of the Graveyard

ALTHOUGH THE TIMING OF THEIR ARRIVAL VARIED GREATLY FROM REGION to region, the day the Yankees came was always a traumatic, tension-filled moment for those awaiting enemy occupation. While some terrified Southerners fled to the mountains, swamps, and woods, most simply stayed put. Mary Chesnut was one. "We are going to stay. Running is useless now. So we mean to bide a yankee raid, which they say is imminent. Why fly? They are everywhere. These yankees—like red ants—like the locusts and frogs which were the plagues of Egypt."[1]

While tales of Northern crime and savagery had rung harshly in Southern ears for years now, when the moment of truth finally came, most Rebels simply hoped for the best . . . and prayed against the worst.

"Everybody is cast down and humiliated . . . ," Eliza Andrews of Georgia wrote in her journal. "We are all waiting in suspense to know what our cruel masters will do with us."[2]

"We were all very excited," said South Carolinian Floride Clemson, whose family was made so nervous by the enemies' approach that they slept for three nights with their clothes on. "We had everything burried, but were dreadfully afraid of personal insults."[3]

As the young woman noted, although frightened even unto insomnia, most families nevertheless took the sage precaution of burying valuables and keepsakes in gardens, fields, and woods. Fretful parents sent little children to areas less exposed. Many slave owners, fearing the damning evidence when the "abolitionists" came calling, decided then and there to set their slaves free. Recalled a young bondswoman, Mary Anderson:

Floride Clemson
CLEMSON UNIVERSITY LIBRARIES, SPECIAL COLLECTIONS

> At nine o'clock, all the slaves gathered at the great house, and Marster and Missus come out on the porch and stood side by side. You could hear a pin drop, everything was so quiet. Then Marster said, "Good morning," and Missus said, "Good morning, children." They were both crying. Then Marster said, "Men, women, and children, you are free. You are no longer my slaves. The Yankees will soon be here."
>
> Marster and Missus then went into the house, got two large armchairs, put them on the porch facing the avenue, and sat down side by side and remained there watching.[4]

Therein generally followed a period of unusual, uneasy silence, a time said Eliza Andrews, as if a "secret pestilence" were spreading over the land.[5] It was then, during the calm before the storm, that all the terrible reports of Yankee barbarity and cruelty came flooding back to haunt the women and old men yet remaining in Southern households. Well might some Rebels recall in horror accounts such as appeared in the *Richmond Examiner,* accounts of Yankee prisoners being marched through Southern streets near the end of the war:

> They appeared the scabs, scavengers, and scum of all creation; not a face or feature on which was not written "thief," "murderer," "house burner," and "woman ravisher." Never since the war began has such a crew of hell-born men, accursed and god-forsaken wretches, polluted the air or defiled the highways of Richmond with the concentrated essence of all that is lecherous, hateful and despised.[6]

Slaves, too, often suffered as much as or more than their masters from such visions. Wild rumors along the plantation grapevine and midnight horror stories that grew more lurid with each telling told of "abolition demons" coming south to "kill & eat everyone."

"They told the slaves that the Yankees had horns," one frightened black girl remembered.[7]

In the midst of such terrifying thoughts, those awaiting the onset were occasionally startled by seemingly inexplicable phenomena. Sometimes it was flocks of birds flapping their wings madly from the woods. Other times, for no apparent reason, deer and other wild animals stampeded in terror over fields. One slave recalled seeing squirrels race across the ground, "so thick," he noted, "it looked like a carpet."[8]

And then they came.

"Suddenly," said a lady in Louisiana, "as if by magic, the whole plantation was covered with men, like bees from an overthrown hive; and as far as my vision extended, an inextricable medley of men and animals met my eye."[9]

"Men in blue tramping everywhere," a woman in North Carolina remembered, "horsemen careening about us with no apparent object, wagons crashing through fences as though they had been made of paper. The Negroes stood like dumb things, in stupid dismay. . . . The only feeling was one of awe."[10]

Although some Federal units, under good officers, were disciplined and well behaved, many were not. The Louisiana woman continued:

> In one place, excited troopers were firing into the flock of sheep; in another, officers and men were in pursuit of the boy's ponies; and in another, a crowd were in excited chase of the work animals. The kitchen was soon filled with some, carrying off the cooking utensils and the provisions of the day; the yard with others, pursuing poultry and firing their revolvers into the trees. They penetrated under the house, into the out-buildings, and went into the garden, stripping it in a moment, of all its

> vegetables, and trenching the ground with their bayonets, in search of buried treasures. . . .
>
> . . . Passing through the house, my attention was attracted to a noise in the parlor. I opened the door, and was just in time to see two soldiers springing out of the window, in possession of some books and daguerreotypes they had taken from the table. Securing the windows, I turned to other parts of the house. In the children's room, I found a trunk broken open, and its contents strewn upon the floor.[11]

"Right into the house, breaking open bureau drawers of all kinds faster than I could unlock," wrote 17-year-old Janie Smith of North Carolina. "They cursed us for having hid everything and made bold threats if certain things were not brought to light. . . . They took Pa's hat and stuck him pretty badly with a bayonet to make him disclose something. . . . Every nook and corner of the premises was searched and the things that they didn't use were burned or torn into strings. . . . The house was so crowded all day that we could scarcely move."[12]

"One young villain came in," recalled a South Carolina woman, "fastened the doors, demanded our watches, and using the most profane language and terrible threats, ordered us to confess where our gold and silver was buried; [he] laid his hands on Pauline's shoulder and mine, while we obediently emptied our pockets."[13]

After terrorizing and robbing the women, the thief then stripped the old man of the house to his waist, searching for money.[14]

"I had heard that the officers would protect ladies," said Janie Smith, "but it is not so. Sis Susan was sick in bed and they searched the very pillows that she was lying on."[15]

"It was bedlam let loose," another female victim added.[16]

The horror and the deadly uncertainty of the moment was vividly described by Dr. John Adger, who was at home hobbling about on a crutch:

> One of the party . . . demanded my watch. I gave it to him but said, "Does your government send you all through this country to rob private citizens?" Said he, "Do you suppose I would go riding all about here and not take anything home to my family. . . ?"
>
> I followed this man around about as well as I could with my crutch, and pretty soon found myself walking with him through one side of my wide piazza, and down the back steps,

> where his horse was standing hitched. The man started to mount. As he did so, my back was turned towards him, and I heard his gun go off. Startled at the sound, I turned to look, and saw the man . . . falling head foremost from his saddle, with the blood pouring in a stream from a wound in his throat. The sound of the gun made several others rush to the scene, and two of them raised their guns and were about to shoot.
>
> My daughter . . . was in the piazza, the only witness to what had happened. She cried out to them, "He shot himself. . . ."
>
> I called out, "Don't you see this man is bleeding to death? Come here, some of you, and lift him up." Three of them obeyed. As soon as they raised him it was plain to see that, as he mounted his horse, his gun discharged, the bullet entering his throat, and coming out at the top of his head. Instantly, they dropped his head, and all three began promptly to empty his numerous pockets which were full of plunder.[17]

Unlike white families, blacks were greatly relieved to discover that far from having horns, the Federals were actually human . . . and often very friendly.

"We were scarder of them than we were of the devil," admitted a young slave, Andrew Goodman. "But they spoke right kindly to us colored folks. They said, 'If you got a good master and want to stay, well you can do that, but now you can go where you want to, cause there ain't nobody going to stop you.'"[18]

"Slaves were whooping and laughing and acting like they were crazy," a suddenly free Mary Anderson reminisced. "Yankee soldiers were shaking hands with the Negroes and calling them Sam, Dinah, Sarah, and asking them questions. They busted the door to the smokehouse and got all the hams. They went to the icehouse and got several barrels of brandy, and such a time. . . . The slaves were awfully excited. The Yankees stayed there, cooked, eat, drank, and played music."[19]

Not all Northern soldiers were so convivial, however. In fact, many Yankees cared little whether the victim was black or white. According to one source:

> Eben dressed himself in his best and went at a run to meet his Yankee deliverers, so he said. At the gate he met a squad coming in. He had adorned himself with his watch and a chain. . . . He knew the Yankees came to rob white people, but he thought they came to save niggers.

> "Hand over that watch!" Minus his fine watch and chain, Eben returned a sadder and a wiser man. . . .
>
> "Why? You here? Why did you come back so soon?"
>
> "Well, I thought maybe better stay with ole Marster that gave me the watch and not go with them that stole it."[20]

Another slave recounted:

> I was setting on the steps when a big Yankee come up. He had on a cap, and his eyes was mean.
>
> "Where did they hide the gold and silver, nigger?" he yelled at me.
>
> I was scared, and my hands was ashy, but I told him I didn't know nothing about nothing; that if anybody done hid things, they hid it while I was asleep.
>
> "Go ask that old white-headed devil," he said to me.
>
> I got mad then, 'cause he was talking about [my mistress], so I didn't say nothing, I just set. Then he pushed me off the step and say if I didn't dance, he going to shoot my toes off. Scared as I was, I sure done some shuffling.[21]

And an Alabama editor reported:

> There was . . . a large number of negroes who came up grinning and rejoicing, to shake hands with their friends the Yankees. The deluded wretches thought the day of jubilee had come, and they were going to have things their own way. They were slightly mistaken. . . . Many of them . . . were driven off by the troopers, who used the flat of their sabers without stint over the pates of the darkies.[22]

"They were treated, if possible, worse than the white folks, all their provisions taken and their clothes destroyed and some carried off," remarked Janie Smith.[23]

Despite the rough handling some blacks received, many could not resist the call of freedom and eagerly rushed off with their liberators. "All departed in search of freedom, without bidding any of us an affectionate adieu," wrote a white woman from Georgia.[24]

Not only did many former slaves leave their white families without a backward glance, but some left black families as well. Mary Chesnut related the haste of some Negro mothers, in their frantic race to follow the

Yankees. "Adam came in exultant," she wrote. "Oh, Missis, I have saved a wagon load of babies for you. Dem niggers run away an' lef' dem chillun all 'long de road."[25]

But while many slaves left, to the great surprise of the conquerors many remained. Having lived and worked on the land for generations, thousands of negroes refused to be coaxed from their ancestral homes.

"I know I is free," said a South Carolina black to his former white owner, "but you needn't think I is gwine to do like de rest of de niggers . . . fur I ain't gwine to leave you and ole Mistis as long as you will let me stay wid you and de chillun."[26]

As the Union forces poured in to occupy the South, the "fidelity of the negroes" was one of the few proud and precious moments for white Southerners. "There seems not a single case of a negro who betrayed his master," noted Mary Chesnut.[27]

The words of one old Georgia bondsman to his mistress were typical:

> I told you at de very fust I was gwine to stand by you. Dase been here twice, did I tell 'em on you? Den what makes you think I'd eber do it? Think I'd leave my children and you for dem? No, I feels anxious, when dase here, for you and for fear dey might burn our things. But if a million of 'em was to come I wouldn't go with 'em. No, no Miss Martha, I tells you fust and I tells you last I'se gwine to stand by you.[28]

"When you-all had de power, you was good to me, and I'll protect you now," another freedman explained to his old master. "No niggers nor Yankees shall touch you. If you want anything, call for Sambo. I mean, call for Mr. Samuel—that's my name now."[29]

Indeed, for some white Southerners, the difference between life and death—or worse—often rested on the fidelity of former slaves. Mary Chesnut described the experience of a friend, Mary Kirkland, reportedly the most beautiful woman "on this side of the Atlantic."[30]

> Monroe, their Negro manservant, told her to stand up and keep her children in her arms. She stood against the wall, with her baby in her arms and the other two as closely pressed against her knees as they could get. Mammy Selma and Lizzie stood grimly on each side of their young Missis and her children. For four mortal hours the soldiers surged through this room. Sometimes they were roughly jostled against the wall. Mammy and Lizzie were staunch supporters and the Yankee soldiers reviled the

> negro women for their foolishness in standing by their cruel slave-owners. And they taunted Mary with being glad of the protection of her poor, ill-used slaves. Monroe had one leg bandaged and pretended to be lame so that he might not be enlisted as a soldier.
>
> He kept making pathetic appeals to Mary.
>
> "Don't answer 'em back, Miss Mary. Let them say what they want to. Don't answer them back. Don't give 'em any chance to say you are impident to 'em."
>
> One man said to her: "Why do you shrink from us and avoid us so? We did not come here to fight for negroes. We hate them. . . ."
>
> Outside they said, "She was an insolent rebel hussy who thought herself too good to speak to a soldier of the United States." Some of them said, "Let us go in and break her mouth." But the others held the most outrageous back.
>
> Monroe slipped in.
>
> "Missy, for God sake, when they come in, be sociable with them. They will kill you."[31]

As Mary Kirkland was about to find out, had Southerners only one call by their conquerors to deal with, it would have been devastating enough. Often, however, other units followed close on the heels of the first. Eventually a pattern developed. Recounted one man:

> They were regularly organized. First squads demanded arms and whiskey. Then came the rascals who hunted for silver and ransacked the ladies' wardrobes and scared the women and children into fits. . . . Then came some smiling, suave, well-dressed officers who regretted it all so much. And then, outside of the gate, officers, men, bummers, divided even—share and share alike—the piles of plunder.[32]

The raids and rumors of raids were so traumatic to Clarissa Bowen that the tired, terrified woman miscarried. "All was over and we knew that God had taken from us the desire of our hearts—our much prayed for and longed for treasure," the South Carolinian wrote in her journal, June 1865. "O, it was hard, very very hard to give up our beautiful boy. . . . Our hearts are sore and this is too sacred a sorrow to be talked or written about. My recovery has been slow, being constantly retarded by fear of the Yankees."[33]

"Still another batch of Yankees . . . ," a weary Eliza Andrews scribbled in her diary.

> One of them proceeded to distinguish himself at once, by "capturing" a negro's watch. They carry out their principles by robbing impartially, without regard to "race, color, or previous condition." 'Ginny Dick has kept his watch and chain hid ever since the bluecoats put forth this act of philanthropy, and . . . old Maum Betsy says that she has "knowed white folks all her life, an' some mighty mean ones, but Yankees is de fust ever she seed mean enough to steal fum niggers."[34]

Not surprisingly, after suffering through several such visits, most plantations and farms had little more to offer. "We were left almost destitute," said one stunned and suddenly impoverished lady.[35] "Our poverty," noted another victim, "is now our protection."[36]

Eventually, the highways of the South began to resemble scenes from antiquity and the plundering hordes of Mongolia. Observed one man:

> The road was filled with an indiscriminate mass of armed men, on horseback and on foot, carts, wagons, cannon and caissons, rolling along in most tumultuous disorder, while to the right and to the left, joining the mass, and detaching from it, singly and in groups, were hundreds going empty-handed and returning laden. Disregarding the lanes and pathways, they broke through fields and enclosures, spreading in every direction that promised plunder or attracted curiosity. Country carts, horses, mules and oxen, followed by negro men, women, and even children, (who were pressed into service to carry the plunder) laden with every conceivable object, were approaching and mingling in the mass from every side. The most whimsical scenes presented themselves, at every step: horses and even gentle oxen, were pulled, pushed, and beaten along towards this seething current, with pigs, sheep, geese, ducks, and chickens swinging from their backs, fluttering, squealing, and quacking, while the burthened animals, in bewildered amazement, were endeavoring to escape from their persecutors.[37]

When the blue tide finally receded and moved off to garrison the cities and towns of the South, it left behind in its wake a land "as silent as a graveyard."[38]

What little the South had not lost in war, it now saw vanish in "peace."

CHAPTER 12

The Road Back

"THE TROOPS ARE COMING HOME," RECORDED A WOMAN IN SOUTH Carolina.

> For four years we have looked forward to this day—the day when the troops would march home. We expected to meet them exulting and victorious. . . . Then we determined, after our independence was acknowledged and the time came for Gen. Lee to disband his army, to go on to Richmond to see the glorious sight, to see the hero take leave of his brave victorious men. The army is disbanded now—oh! Merciful God!—the hot tears rush into my eyes and I cannot write.[1]

The road to peace was a far harder journey than had been the one to war. Hope for victory had been replaced by the hope of simply reaching home alive. Bravado subsided into resignation; steps were slowed by wounds and time and the awful burden of having been vanquished.

For many, as soon as word of surrender came, the journey commenced. "The soldiers began to scatter," recalled a former body servant. "They were a sorry looking bunch of lost sheep. They didn't know where to go."[2]

They didn't know where to go. Truer words were never spoken, especially for those Rebel soldiers released from Northern prison camps, far removed from their homeland. "My first impulse was that I would never go home again," one disheartened young Rebel wrote as he prepared to leave prison.[3] Ironically, a large percentage of soldiers heading home at war's end were coming not from the battlefields of the South, but from the prison camps of the North.

"Their prison gates opened to restore them, not to affluence and gratulation, but to hunger and nakedness," a sympathetic New Yorker observed of prisoners freed from Elmira. "I weighed 140 lbs when I went in this prison," commented a Confederate on the camp at Fort Delaware near Philadelphia, "and weighed only 60 lbs when I came out." Most prisoners, like this man, were turned loose with little on their backs and virtually nothing in either their pockets or their bellies.[4] Consequently, thousands of released Rebels were forced to scout odd jobs in the vicinities of their old prisons in the hope of buying food and earning enough money for transportation home. From New York City, a witness wrote:

> A squad of ragged fellows may be seen on every square. They are sunburnt and scraggy of beard. They wear their dry, straight hair very long. . . . Their clothes are of a dirty gray or a dirtier butternut, and they are very independent in the matter of shoes, some wearing a boot and a slipper. . . . They are here by thousands, broken, hopeless, and penniless, waiting to go to their ruined homes, but so fearful of meeting the changed spectacle that they dally and tarry, and look up to the high marble edifices and the lace curtains in our beautiful homes as if they were quite hungry and astray, and spoke another language than ours.[5]

Released from the prison at Fort Delaware with no transportation nor the means to obtain it, Matthew Jack Davis and his emaciated companions were forced to shift as best they could. For days, the ragged men roamed aimlessly, not knowing where to go or what to do. Although they were able to acquire new garments in Philadelphia, the clothes were ill fitting, far too short and tight. The men looked ridiculous and knew it, and reinforcing this feeling, a crowd of street urchins followed at their heels laughing and jeering. "Our appearance on the street was equal to a circus," Davis admitted.

Once in the countryside, the weary Rebels went from "farm house to farm house in quest of employment but met only with rebuffs, insults and abuse. When we asked for 'bread' they gave us a stone."

Sleeping in the woods, nearly starved, discouraged beyond all hope by their treatment in Pennsylvania, the men finally encountered about twenty discharged Federal soldiers camped for the night. "They hailed us," remembered Davis, "and when they learned who we were they took us in and treated us like brothers, and fed us. Next morning they gave us a haver-sack well filled with crackers and bacon, bade us good-bye and started us on our journey with a better opinion of our fellow man than we had entertained in some time."[6]

J. T. Bowden, a thousand miles from his home in Texas, penniless, knowing no one, was informed by a Federal officer that there was no transportation available for paroled Rebel prisoners.

"I'll be damn if that is right," another Yankee exclaimed upon learning of the situation. Sharing his rations, as well as his tent, the Northerner even took the Confederate on board the train contracted to carry his regiment. The conductor had a few words with the soldier, explaining that the train was designated to carry Federals and Federals alone. Staring the man into shame, the angry Yankee threatened to leave the car if his friend could not ride. The conductor at last relented.

When their journey together had gone as far as it could, the good-hearted Northerner offered to loan the grateful Southerner enough money to finish his trip.[7]

Unlike the soldier above, William Baldridge was provided a train trip home following his release from Johnson's Island Prison Camp—but no food for the four-day journey. "By the kindness of citizens of Sandusky, Ohio, we were given about two days rations," the thankful soldier wrote.[8]

Unfortunately, some Confederate soldiers stranded in the North would never make the journey home. Languishing in one Northern prison camp, John Jones composed a song for the comfort of his family in the mountains of Virginia—a hopeful lament:

> It may soon be this war will end
> and prisoners all set free
> And volunteers returning home
> O shout for victory.[9]

But the war's end did not bring victory or the sergeant to his home. He died in prison one month after Appomattox.

> If im called home while I am gon
> Shed not a tear for me
> But tell to all my friends around
> I died for liberty.

Another soldier, Jesse Edwards, visited home more than most men during the war. Since his family lived in southwestern Virginia, it enabled the father and husband to keep a closer watch on the business and affairs of the farm. And even in the interim, Jesse had often written to his wife, Betty, directing her in the details—little things, mostly, like putting hay over seed potatoes so they would keep through the winter. While he was yet ill,

John Jones
RANDY LEONARD COLLECTION

Edwards was captured in the last days of the war and confined at a hospital attached to Fort Monroe. In his last letter to Betty, who was pregnant and tending several small children, Edwards spoke of his plans:

> My Dear Wife,
> I am very low but I have put down my name for to start home in the morning and if I die on the way I prefer making the start to staying here any longer. . . . If I die on the way to Richmond and was buried in the beautiful James River don't you greave about that. My boddy would sleep as peacible as if laid in the family graveyard.

The letter remained unfinished and unsigned. Three days later the chaplain wrote to Betty, informing her that Jesse had died. "He was well cared for," expressed the minister, "neatly laid out and interred in this Hospital burying ground with Christian ceremony and proper honors. . . . A lock of his hair was reserved, which you will find enclosed."[10]

Like thousands across the land, Jesse Edwards's baby girl was born a few weeks later, with her father cold and in the grave.

Many soldiers, like Edwards, remained in hospitals, too sick for the journey home. In late April 1865, a bedridden Nicholas Wesley Miller wrote to his father in Georgia. Hospitalized at Petersburg, the young captain's leg had been amputated just above the knee:

> My leg sloughed off a little soon after it was amputated which threw me back some. I have suffered a great deal and still suffer some nearly all the time. I get very good attention and am attended to by our own Surgeons who staid here with the wounded. The ladies are also very kind to bring us everything they think we want to eat.[11]

The next day, in a much weaker hand, Miller wrote the last lines of his letter: "I hope it is the Good Lord's will that I will soon be well enough to get home and see you all again."[12]

Because of his winning ways and sensitive nature, Miller had become a favorite not only with the local women, but with even the Northern nurses. On June 5, 1865, a volunteer at the hospital felt compelled to write to Miller's wife, offering whatever small comfort she could to the now-widowed woman . . . and also to ease the pain she felt herself:

> His thoughts would wander to her, he so dearly loved, yet who was so far distant, in this hour of trial and suffering; he often spoke of you in the tenderest manner, and almost the first thing he did, when I found him in the hospital was to show me your likeness, which was lying by his side. . . . "Tell her I love her dearly, she has been a good wife to me—and she must meet me in heaven." This was the last conversation I had with him, but oh! Is it not rich in comfort and hope to you—for myself it was a privilege to sit by his side, and rate the gradual departure of a spirit so full of holy assurance and love. . . . I am, dear Mrs. Miller,
>
> Your Stranger-friend[13]

For those who were capable of making their way to the rails and rivers, the sometimes long, sometimes dangerous, but always uncomfortable journey home truly began. In their efforts to move men as quickly as possible, neither comfort nor safety were priorities of the victors. A recently released Rebel watched his comrades "being packed on a vessel . . . like . . . sardines in a box." They had been "buffeted about on boats and stock cars ever since they had left prison," related the soldier, "fed just often enough to keep them alive, and fed too like hogs."[14] Given the conditions, accidents were bound to happen.

Though no disaster compared with the sinking of the *Sultana,* in which as many as eighteen hundred released Yankee prisoners were lost, Confederates had smaller, more frequent tragedies. One such incident involved the *Kentucky.*

"The Kentucky was a very old boat," wrote a correspondent, "and I understood she was leaking at the time the troops (nine hundred in number) were loaded aboard her, and that she had been condemned several times as unfit for use any longer."

On the evening of June 9, while navigating the Red River in Louisiana, the *Kentucky* struck a bank and soon sank. "For some reason yet to be explained," wrote a Memphis editor, "the soldiers were permitted to remain asleep, in fancied security, while the boat had thus filled with water and was sinking; and thus nearly all of them were carried under with the boat."[15]

"Such was the confusion and terror, occurring as this did in the night, and while the men were asleep, that when they emerged from their dreams they thought of nothing but self preservation," said a witness. Though this was true in the main, there were accounts of heroism. Many soldiers "exerted themselves to save the ladies."[16] Braving the dark water, another man succeeded in rescuing a child who had been swept away by the swift current.[17]

As many as two hundred paroled Rebel soldiers died during the disaster. Survivors argued angrily that the entire affair was the result of "criminal indifference."[18]

The rivers were no more perilous than the rails. In Virginia, the railroad was so devastated that it took five days to travel from Richmond to Lynchburg, a distance that might easily have been walked in the same time.[19] One soldier considered himself lucky to have survived a train crash that killed several men. Another returning Rebel swore that the Yankees had intentionally tried to wreck the train he was on. There were numerous other mishaps.[20]

Women who were waiting at home, like Anne Frobel, were heartsick and horror-struck by the accounts of accidents they saw in the papers.

> I cannot under stand how it is that so many Confederate prisoners being sent home are lost. In every paper we see now there is some terrible account of disaster to Confederates[.] At one place a boat was snagged and two, or three, hundred drowned. Then a train ran off the track, and a great number killed[.] The last

> account was of a boat load, between Ft Lookout and Savanna being scalded to death by the steams being turned on them (accidentally, of course)[.][21]

Anne's concerns were not without foundation. I. G. Bradwell and his weary comrades, hoping to catch a train in Danville, Virginia, were disappointed and forced to wait indefinitely for transportation. The men took advantage of the delay to rest, recuperate, and cook rations for the remainder of their trip. Filling a wash pot with water, throwing in some peas and a shoulder of salty ham, the ravenous group then began the agonizing wait for their meal to cook. Made impatient by the aroma, some could not sit still and wandered over to the nearby arsenal to scavenge powder and lead. A short time later, as Bradwell and his friends sat around the campfire, they felt the ground beneath them quake.

"We were startled by a tremendous explosion that shook the entire town," recalled the soldier, "and pieces of shell began to drop about us and everywhere in the city. Soon we saw men running with stretchers toward the scene, bringing mangled boys and soldiers away." Somehow a spark had ignited gunpowder in the arsenal, blowing to bits not only the building, but the crowd of people inside.

"How many of our brave soldiers perished in this unfortunate catastrophe," Bradwell said sadly, "no one will ever know."[22]

Continuing his journey—put on, then off more rundown trains than he cared to count—Bradwell was again loaded onto one of those "old ramshackle cars that had done duty during the whole war without repair."

"We were packed in them and on top . . . ," he recalled. "When we reached Blackstock Station, in South Carolina, in the darkness our engine ran into a freight car standing on the track, and the top of the one on which I was riding broke in, dumping us down on our companions sleeping below."

"We now decided," Bradwell said, "to abandon the railroad."[23]

"The hardships of railway travelling . . . have not been exaggerated," another man complained. "Rails worn out, shaky, creaking trestle-works, the slow, thumping motion, the frequent transfers from dirty cars . . . the long delays."[24]

Four other men were compelled to wait a month for the railroad to be repaired from Atlanta to Chattanooga. "We were all crippled," explained one soldier, "and disabled by wounds received in the service."[25]

Crippled men waiting for crippled trains—such was the South following the war. No matter what their condition or circumstances, however, the one thing every man carried back with him was a sense of defeat.

On his way home, one former Rebel prisoner, Matthew Jack Davis, paused just long enough in Washington to witness the Grand Review. What he saw in the city must have stirred more emotions than he had words to express. Near starvation, his clothes tattered, dreading what he might find when he reached home, and above all, humiliated by defeat, Davis gazed upon the conquering blue host as they made their coveted victory parade through the flower-strewn streets of the capital. For two days, amid a roar of cheers and a sea of waving handkerchiefs, the columns of the victors appeared to go on and on forever. But what left an indelible impression upon the young man was not the shiny weapons of his former foe, or their bold blue uniforms, or even their numbers. Instead, what was most impressive to Davis was the spring in their step, the strength in their arms, and the incredible air of health and vitality surrounding them. Contrasted with his own weak and pitiful self, nothing could have brought home more the inevitability of defeat to this young man than this display of confidence and might. There could have been no other outcome—the South had lost because it could not win.[26]

CHAPTER 13

Glorious in the Dust

THEY TRAVELED BY ONES AND TWOS BECAUSE IT WAS EASIER TO BEG FOOD, and by tens and twenties because of outlaws and Yankee raiding parties. In every conceivable condition, men struggled to reach their homes.

Hundreds hobbled home on crutches. "I walked on my crutches from Vicksburg, Miss., to Mount Prairie, Tex."[1]

Pathetically, a few men staggered back alone. "I walked two hundred miles, having a wound in the abdomen. I came near dying having contracted gangreen."[2]

Others were carried by comrades. A Louisiana regiment chose to march homeward in formation, caring for and feeding its members as it went, then dropping them off one by one as they reached their homes.[3]

The farther men traveled from Appomattox, the more hostile it seemed the environment became. In New Orleans for processing, one Rebel recounted, "we passed through a rough crowd of soldiers, most of whom seemed to [be] foreigners. One big fellow said, 'The last damned one of them ought to be hanged.'"[4] Elsewhere, men who had been allowed to keep their sidearms and horses had them taken by occupying troops.

Such was the case when one group arrived in Strawberry Plain, Tennessee. "We met [an officer] . . . of the Union Army. He demanded our horses," recalled an irate veteran. "We took our sidearms to pieces and threw them in the river. Stampeded our horses and came home on train."[5]

Another man who lost his mount at Strawberry Plain recalled that he and his comrades were put into boxcars and taken to Knoxville, where they were ordered off and "marched thro the street." Shortly, the humiliated

Rebels were put back on those same boxcars for the remainder of their journey. Just as unlucky was John Barron, who started for home riding in a wagon drawn by a team of mules. The animals were taken by Yankee soldiers along the way, forcing Barron to reluctantly leave his coveted vehicle and walk.

"A Wisconsin man took my jacket from me, a Rhode Island man took my cap," Thomas Perkins noted matter-of-factly concerning his walk home.[6] And so, little by little, many were despoiled of their pathetic possessions.

A South Carolina soldier's only valuables at war's end were a blanket and a dinner plate. By comparison, at least one Texas soldier was lucky. "After two years of the war, I returned home with a ten dollar bill [and] two enfield rifles." The Texan's luck did not hold, however, for the money was Confederate, and his two weapons were soon confiscated.[7]

Some returning Rebels traveled more naked than not, with string, twine, even thorns holding together bits and pieces of their garments. "One soldier's clothing was so bad that it wasn't decent," commented a sympathetic woman. "A comrade gave him a silver dime and they had the great luck to get a half worn pair of jeans pants at a small farmhouse in the piney woods. Those pants the soldier wore home."[8]

An Alabama woman cited another account of the challenges of staying clad:

> A brother-in-law of mine, who became bare as to pants . . . had recourse to his army blanket, and having no scissors with which to cut the blanket he used his pocket knife for that purpose. He sharpened a stick with his knife to make holes in each half of the blanket, which he tied up separately with the raveling of the blanket; making each leg of the pants separately. They were tied around his waist with a string.[9]

Marching home through Texas, a soldier recounted another incident:

> In passing a house while the inmates were at dinner, notice was made of one of our boys that was passing by, barefooted; the man of the house asked a few questions of some one of the command that was in the rear; when mounting his horse he followed the Company, and halting the barefooted soldier, he takes the shoes off of his own feet and gave them to "Dick," and turning his horse, he rode home shoeless.[10]

There were many such acts of kindness, which assured these troops that their sacrifices had been deeply appreciated. A veteran traveling through Mobile was befriended by an innkeeper. Upon learning that the soldier was sick and penniless after having served four years in the army, the kindly hotel owner opened his heart.

> "You shall have two instead of one servant to attend you."
>
> "But I have no money," urged the veteran.
>
> "Then . . . you shall have wine for dinner and I will loan you enough to take you home.
>
> The soldier stared at the landlord and in speechless amazement and gratitude turned his face to the wall.[11]

Although painful to some and an embarrassment to others, for a few of those Rebel soldiers traveling home, the journey provided many of the most unforgettable experiences of the war. Such was the case for William Fletcher, on the road to Texas.

While passing through Alabama, Fletcher and his companion rode up to a house one day and noticed that several rats were roaming over the yard, seemingly oblivious to the presence of humans; some even scampered near an old dog unmolested. The family, which included two teenage daughters, explained that the Yankees had raided and burned a Confederate commissary nearby filled with corn. During the destruction, numerous rats had fled to the farm. Finding the new home much to their liking, the animals continued to multiply until they had devoured almost everything in sight. Not only did they consume much of the grain supply, but the rats had even gobbled down the family's chickens.

"The rats had eaten all but one old cock that . . . had roosted well up in a tall tree and as yet they had not been able to get him," the Texan remembered. "The occupants of the house next to them had a sow with six pigs a few days old and they had all been eaten."

The combination of rats to rid and young ladies to spark inspired the two men to come calling that evening and join the "civil war" on rodents. Although stunned by the number of rats, the soldiers, with the aid of the family, quickly went to work trapping the animals in sacks before killing them. "The rats were not cowed . . . and several times I jumped backward to keep a grinning rat on a barrel or box from jumping on me," noted Fletcher.

As the soldier and a young lady were struggling to secure the end of a writhing sack, a rat escaped from the bag "and was making fast flight up

Image of Defeat U.S. MILITARY HISTORY INSTITUTE, CARLISLE BARRACKS

her clothes. She was up and dancing all kinds of steps," said the Texan, laughing. "She finally got rid of the rat and quieted down."[12]

Conceding defeat in their efforts to eliminate all the rats, Fletcher and his companion continued their journey until they reached Mississippi and a family interested in horse trading. After business was transacted, the soldiers were wined and dined until a late hour. "The past and future was no part of our rejoicing—it was the present and we made each minute count," Fletcher reminisced fondly. "We hugged, danced, sang and halloaed to our soul's content."[13]

Returning soldiers were not always met with such hospitality by their countrymen. On his way home to South Carolina, Sgt. William McClinton and his comrades sought shelter one evening from an approaching storm. When the soldiers asked a farmer for permission to sleep in his barn, the "surly landlord" pointed instead to a miserable, rundown shed. Disheartened as they were, the bone-weary travelers nevertheless gladly accepted and were soon sound asleep. During the night, the storm struck and high winds shook the frail shed. When one fierce blast dislodged a beam, it crashed down onto the chest of the sleeping sergeant, crushing and killing him instantly.[14]

If not excusable, the reluctance of some civilians to take in this wretched assortment of soldiers is nonetheless understandable. Four years of war and want had ravaged these men. The "poor, ragged, starved, and dirty remnants" of the army gravitated to town squares across the South to ask for water, beg a bite to eat, and above all, to rest before pushing on. And the picture was always the same:

> The sidewalk along there is alive with vermin, and some people say they have seen lice crawling along on the walls of the houses . . . at the spring in our grove . . . lice have been seen crawling in the grass, so that we were afraid to walk there . . . Poor fellows. . . . These men were, most of them, born gentlemen, and there could be no more pitiful evidence of the hardships they have suffered than the lack of means to free themselves from these disgusting creatures.[15]

The only way to rid oneself of the lice, discovered a soldier, was to rid oneself of one's clothes. Upon getting a new suit and a bar of soap, the dirty soldier took his old rags and "cast them with all the living things they contained into the Savannah River to float on and out to the Atlantic Ocean."[16]

The closer men got to home, the more self-conscious many became of their condition. Wounds, dirt, disease, rags—the visible signs of defeat could plainly be seen by all. Inside most soldiers, however, a struggle vastly more painful was being waged. Wrestling with their own thoughts, some attempted to understand what they had been through while others tried to deal with their disgrace and how they would be received at home.

"I am . . . upon the soil of Alabama. But how different are the circumstances . . . under which I expected to return to my native state," said Edward Crenshaw sadly. "It is very humiliating."[17]

"And so the war is over . . . ," a soldier from Mississippi reflected. "As a people, we have failed."[18]

John Russell Dance, paroled with Nathan Bedford Forrest's troops, felt that same sense of shame. "I did not want to go home," he said, "felt like I never wanted my people to see me. We had failed and laid down our arms."[19]

"I'll be damned if I ever love a country again," vowed another veteran.[20]

Just as many soldiers had helped one another cope with the humiliation of defeat, so too did most men continue to depend upon one another even in the journey home. Bonds stronger than blood had been formed in the furnace of strife and the cold mud of adversity. Thus, after years of comradeship, their partings, perhaps forever, were the saddest leg of the journey. Wrote Frank Mixson:

> The nearer we reached this fork of the road the more serious we would become. We had eaten and slept together for nearly three years—had shared privations together, and in prosperity we divided with each other; and now, we were on the verge of parting, perhaps never to see each other again. . . . At last, we arrived at the parting place, and, by common instinct, we determined to make the parting short. Jim took the bolt of jeans from his shoulders, where he had it slung, told me to pull it out, and then, doubling it in the middle, cut it in two. *This was all.* Without saying a word more, we shook hands and turned off quickly.[21]

Without the support of their fellow soldiers, many were now left alone to face civilians along the way—civilians who had counted on them to win their independence.

"I felt ashamed, but knew not what to say," confessed one soldier after he told two weeping women in Virginia that he was headed home.

> When I looked at the[ir] old horse and buggy, in fact the entire outfit, I thought, in the name of Heaven, what more would you have us do? I could not tell them the cause was lost, but

> said we were going home and when our great commander, Gen. Lee, needed our services, we would rejoin him. They smiled through the tears. "Oh, we knew you would never give up the cause!"[22]

Ironically, the mere fact that the cause had lasted so long against such unequal odds made the sight of these returning soldiers even more precious in the eyes of their friends and loved ones. The men were heroes, and no matter how dirty and diseased and despondent they were, appreciative Southerners saw beyond appearances. Said one young woman sadly but simply, "They have a noble bearing."[23] "Even dirt and rags can be heroic sometimes," another lady reflected.[24]

And thus, wrote Eliza Andrews in her journal, "the shattered remains . . . are beginning to arrive. . . . They looked so weary and ragged and travel stained. Many of them, overcome with fatigue were lying down to rest on the bare ground by the roadside. I felt ashamed of myself for riding when they had to walk."[25]

A woman in Virginia felt similar shame at enjoying any such comfort while these men were so deprived. She rode in a carriage supplied by Northern authorities, and as the vehicle neared the "dusty Confederate soldiers," they stood aside to let it pass. "I was cut to the heart by the spectacle," the lady recalled. "Here was I, accepting the handsome equipage of the invading commander—I, who had done nothing, going on to my comfortable home; while they, poor fellows, who had borne long years of battle and starvation, were mournfully returning on foot, to find, perhaps, no home to shelter them."[26]

"Could you have seen . . . ," wrote another woman to her sister, "it would have wrung your very soul. . . . I felt as if I could lay my head in the dust and *die!*"[27]

"How different from the home coming which they planned when they left us," reflected a South Carolina schoolgirl.[28]

The heartbreaking sight of these soldiers caused many households, like that of Eliza Andrews, to open their nearly empty cupboards:

> It is impossible to refuse anything to the men who have been fighting for us. Even when they don't ask for anything, the poor fellows look so tired and hungry that we feel tempted to give them everything we have. . . . Numbers of them come to our door every day, begging for bread, and it almost makes me cry when a poor fellow sometimes pulls out a piece of rancid bacon from his haversack and offers it in pay. Mother will never take anything from a soldier.[29]

Priscilla Bond
LOUISIANA STATE UNIVERSITY
SPECIAL COLLECTIONS
HILL MEMORIAL LIBRARY

Howard Bond
LOUISIANA STATE UNIVERSITY
SPECIAL COLLECTIONS
HILL MEMORIAL LIBRARY

For loved ones waiting at home, the times were tense. With communication and transportation at a virtual standstill, the waiting became almost unbearable, especially for impatient young couples in love.

"Do not look for me till I come," Sgt. Edwin Fay instructed his worried wife, noting that he had not accepted parole and was in danger of being arrested.[30]

Priscilla Bond was brightened to receive a letter from her husband in May 1865. But with rumors of continued resistance and Howard's own unwillingness to give up the cause, days and weeks passed without any further word. Stung by the unkind remarks of neighbors, the mind of the distracted young woman began to reel, and she wondered if her husband intended to return at all. "My heart is filled with so much troubles about Howard. . . . Everything goes to prove he has deserted me," Priscilla confided to her diary. "O my heart feels at times as though it would break."

With other soldiers arriving and still no word of Howard, she became frantic: "I feel sure he has gone to Mexico. I have suffered a great deal in mind and have nearly been made crazy. . . . I took off my wedding ring today. It almost felt like a snake around my finger. If he has gone to protect his own life at the expense of mine, I say I have no further use for such a man." Snapping shut her diary, the distraught woman thereupon ripped in two her treasured photograph of Howard.[31]

Weeks later, Priscilla received welcome news. Far from fleeing without her like a coward, Howard had been badly burned at the end of the war. He was now fully recovered and would be home soon. With this "blessed news," all her earlier doubts vanished. "I feel as though about 50000 lbs were lifted from my heart," she wrote in relief.[32]

Also weary of waiting for her husband was Myrta Lockett Avary. Unlike Priscilla, however, Myrta decided that if Dan did not arrive home the very next day, she would set off in search of him. Miraculously, he did indeed appear the next day. While handsome to her tear-filled eyes, the returned soldier would have been a spectacle to almost anyone else:

> He wore a pair of threadbare gray trousers patched with blue; they were much too short for him, and there were holes which were not patched at all; he had no socks on, but wore a ragged shoe of one size on one foot, and on the other a boot of another size and ragged too; he had on a blue jacket much too small for him—it was conspicuously too short, and there was a wide margin between where it ended and his trousers began, and he had on a calico shirt that looked like pink peppermint candy. Set

> back on his head was an old hat, shot nearly all to pieces—you could look through the holes, and it had tags hanging around where the brim had been. He was a perfect old ragman except for the very new pink shirt.
>
> "My dear Dan," I said, "what a perfect fright you are! What a dreadful ragtag and bobtail!"[33]

Also tormented by the waiting was Sara Little. Sara had married while her husband was home on leave, and thus their time together had been brief. The young bride became despondent in his absence, lying on the bed and sobbing for hours.

> One Sunday when I was on the bed crying, a little white girl kept by my mother came to my room and looking out of the window up the long avenue toward the road, Carrie said to me, "Mrs. Little, there comes Dr. Little, riding horseback." I thought she was mistaken and I didn't even get up until my mother came in and told me that Carrie had told the truth. Then I was so happy that I couldn't get up. I just cried for joy until he came to me and we took each other in our arms.[34]

So anxious was Jesse Loving to reach his wife and the baby he had never seen that he traveled nearly forty miles the first day. When he finally rode up to the gate and yelled, "Hello," a voice replied, "Who is that?" Playing upon his own name, the husband answered, "your Loving Jesse." Loving described what followed:

> My Black Eyed Ellen came tearing out to this gate like a cyclone, and after the Hugging and Kissing Bee was over we unsaddled Black Charlie, and staked him on the Bermuda Grass in the yard. We then entered the Home, and the first thing on the Program I was introduced to Master William Wilshire Bomar Loving. This youngster was Five months and eleven days old.[35]

Fearful of retaliation and perhaps prison, E. Porter Alexander had obtained the necessary documents to emigrate to Brazil. When the general learned that he had a baby only weeks old, however, he could not reach his wife fast enough. "She knew the rush of my feet up the stairs the moment she heard it," recalled Alexander, "and as I opened the door she was in the middle of the room advancing to meet me."[36]

When young Milton Ryan reached Hickory, Mississippi, after a long trip from a Northern prison camp, his tired, weakened legs took new life: "I struck a trot for home, a distance of twelve miles. In two hours I was in the arms of my dear mother." William Bevens of Jacksonport, Arkansas, was another grateful son. "Mother would look at me for hours and could not talk for joy," remembered the young Rebel. "Her dear soul was never happier than now with her dear soldier boy safe at home."[37]

"Oh! how glad I am to get home once more," exclaimed another man after a journey filled with sickness and danger. "Thank God for this great blessing. May I prove a better and more zealous laborer in His vineyard than I ever have before."[38]

For some, however, the anticipation of reaching home was tempered by the dread of what they would find. Said Frank Mixson, "We had been passing the burnt houses, done by Sherman in his march and we did not know what we might find at our homes."[39]

After an eventful journey of hundreds of miles, William Fletcher finally arrived at his home in Beaumont, Texas, to find that his brother and stepmother had died of yellow fever.[40] Another veteran arrived the day after his youngest sister was buried, knowing nothing of her death until his homecoming.[41] Yet another soldier found his father on his deathbed and unconscious. "When told that 'Willie' had come home," reminisced the son fondly, "he opened his eyes and his arms and held me in a long embrace, and was never conscious again."[42]

And for many others returning home, there was awful anxiety of what they would *not* find. Upon reaching home at twilight and observing the lamplight's glow of his home, D. J. Cater's happy thoughts were also tempered with sadness:

> I cannot tell of my own feelings as I dismounted at the gate and heard the "faithful" watch dog's bay deep mouth welcome. I knew welcome awaited me, not as a returning prodigal, but as the only one left of the three this home had furnished as soldiers to the Confederate States Army. I knew there would be joy, but with that joy would be sadness because my presence would bring recollections of those who did not return.[43]

"My brothers have all been killed and relatives not a few," lamented an Arkansas soldier. "Fathers, husbands and sons all—all gone." So many families were torn asunder by the war, and so great were the dislocations, that for weeks and months, thousands were in motion throughout the South searching for lost loved ones. One Mississippi newspaper requested help for a frantic veteran searching the Southland for his seven-year-old daughter, orphaned when her mother died unannounced in Louisville, Kentucky.[44]

When her boys failed to return with the rest, another desperate parent ran a classified ad: "Mrs. Mary Arthur wishes to know the fate of her sons. . . . Any information . . . will be joyfully received by a disconsolate mother."[45]

A woman in Delaware wrote to an acquaintance in Virginia, hoping for word of her husband. "My last news of him was a letter dated March 20th at Richmond, when he was not yet released from parole. . . . Any information," pleaded the desperate wife, "will be thankfully received."[46]

Another man succeeded in tracing his missing brother, but discovered to his grief that he had fallen in the last month of the war. Traveling to the battleground near Selma, Alabama, in hopes of bringing his brother's body home for burial, the man soon realized he could not afford to ship a coffin. "He put the bones in his large traveling bag," said a shocked observer, and thus carried them home.[47]

For Jacob Hildebrand, religious beliefs had made his son's decision to join the Confederate army doubly painful. Learning that his boy was sick and injured at war's end, Hildebrand set out to bring his child back and care for him at home. When the old man arrived at the army camp, he found, to his agony, that his son had been buried two weeks earlier, without benefit of coffin.

"I took him up & made one for him," the grief-stricken father wrote in his journal. "We buryed him in the Graveyard at the Mennonite Church. . . . Oh my son how I miss you—May God in his mercy grant us Grace that we may meet you in Heaven where there will be no more war & blood shed."[48]

Although the experiences of those at home and those arriving varied greatly, some scenes, similar to the following, were repeated again and again in countless towns throughout the defeated South:

> A single horseman turned slowly into deserted Franklin Street. Making no effort to urge his jaded beast, travel-stained and weary himself, he let the reins fall from his hands and his head droop upon his chest. It was some time before any one noticed that he wore the beloved gray. . . . Like electricity the knowledge ran from house to house. . . . Windows, doorsteps and curbstones became alive . . . each woman had known him from childhood. . . . Each longed to ask for husband, son, or brother; but all held back as they saw the dropped head, and felt his sorrow too deep to be disturbed.

At last, one fair wife, surrounded by her young children, stepped into the road and spoke. The ice was broken. The soldier was surrounded; fair faces quivering with suspense looked up to his, as soft voices begged for news of—"somebody's darling;" and tender hands even patted the starved beast that had borne the hero home! The broad chest heaved as [if] it would burst, a great sob shook the stalwart frame, and a huge teardrop rolled down the cheek. . . . And then the sturdy soldier—conquering his emotion but with no shame for it—told all he could and lightened many a heavy heart. And up to his own door they walked by his side, bareheaded and in the roadway, and then they left him alone to be folded in the embrace of the mother to whom he still was "glorious in the dust."[49]

CHAPTER 14

The Year of Jubilo

FOR MANY REBEL SOLDIERS, A BITTERSWEET DUTY AWAITED THEM ON their return home. Remembered former slave Andrew Goodman:

> When Marse Bob came home, he sent for all the slaves. He was sitting in a yard chair, all tuckered out, and shook hands all around, and said he was glad to see us. Then he said, "I've got something to tell you. You are just as free as I am. You don't belong to nobody but yourselves. We went to war and fought, and the Yankees done whipped us, and they say the niggers are free. You can go where you want to go, or you can stay here just as you like." He couldn't help but cry.
>
> The niggers . . . didn't know much what Marse Bob meant. They were sorry about freedom because they didn't know where to go and they had always depended on old Marse to look after them.[1]

"The niggers bellered and cried and didn't want to leave Massa," reminisced former bondsman John Sneed of Texas. "He talked to us and said as long as he lived, we'd be cared for."[2]

Another slave recalled her master coming into the yard with his hands clasped behind him, his head lowered, asking the people to gather round him. There were tears in his eyes. "I love every one of you," he finally said. "You've been faithful, but I have to give you up. I hate to do it, not because I don't want to free you but because I don't want to lose you all."[3]

This devotion to slaves was not uncommon. Returning Rebel soldiers were grateful for the loyalty shown them and their families during the war, and in turn felt obliged to care for their former bondsmen. "We left our homes and our helpless ones in the keeping of the Africans of our households, without any hesitation whatever. We knew these faithful and affectionate people too well to fear that they would abuse such a trust," George Cary Eggleston explained.

> They might have been insolent, insubordinate, and idle, if they had chosen. They might have gained their freedom by asserting it. They might have overturned the social and political fabric at any time, and they knew all this too. They were intelligent enough to know that there was no power on the plantations capable of resisting any move they might choose to make.[4]

Martin Jackson and his father were just such trusted servants. Both had gone to war with their master. And although, like many blacks, they secretly prayed for the North to win, they did not want to see white Southerners destroyed in the process. Martin's father often reminded him "that the war wasn't going to last forever, but that our forever was going to be spent living among Southerners, after they got licked."[5]

Not surprisingly, many newly freed slaves were at first confused by their sudden status. Many were uncertain about "this land called 'freedom.'"

"We was afraid to move," explained a former bondsman. "Just like terrapins or turtles after emancipation. Just stuck our heads out to see how the land lay."[6]

At least one former slave advised his friends to stay put: "Stay wid your massa and work, he'll feed you and clode you, but you come to town and gits your freedom, 'tis like Confederate money, de more you hab, de wuss it is."[7]

A man traveling through the South noted that generally the house servants stayed and the field hands left.[8] Whether it was the closer bonds of family or their more comfortable circumstances, those who had served inside homes did tend to remain. "Our negroes have acted so well through all these troublous times that I feel more attached to them than ever," Eliza Andrews admitted. "I had a long talk with mammy on the subject to-day, and she says none of our house servants ever had a thought of quitting us."[9]

Mandy Hadnot and her mother "paid no attention" to freedom, staying and working as usual. When Mandy's mother died shortly thereafter, her worried mistress quickly became a surrogate, caring for the young woman after she was badly burned in a fire. The old lady, said Mandy, "read the Bible and prayed for me to get healed up and not suffer. She cried right along with me when I cried, cause I hurt so."

When the black girl decided to marry, her mistress planned the affair:

Those Who Stayed

UNIVERSITY OF NORTH CAROLINA LIBRARY, CHAPEL HILL

We married right in the parlor of the master's house. The white man preacher married us, and mistress gave me away. Old mistress helped me make my wedding dress out of white cotton. I had pretty, long black hair and a veil with a ribbon around the front. The wedding feast was strawberry ice cream and yellow cake. Old mistress gave me my bedstead, one of her prettiest ones, and the set of dishes and glasses we ate the wedding dinner out of. My husband gave me the traveling dress, but I never used that dress for three weeks, though, cause old mistress cried so when I had to leave that I stayed for three weeks after I married. She was all alone in the big house, and I think it broke her heart.

The bonds forged between these two women would not be broken by distance. Mandy had lived away only a short time when the old woman summoned her back to the home:

> I went to see her and took her a peach pie, cause I loved her, and I knew that's what she liked better than anything. She was sick, and she said, "Mandy, this is the last time we're going to see each other, cause I ain't going to get well. You be a good girl and try to get through the world that way." Then she asked me to say the Lord's prayer with her just like she always made me say it for a night prayer when I was a little gal. I never saw her no more.[10]

Other former slaves shared similar experiences—freedom didn't make much difference. John McCoy's master told him, "John, you can go out in the field if you want to, or you can get out if you want to, cause the government says you are free. If you want to work I'll feed you and give you clothes but can't give you any money. I haven't got any." Replied McCoy, "I didn't know what money was anyhow, but I knew I'd get plenty of victuals, so I stayed."[11]

Other blacks, sure of their important role in the everyday scheme of things, also chose to ignore freedom. After accompanying her master and mistress to announce to the other slaves that they were free, one woman said under her breath, "Thank Gawd ahse a mammy an' don't hab to be free." When her mistress insisted she was indeed free, the woman was adamant:

> "Naw, ma'am!" was the emphatic denial. "Ah jes nachelly don't wanna be one uf dem on-de-loose cullud folks. Ah belongs to quality an' cain't nobody put me out in de streets. NOBODY!" Her head violently bobbed up and down in emphasis, and her eyes peered sternly at her mistress and master. "You heah dat, Marse Williams? NOBODY! An' dat's a FAC'!"[12]

Like this woman, others who served as mammies often held powerful, and usually beloved, places in many Southern homes. "Mammy," one little white girl gushed, "you ain't black, you'se chocolate and I love chocolate best of all."[13]

And like their domestic counterparts, even some field hands clung to their old homes—a few for sentiment's sake, others for purely pragmatic reasons. One Texas planter begged his slaves to linger "till we get the crops laid by." A freedwoman recalled that the men "talked it over a-twixt themselves" and decided to hold. "They said we might as well stay there as go somewhere else, and we had no money and no place to go."[14]

For those hands willing to stay put, many homes ravaged by war would not support them. One planter, who had lost not only his fortune but his three sons to the war, also lost his will to go on. As the home and crops began crumbling, former slaves, one by one, just left. The last to leave recounted the poignant picture:

> The last time I seed the home plantation I was a standing on a hill. I looked back on it for the last time through a patch of scrub pines, and it looked so lonely. There wa'n't but one person in sight, the massa. He was a-setting in a wicker chair in the yard looking out over a small field of cotton and corn. There was four crosses in the graveyard in the side lawn where he was a-setting. The fourth one was his wife.[15]

But for everyone who wanted to stay, there was another more than willing to leave. Many blacks were caught up in the frenzy for freedom and wanted to celebrate, to move, to *feel* free.

"Many who are well treated, & much better off than they can be by their own exertions, are going away," noted one diarist. "They all want to go to the cities. . . . The fields have no attraction."[16]

"Some of them came up with tears in their eyes to shake hands with me and say good-bye," remembered one Virginia planter:

> "Sorry to lef' you, massa; good-bye, massa!"
>
> "But why do you go, Toby . . . what makes you leave?" I said.
>
> "Oh, sah, we 'bleege to go, sah."
>
> "Well, what is it obliges you? Do you expect to find a better place than this? Haven't you always been well treated here?"
>
> "Yes, massa, but we 'bleege to go, massa."
>
> So they went, and I have been working my crops with Negroes that I have hired, and I suppose somebody else has hired mine.[17]

Grown skeptical by tales told over the years of "Jubilo," others sought proof of their freedom before they left.

"I went down to Augusta to the Freedman's Bureau to see if 'twas true we was free. I reckon there was over a hundred people there," one former slave recalled. "The man got up and stated to the people: 'You all is just as free as I am. You ain't got no mistress and no master. Work when you want.'"[18]

"Everyone was singing. We were all walking on golden clouds," rejoiced freedman Felix Haywood. "Hallelujah! Everybody went wild. We all felt like heroes. . . . We were free. Just like that, we were free."[19]

After hearing the sheriff read the notice of freedom to a crowd in Austin, Texas, June 24, 1865, Amelia Barr rushed home to tell her slave that she was free. Harriet was found sitting quietly in the kitchen looking out the window to the east; freedom, she had been told, would someday come from the east. On the floor playing with empty spools was Harriet's one-year-old daughter. Barr had often observed that the mother seemed indifferent to her baby. Finally, the white woman interrupted the reverie of the black:

> "Harriet . . . you are free, Harriet! From this hour as free as I am. You can stay here, or go; you can work or sleep; you are your own mistress, now, and forever." She stepped forward as I spoke, and was looking at me intently, "Say dem words again, Miss Milly!" she cried, "say dem words again." I repeated what I had told her, making the fact still more emphatic; and as I did so, her sullen black face brightened, she darted to her child, and throwing it shoulder high, shrieked hysterically, "Tamar, you'se free! You'se free, Tamar!" She did not at that supreme moment think of herself. Freedom was for her child; she looked in its face, at its hands, at its feet. It was a new baby to her—a free baby.[20]

Jubilee was in the air. A Negro woman baptized at Huntsville, Alabama, came from the water shouting, "Freed from slavery, freed from sin, bless God and General Grant."[21]

Eda Harper, who had been a slave in Mississippi, remembered the day a white man came to the fields and made the announcement. Upon hearing the news, her mother-in-law dropped her hoe and "danced right up into old master's parlor. She went so fast a bird could of sot on her dress tails. . . . That night she sent and got all the neighbors, and they danced all night long."[22]

Black women colorfully paraded their freedom, noted a spectator, with red silk parasols and "artificial waterfall[s] of fair blonde hair . . . from the most respectable old 'mammy' to the rawest Dinah in the cornfield."[23]

With freedom came great expectations. "We thought we were going to get rich like white folks," said a former bondsman. "We thought we were going to be richer than the white folks, because we were stronger and knew how to work and the white folks didn't."[24]

After generations of talk about freedom and reaching the "promised land," many blacks set off in search of it. Most believed they would find it in a city. "Nearly every family in Aiken has lost some, many all their servants," wrote South Carolinian Henry Ravenel.[25]

A freedman described the desire of fellow blacks to leave the farms and plantations that had been home for generations. "Nobody took our homes," he explained, "but right off, colored folks started on the move. They seemed to want to get closer to freedom, so they knew what it was—like a place or a city."[26]

On a steamboat near Natchez, John Trowbridge encountered many such pilgrims, "ill-clad, starved looking, sleeping on deck in the rain, coiled around the smoke pipe, and covered with ragged bedclothes."[27]

When blacks reached cities they found a new world of wonder and excitement awaiting. No longer restricted by passes or curfews, the freed people came and went as they pleased, entering stores, shops, saloons, and theaters at anytime of the day or night. In their mania for movement, many mistook liberty for license, as a Louisiana editor makes clear:

> They have come . . . as they would come to the promised land, expecting all their wants to be supplied and to be supported in luxurious idleness. . . . They . . . seem to believe that like Selkirk of old, they are monarchs of all they survey, and can act at will, without being held responsible for any misdemeanor. . . . The main complaint of our town people is that these Freedmen . . . are continually going in their private yards, kitchens, dairies, and wash-rooms with perfect impunity, frequently very insulting if even *asked,* not ordered to leave the premises, if they do leave, do it sullenly and abusively.[28]

Although cities provided numerous outlets to satisfy curiosity and exercise liberty, many former slaves quickly discovered that freedom of movement did not necessarily mean freedom from want, worry, and above all, work.

"Lawdy, Cap'n, we aint nebber been what I calls free," explained one confused freedman, Walter Calloway. "'Cose ole marster didn' own us no mo'. . . but iffen dey all lak me day still hafter wuk jes' as hard an some time hab less dan we useter hab."[29]

Echoed Sarah Debro, "I was never hungry till we was free."[30]

Already strained by defeat to feed its own population, no Southern community was prepared for the great black migration to the cities. "There are between 4,000 and 5,000 negroes congregated at Columbus, KY, and they draw their rations regularly from Uncle Sam," reported a Kentucky newspaper.[31] In Tennessee, the situation was even more dire. "There are said to be 16,000 blacks in Memphis," wrote one editor. "12 to 14,000 will be objects of charity this fall and winter, and 1,000s will starve."[32] The Freedman's Bureau in Alabama predicted that 30,000 would perish over the winter in that state alone.[33] In Washington County, Texas, ten thousand freedmen were adrift with nowhere to turn except the government or public charity.[34] In Alabama, an apparent case of cannibalism was reported, in which the partially eaten body of a Negro was found in a wooden box. Rampant starvation among the freedmen was given as the cause.[35]

"I don't know what is to become of the free negroes," mused a Georgia woman. "Every vacant house in town is packed full of them, and in the country they are living in brush arbors in the woods, stealing corn from the fields and killing the planters' stock to feed on. . . . Some of them have no shelter but an old blanket stretched over a pole, or a few boards propped against a fence."[36]

Given the crowded conditions, small pox, cholera, as well as "malignant and loathesome secret diseases," swept through black communities, killing hundreds.[37] Accounts of blacks dying in the streets, their bodies left there to be kicked out of the way while they rotted, appalled both races. "Many were found on the river banks dead in hogsheads where they had gone for shelter," remembered a young girl near Montgomery.[38]

A traveler on his way to Atlanta saw a freedwoman lying dead beside the road, two children standing over her. "I asked what had been the matter with her," the man wrote. "The reply from one of the little girls was, 'She perish to def, sir; but she free dough.'"[38]

"My father was dead . . . ," said former slave Fountain Hughes. "My mother was living but she had three, four other little children, an' she had to put them all to work for to help take care of the others. So we had . . . [it] worse than dogs has got it. . . . My mother hunted places and bound us out for a dollar a month."[40]

"Miss Clarice," sobbed a black mother as she embraced her former mistress, "I wish to goodness dat you'd tek . . . de chillun! Leastways I mek you a present of de chillun. Dey tells me dat's we'se all free, but I can' mek out how I'm guine raise 'em if you don' help me! I reckon you ain' guine refuse me, is you?"[41]

Following accounts such as the above, even some Northerners, including the editor of the *Boston Journal,* acknowledged the failure of freedom as it now existed. "His status as a man capable of labor and needing bread is of more urgency to him than his recognition as a citizen," the *Journal* observed. "In fact, he must be kept alive in order that he may vote. While we are camly [*sic*] discussing political philosophy, he is hastening to his grave; he implores food, we promise him the ballot."[42]

"We have turned . . . loose four million slaves without a hut to shelter them or a cent in their pockets," thundered Thaddeus Stevens on the floor of the U.S. House of Representatives. "The infernal laws of slavery have prevented them from acquiring an education . . . or of managing the ordinary business of life. This Congress is bound to provide for them until they can take care of themselves. If we do not . . . we had better have left them in bondage."[43]

By late 1865, extermination of the black race in America loomed as a distinct possibility in the minds of many and some voiced fears that Negroes would soon disappear from the South.[44] New Yorker Calvin Fay, however, saw total extinction as not only a possibility, but a highly desired goal. Writing from Atlanta to a friend, the architect referred to blacks as the "most troublesome element in our population."

> They are the most worthless, lazy, filthy, thieving set of vagabonds that you can conceive of. They have been turned loose upon us without any idea of making a living for themselves. Their idea of freedom is to have plenty to eat and nothing to do. They flock to the cities, where they get some protection and assistance in stealing from Yankee soldiers. I see nothing ahead for them but extermination.[45]

In the harsh light of freedom, some blacks did look back through rose-tinted glasses to more comfortable times. All wanted freedom, but not at the price of food, shelter, and safety.

> Dere is no sich kindness dese days betwixt de boss and them dat does de work. All de slaves worked pretty hard sometimes but never too hard. They worked wid light and happy hearts, cause they knowed dat marster would take good care of them; give them plenty of good vittles, warm clothes, warm houses to sleep in, when de cold weather come. They sho' had nothin' to worry 'bout.[46]

At Tallahatchie County, Mississippi, one freedman, despairing over his current condition, petitioned the probate court that he might be allowed to sell himself back into slavery.[47] Although few went to such extremes, among thousands there was a longing and looking back to a time when the details of day-to-day life were handled by others.

Freedom: Life Continues KANSAS STATE HISTORICAL SOCIETY, TOPEKA

Typical of those who returned to their plantations was a slave named Lewis. During the euphoria of freedom, Lewis had gone to his former master and explained that even though he had been treated well, he wanted to move away and "feel entirely free and see what I can do by myself." Recalled his former mistress:

> Mr. Clayton said, "Very well, Lewis, that is all right, move when you please; but when you leave, nail up the door of your house and leave it until you want to come back. No one will go into it." . . . The next fall, when Lewis made his appearance, very much dejected[,] Mr. Clayton said, "How are you, Lewis? How are you getting on?"
>
> "Bad, Mars' Henry. I have come to ask ef I cen go into my house again."[48]

Other slaves, equally dismayed by the reality of freedom, also returned. "Mammy came back the other day with tears in her eyes and begged help," wrote Isabel Maury of Richmond to a cousin. "We got her a good home and I'm sure we will never let her want bread when we have it. She told us of hundreds in her condition—and they cannot get work and Southern people haven't got the means to help them.[49]

Not every black who returned home asked to be taken back. Some had other motives. According to John Trowbridge:

> The judge told a story of a free Negro to whom he had often loaned money without security before the war. Recently this Negro had come to him again and asked the old question, "Have you plenty of money, master?"
>
> "Ah, James," said the judge, "I used to have plenty, and I always gave you what you wanted, but you must go to somebody else now, for I haven't a dollar."
>
> "That's what I was thinking," said James. "I haven't come to borrow this time, but to lend." And, taking out a fifty-dollar note, with tears in his eyes he entreated the judge to take it.[50]

Another former slave, sent by his mistress to study music abroad before secession, came back after the war to find the old woman a destitute widow. "He went to work manfully to support her," said a neighbor, "and has eventually been able to give her a home." In New Bern, North Carolina, several prosperous servants returned to pay delinquent taxes on their late masters' properties.[51]

Although blacks who returned arrived in differing conditions, it would be wrong to assume that anyone preferred slavery over freedom.

According to one former slave, John Quincy Adams, who had lived on a farm near Winchester, Virginia:

> Some of our friends ask, "how were you treated in the South[?]" "Well," I would say, "very well in some respects." They say, "well, if I had been in your place I would have stayed there." This is what I would say to them, "the place is vacant yet; you can go and fill it if you want to," and I never saw one who wanted to fill it. I will just say that all of them that want my place in the South can have it, for I do not want it—I had it too long already.[52]

"I have asked over a hundred negroes . . . if they wanted to go back and live with their old masters as slaves, or if they know any negro who did desire to return to that condition," reported Sidney Andrews on his journey across the South, "and I have yet to find the first one who hesitates an instant in answering, 'No.'"[53]

Whites, however, viewed the plight of Negroes as a mitigation of slavery.

"Poor Negroes! I pity them in the delusion & ruin the yankee had forced upon them," a man in Kentucky wrote. "If changing the status of the race be God's will I say Amen—but to my eyes certain ruin awaits the race under the new programme. Many of them remain with their masters. Many return & beg to be taken back as they were before—but the majority are restless—indolent, discontented, seeking constant changes—& not knowing what to do with their freedom."[54]

"The negro is nothing like so free as before," reflected another white man, "except in name."[55]

Freedwoman Patsy Mitchner summed up the plight of blacks before emancipation and after: "Slavery was a bad thing, and freedom, of the kind we got . . . was bad. Two snakes full of poison. . . . Both bit the nigger, and they both was bad."[56]

CHAPTER 15

Swallowing the Dog

> But for the assassination of Mr. Lincoln, I believe that the great majority of the Northern people, and the soldiers unanimously, would have been in favor of a speedy reconstruction on terms that would be the least humiliating.
>
> —Ulysses S. Grant

IT WAS THE MOST DESPISED WORD IN THE SOUTH. A FEW TOOK IT "AS IF IT was nothing more than a Glass of Lemonade."[1] Others refused as if it were arsenic. It forced people to reexamine their priorities: principle or bread? They reconsidered what it meant to give their word of honor. For loyal Confederates, it was likened to "swallowing the dog."

The Oath of Allegiance to the United States became a staple of the Confederate diet. In exchange for the privilege to vote, to transact business, to acquire rations, to perform marriage ceremonies, or even to get married, Rebels were forced to gulp down their pride and utter these words: "I do solemnly swear that I hereby renounce all countenance, support and allegiance to the so-called Confederate States of America."[2]

For a people left crushed and crippled, the requirement of the oath was like pouring salt into an open wound. "I think the exaction of this oath cannot be justified upon any grounds whatever whether as of admonition and warning for the future or as punishment for the past," wrote Henry William Ravenel from South Carolina. "It is simply an arbitrary and tyrannical exercise of power."[3]

The *Western Democrat* in Charlotte summed up the situation for most ex-Confederates: "Those who expect to follow any occupation in the country have no alternative but to take the oath."[4]

Paroled soldiers were denied transportation home unless they took the oath. Discharged at Lynchburg, William Carroll walked to Winchester for his parole and free transportation back again. The Virginian refused to swear allegiance and had to walk home. A Kentucky soldier paroled in South Carolina was informed that he could not leave at all, until the oath was taken. Likewise, in Richmond, "a parole bearing any significance was ignored," wrote an observer, unless its owner took the oath. "Many men . . . were reduced to distress and almost starvation by the refusal of transportation."[5] Even civilians were afraid to travel without taking the oath, knowing they would not "be protected against violence or injustice of any kind."[6]

For many Confederate prisoners, liberty itself hinged on taking the oath. A young man imprisoned in the waning days of war remained so through May because of his refusal to swear allegiance to a country he had been fighting against for years. Understanding his dilemma but frantic to see him, a sister implored the boy to reconsider:

> *Do not again refuse* when the opportunity presents itself. God judge me if I do wrong in writing thus to you. If you have suffered, believe me it has cost your sister no little pain to do that which I would rather have died than done twelve months ago! Let you act as you may, you will ever command the respect of your friends. Your character is too well established to be assailed after four years of strict adherence to duty, should you deem it advisable to bury all hopes and become a good "citizen" of the United States of America. A man of sense ought to yield everything for duty's sake, and "obey the powers that be." Don't imagine that those who love you so dearly will ever blush for your conforming to unavoidable circumstances. Come home, then, my darling, for home needs you as well as you need it.[7]

A man living near Tullahoma, Tennessee, was required to report to headquarters once a month, then sent to Nashville to report daily. "They finally got tired of that, I suppose," recalled the disgusted soldier, "and they sent me to the penitentiary for safe keeping." Finally, after weeks of imprisonment, the man swore the oath and was released, but was still forced to walk over sixty miles home.[8]

Even civilians faced the same dire consequence for their obstinacy. A woman living in Selma recalled that "everybody was required to take the oath (how I hate that word), and every one who refused was imprisoned."[9]

Swallowing the Dog LIBRARY OF CONGRESS

A group of women in Tennessee, who had organized during the war to take clothes, medicine, and provisions to several companies serving from their area, were among those arrested. Guards walked them for hours, through mud over their shoe tops, to an awaiting steamer that transported them to Chattanooga. "They were marched up to the provost marshal's office like a lot of criminals and required to take the oath of allegiance," said a man who knew the ladies.[10]

Some reasoned that being forced to swear to such an oath made it acceptable to break it. One woman admitted that she "would break it as readily as she would take it," without violating her conscience.[11] Skeptical Yankees observed this insincerity. "They [will] take loyalty like gin and sugar," one colonel remarked, "and pass it off just as easy."[12]

An angry George Wise, when faced by the oath, sought the advice of his former commander, General Lee. "I feel that this is submission to an indignity," complained Wise. "If I must continue to swear the same thing over at every street corner, I will seek another country where I can at least preserve my self-respect." Lee responded, according to Wise, sadly and quietly: "Do not leave Virginia. Our country needs her young men now." When young Wise informed his father that he had indeed taken the oath, the former governor of Virginia declared that the son had disgraced his family. Upon learning that General Lee had encouraged his son to do so, the old man quietly retracted his statement.[13]

"I have my pardon in my pocket, and have taken the oath three times," said a man in Albany, Georgia, "but I'll be damned if I a'nt as big a Rebel as I ever was!"[14]

No matter how many times they swallowed the dog, the taste was always foul, and compelling Southerners to swear allegiance over and over required great ingenuity. There was seemingly no end to the inducements Federals contrived to coerce oath taking. In Columbus, Georgia, ladies were initially required to take the oath in order to receive their mail.[15] Elsewhere in Georgia, letters were opened, in order to test the sincerity of Rebels who *had* taken the oath. "This, I am told, is now frequently done . . . so we will have to use great prudence," a woman wrote furtively to family members in Atlanta. "Alas, for our humiliated and degraded condition!" Some Southerners began hiding their diaries from prying eyes, for fear their true feelings would be discovered.[16]

Another man who wearied of taking oath upon oath to every county, state, and Federal entity imaginable, and who worried about his mail being opened, was Moses Evans.

> Painesville, Amelia Co. VA
> United States in North America
> Western Hemisphere, Earth,
> Solar System No ——, Nebula No ——,
> Universe
>
> My dear Sister Mary;
>
> With the above patriotic heading, I suppose that I may safely write somewhat explicitly. As soon as President Johnson has established, at the point of the bayonet, the respective numbers of our solar system and Nebula, I will fill the above blanks with pleasure, and in the true Union spirit.[17]

In the minds of Southerners, it was doubly insulting to exchange the oath for food. "It was most heart-rending," observed Cornelia Spencer, "to see daily crowds of country people, from three score and ten down to the unconscious infant carried in its mother's arms, coming into town to beg for food and shelter, to ask alms from those who had despoiled them."[18] One poorly educated woman in this circumstance went to the local provost and inquired if she could draw rations. The officer asked if she would take the oath. "Thank you, sir," said the lady, "there is my cart—please put it in that."[19]

"Poor soul she thought it something to eat, and she did not miss it far," one man sagely noted upon hearing the story. "It is an article all have now to eat and digest as best they can."[20]

Another naive young woman who applied for rations was asked if she had sworn the oath. "No, indeed, sir," the girl replied emphatically, "I never swore in my life." When told again by the amused agent that, in order to obtain food, she must swear the oath, the reluctant girl acquiesced. "Well, sir," the shy, young woman finally responded as she stared at the ground, "if you will make me do such a horrid, wicked thing[,] GOD-DAMN the Yankees!"[21]

Resolved to take the oath in order to feed her starving family, a mother at Petersburg was relieved when the commanding officer did not require it. Fantasizing about the dinner her family would enjoy, the lady was brought back to reality when a servant returned with the "feast"—musty meal with hairy caterpillars. The rations included fish, as well, but it was so rank and repulsive that the servant buried it rather than take it into the house. The woman's only consolation was the fact that she had not sworn falsely to receive such wretched fare.[22]

Young Emma Le Conte was one of many who declared they would starve before taking the oath, and given the quality of rations in some areas, the decision may not have been a difficult one.[23]

Southerners were forced to swear the oath for spiritual food, as well. Even their God had been supplanted by a cold and distant Northern deity, at whose altar they resentfully laid sacrifices. At Richmond, ministers could not perform wedding ceremonies unless they had taken the oath. And couples could not marry without first swearing allegiance.[24]

Given the situation, working in the ranks of the clergy became a high-risk occupation. Reading of events unfolding in Missouri, Washingtonian William Owner was outraged that five Catholic priests were arrested and thrown into a cell "with two burglars and a nigger ravisher."[25] Again, their only crime was refusing to swear the oath.

At Charleston, Rev. Alexander W. Marshall omitted prayers for the president from his service, an oversight that went unreported for some time. When Brig. Gen. John P. Hatch finally learned of the misdeed, he ordered the minister exiled and his property confiscated. Hatch left no doubt as to his future course should parishioners forget "their duty to their country" by not informing on any "disloyal priest." "They . . . will hereafter be marked persons," announced the general menacingly.[26]

Alfred S. Hartwell, while military commander in Columbia, attended a local church and warned the minister that his building would be boarded up if the prayer for the president was not used. The frightened preacher complied with the order but rushed through the prayer "as if the words choked him," observed a parishioner. "At the end not one Amen was heard."[27]

Like their Catholic counterparts, when Protestant preachers in Missouri failed to pray for Lincoln, they were arrested and their churches closed.[28] None of these threats were new to Rev. Robert Austin. After serving as chaplain with Rebel forces until they were driven from his state, the Missourian returned to his home and ministry. Upon taking the loyalty oath, Austin tried to resume a normal life. But it was not to be. The preacher encountered relentless harassment at every turn. Occupying soldiers not only burned his churches, but placed his life in constant danger as well. War's end changed nothing. Federal troops again torched his church near Parkville—a church they had already desecrated by using as a stable—and forbade Austin from preaching "under any circumstance." When the minister got word that his assassination was imminent, and when the opportunity to escape to Montana presented itself, he did not dally.[29]

In various denominations, the hierarchy took it upon itself to discipline those clergymen in its ranks who had chosen the wrong side. The General

Assembly of the Presbyterian Church met at Pittsburgh and passed a series of resolutions "practically suspending all . . . ministers until they had repented of the sin of rebellion."

"As those in the south, almost to a man was strong supporters of the Confederacy," explained a devout Tennesseean, "this action declared every pulpit vacant and meant that the North had the right to take over our churches with their property."

Resisting this draconian decree, members of the First Presbyterian Church in Nashville refused to seat a clergyman sent from the North. The Northern minister became belligerent and addressed the crowd, "Gentlemen, you seem to forget that the rebellion is crushed and that Nashville is in the hands of the union army."

A member of the congregation stood and retorted, "Mr. Brown, do you mean to threaten us? Is it your aim to use the military force to compel us to accept you as our minister?"

When the military refused to intervene, Reverend Brown returned to the North.[30]

The Synod of the Methodist Church decided to close five hundred houses of worship in Missouri whose pastors had not sworn the oath. Applauding the dismissal of preachers who had instilled treasonous thoughts into their congregations, a St. Louis newspaper wrote, "We were fearful it would require foreclosure on their worthless souls by the veritable Old Nick himself."[31]

Having the oath forced upon them was not the only form of humiliation suffered by former Confederates. Most melancholy to Southerners was the supplanting of their banner with the federal flag. "The saddest moment of my life," recalled Myrta Avary, "was when I saw that Southern Cross dragged down and the Stars and Stripes run up. . . . I saw it torn down from the height where valor had kept it waving for so long and at such cost."[32]

"Never before," added another woman, "had we realized how entirely our hearts had been turned away from what was once our whole country, till we felt the bitterness aroused by the sight of that flag shaking out its red and white folds over us."[33]

A Georgia woman mourned over the loss of the old "liberty pole." Returned Rebel soldiers had cut it down during the night rather than view the Union flag flapping there.[34] At Winston, North Carolina, a thousand spectators reportedly gathered on the courthouse lawn to watch the raising of the Stars and Stripes. Only a couple months later, however, this item appeared in a local newspaper.

> A DISLOYAL ACT—Some evil disposed person or persons . . . cut down the United States flag and carried it off to parts unknown. It was a mean, low, cowardly, disloyal act, and we hope those engaged in the black deed will be ferreted out and brought to justice. . . . An order was issued offering one hundred dollars reward for the apprehension and conviction of the perpetrators.[35]

Throughout the South, many deeply offended widows crossed the street rather than pass under an American flag draped over the sidewalk.[36]

For returning Rebel soldiers, the order to remove or cover CSA buttons from their uniforms seemed to be rubbing their faces in defeat. Just how strictly these rules were enforced depended upon the fiat of each commanding officer. At New Orleans, Gen. Nathaniel Banks was in charge. Confederates believed that the officer from Massachusetts was particularly vindictive in peace because he had "never won a battle" in war and had been derisively tagged "Stonewall Jackson's Commissary." Rebel soldiers in the city were not permitted to congregate in groups of three or more, and black troops were delegated to cut the buttons from their coats. "I saw squads of them dispersing little gatherings of Confederates," recalled a paroled prisoner, "and I saw coats from which the buttons had been cut."[37]

John Worsham and his comrades thought it so foolish and such a petty concern of the U.S. government that they paid the order no mind. The men were shocked when Yankees stopped them in the streets and snipped off their buttons.[38]

In a Savannah hotel, Whitelaw Reid watched as a drunken Union sergeant cut the buttons from "an elegant grey-headed Brigadier who had just come in from Johns[t]on's army." The officer, Reid thought, "bore himself modestly and very handsomely through it."[39]

"The one thing which humiliated and angered father more than anything else," recalled a Richmond boy, "was to be stopped by a Union sentinel at 9th and Green Streets and have the brass buttons cut off his coat and vest. The poor man had no other clothes than his gray uniform."[40]

No soldier was exempt from this order, no matter what his physical state. Observing hospitalized Rebels in Columbia, South Carolina, a lady commented, "It was sad and touching to see these men, when able to be sitting up in the grounds, cutting off the offending button . . . thus toning down the belligerent gray and transforming themselves into peaceful citizens."[41]

Rebels responded to this outrage according to the whims of their nature. "Some of our boys put their discarded buttons in tobacco bags and jingle them whenever a Yank comes within earshot," wrote Eliza Andrews from Georgia. "Some will not replace them at all, but leave their coats flying open to tell the tale of spoliation. The majority, however, submit in dignified silence to the humiliating decree."[42]

At Tazewell, Virginia, James Whitman seemingly displayed his buttons in open defiance of the rule. When hauled before a Federal commander and asked why he had not removed them, Whitman replied that "the buttons were not U.S. or Confederate buttons but the Virginia, *sic semper tyrannis* [thus ever to tyrants] button, private property." Whitman challenged, "If you think under the order they should be cut off, why not do so now."[43]

Though often humiliated and maddened, these men were luckier than comrades elsewhere. In Nashville, laws prohibited hotels and restaurants from serving men in gray. A former Confederate officer, hoping to have his photograph taken one last time in gray, was arrested and imprisoned for donning his uniform on the streets of Hagerstown, Maryland. At Baltimore, Gen. Lew Wallace forbade even students from wearing their traditional color. Gray, said Wallace, was "offensive." An Illinois newspaper even suggested that henceforth only convicted criminals should wear the now infamous color.[44]

Not only were uniforms, buttons and prayers proscribed, but any other outward manifestation of the former Confederacy was forbidden. Those who foolishly expressed their sentiments in public did so at their peril. One drunk in New Orleans who cried "Hurrah for the Southern Confederacy" during Mardi Gras was sentenced to two years at hard labor in the Dry Tortugas.[45]

Thus, one by one, the victors took possession—body and soul—of the vanquished. Forced to swear loyalty to a hated enemy, their private thoughts censored, their public thoughts punished, the symbols of their nationhood outlawed, their religion and prayers policed—there seemed no haven nor sacred ground.

While the men and women of the South were undergoing their own personal humiliation, the greatest indignities were reserved for the symbol of Southern nationhood. Although his shackles had been mercifully removed, the ordeal of America's leading political prisoner continued.

"Found the prisoner very desponding, the failure of his sight troubling him, and his nights almost without sleep. His present treatment was killing him by inches, and he wished shorter work could be made of his torment."[46] So ran a typical report of John Craven, the federal physician assigned to monitor Jefferson Davis.

"Doctor," the former Confederate president asked Craven:

> Had you ever the consciousness of being watched? Of having an eye fixed on you every moment, intently scrutinizing your most minute actions, and the variations of your countenance and posture. . . ? To have a human eye visited on you in every moment of waking, or sleeping, sitting, walking, or lying down, is a refinement of torture on anything the Comanches or Spanish Inquisitors ever dreamed. . . . This is a maddening, incessant torture of the mind, increasing with every moment it is endured. . . . Letting a single drop of water fall on the head every sixty seconds does not hurt at first, but its victim dies of raving agony, it is alleged, if the infliction be continued. The torture of being incessantly watched is, to the mind, what the water-dropping is to the body, but more effective, as the mind is more susceptible to pain. . . . I confess, Doctor, this torture of being watched begins to pray on my reason. The lamp burning in my room all night would seem a torment devised by some one who had intimate knowledge of my habits, my custom having been through life never to sleep except in total darkness.[47]

"I found him very feeble; prematurely old. . . . He is evidently breaking down . . . ," concluded Dr. Craven.[48] "There must be a change . . . or he would go crazy, or blind, or both."[49]

Hundreds of tourists and curiosity seekers were drawn to Fort Monroe hoping to catch a glimpse of its celebrated charge. One of those was Northern correspondent John Trowbridge, who pondered the life of the prisoner within.

"I . . . looked up at the modest window curtains, wondering what his thoughts were, sitting there meditating his fallen fortunes. Did he enjoy his cigar, and read the morning newspaper with interest?"[50]

CHAPTER 16

Such Damned Rebels

THEATER-GOERS IN MOBILE WERE ENJOYING A RESPITE FROM DAILY CONCERNS—a reprieve from the view of ruin and wreckage in the city. Then the orchestra struck up "Yankee Doodle." Former Confederates hissed and booed. Yankee military in the audience applauded. A minor riot ensued, and many left the performance.[1]

Such scenes were the reality of occupation—the clash of two cultures perhaps more distinctively different after the war than before. As the gray began to fade, blue became increasingly common on the thoroughfares of the South. Try as Southerners might to forget, the signs of defeat were everywhere. Even the same trains that bore ragged Rebels home in one car carried nattily dressed Northern troops in another. Hardly begun to heal from the emotional scars the war had wrought on her family, Kate Foster reflected:

> Both of my noble brothers sacrificed upon our country's altar as far as I can see for nothing. God grant that I may some day feel they were taken for some good. How can I ever love the Yankees as brothers when they made these deep and everlasting wounds in my heart. No, as each day rolls around it is my constant thought how much more do I hate our oppressors to-day.[2]

"All our brave Generals, unequaled soldiers, my own gallant Brothers, was it for this that you died?" sobbed Pauline De Caradeuc. "Subjugation! Never!"[3]

But no matter how fervently Southerners railed against defeat, their desires did not change reality. Thus many chose to ignore it, or at least ignore the blue coats among them. While returning Confederates were met with an emotional homecoming, the conquerors were treated with indifference. "The private soldiers seem good-natured enough," observed a Virginian, "but they are a low order of people, much inferior to our men. . . . The officers are a spruce, dapper-looking set."[4] Despite the war's end and reunification, most Southerners continued to view the North as not only a foreign nation, but a nation with different and decidedly inferior values:

> The more I see of the yankee character the more I dispise & abhor them, how totally different from the southern gentlemen in all their actions. They have as a general thing no politeness, no generosity no feelings of delicacy. I have seen ladies enter the street cars and be compelled to stand while the yankee soldiers & citizens remained seated perfectly unconcerned.[5]

The absence of courtesy evinced by Northerners was observed by many Southern women. Eliza Frances Andrews noted that where the street was thronged with returning Rebel soldiers, they stood like a wall on either side to allow her to pass. A little farther on, she encountered Yankees and blacks, "but not one of them budged." She was forced to walk in the road. "It is the first time in my life that I have ever had to give up the sidewalk to a man!" she disdainfully recorded.[6]

One repulsed woman, a lady who considered herself a "pretty good Christian," stated that if Yankees and "white" people (meaning Southerners) were going to be as one in the hereafter, she much preferred to avoid heaven altogether.[7]

Some Southern women avoided walking near Yankees whenever possible. While attending the local university, Emma LeConte hurried past the sentinels at the campus gate, likening her fear to the "horror of passing . . . a very loathsome reptile."[8] Many ladies eschewed the main avenues for fear of encountering the blue-clad oppressors. Eliza Andrews was disgusted, as were many Southerners, to see Yankees "strut about the streets . . . with negro women on their arms."[9] She heard that the Yankees were determined to insult every Southern woman they saw:

> The white Yankees are getting so rude that ladies are afraid to walk on the streets alone. . . . The only thing they allege against us is that we are such damned rebels we take no more notice of them than if they were dogs, and will not even look toward them when they pass—as if we hadn't the right to turn away from sights that hurt our eyes![10]

John Hatch at his new home, Columbia, South Carolina

U.S. MILITARY HISTORY INSTITUTE, CARLISLE BARRACKS

Some Federals came in closer contact with Southerners than others, as in the case of officers who boarded in the homes of affluent families. "Our houses are all occupied," said a South Carolinian, echoing conditions elsewhere.[11] Most of these officers proved respectful of their hosts, but not all. While visiting her South Carolina plantation, one lady found that a Northern officer had taken possession of her home in Columbia. A short time later, he was joined by Gen. John P. Hatch. Upon learning of these events, the woman hurried back to Columbia and petitioned Hatch to vacate her house.

"He treated her insolently," a neighbor remarked. "She spoke her mind rather freely and he threatened to arrest her. He got spiteful and declared she shall not have her house at all."[12]

Near Macon, a plantation owner offered his home to the newly arrived Northern commander, hoping his family and property would be protected. The officer was "very sullen" during his stay but did maintain strict discipline among his troops.[13]

Even those Federals who behaved like gentlemen often found themselves ostracized and were at a loss to understand why. "The officers occupied parts of many houses," said Thomas DeLeon, "but they were made to feel that the other part, occupied by the household, was private still."[14]

"The Yankees are evidently trying to worry us because they are not taken into society," noted Virginian Joseph Waddell. "No disrespect is shown to them, but cold politeness. The officers ride and walk about, decked off in shining coats, and evidently desire to attract the attention of the ladies."[15]

"Great Heavens! What do they expect?" protested Emma LeConte,

> They invade our country, murder our people, desolate our homes, conquer us, subject us to every indignity and humiliation—and then we must offer our hands with pleasant smiles and invite them to our houses, entertain them perhaps with "Southern hospitality"—all because sometimes they act with common decency and humanity! Are they crazy? What do they think we are made of?[16]

Some Southerners, like Emma, expected the worst from occupation and in most cases their expectations were more than fulfilled. Nevertheless, there were exceptions to the rule. In Tyler, Texas, federal soldiers "keep so quiet we forget their presence," remarked a surprised Kate Stone. "We have not seen them though they came a week ago. . . . We all went to church today expecting to be outraged by a sight of the whole Yankee detachment but not a blue coat was in sight."[17] Eliza Frances Andrews of Georgia received an unexpected "piece of politeness from a Yankee." A chain gang of black "vagrants" was sweeping in front of the dusty military headquarters when an officer ordered a halt to allow the ladies to pass. The girl was so astonished by the gentleman's courtesy that she almost lost her breath.[18]

At Danville, Virginia, occupying forces had been so universally benevolent that citizens sent a letter to Washington thanking them for their "uniform good conduct." Ironically, in this, the last capital of the Confederacy, civic leaders paid tribute to their conquerors: "We deeply regret your removal."[19]

There were other instances of kindness. Amelia Barr, whose home sat in the middle of the Federal encampment in Austin, recalled the humanity of a regimental surgeon. "Lilly fell ill with measles," wrote Mrs. Barr, concerning her daughter, "and one after the other the whole family followed her. What we should have done without Dr. Bacon of the Sixth Cavalry at this time, I cannot imagine. He watched over every sick child with a care and tenderness that probably saved their lives."[20]

Despite these chivalrous acts, fraternizing with Yankees was generally frowned upon. Although Southerners accommodated themselves in the day-to-day dealings with Yankees, beyond the necessities there was little socializing. And, for most respectable Southern women at least, a romantic liaison would have been far beyond the realm of possibility. Available men were never in shorter supply, however, and the number of nubile women never greater. A traveler to South Carolina was shocked at seeing "how few young men there are, and how generally the young women are dressed in black."[21]

Given the situation, it is not surprising that the inevitable occurred—albeit reluctantly in some cases. Writing to her brother, one girl describes the marriages of "several furiously rebellious ladies with Federal officers." Four postscripts were then playfully added to the letter, concerning a Union captain who had been boarding with her family:

> P.S.1.—Do you think it would be a violation of my Southern principles to take an occasional ride for my health with the Captain? He has such a nice horse and buggy. You know there can be no possible harm in that.
> P.S.2.—That impertinent fellow actually squeezed my hands as he helped me out of the buggy this evening. We had such a delightful ride. I want you to come home and protect me, Tom, as I don't like to live this way much longer.
> P.S.3.—If ever I should marry a Yankee (but you know my principles too well for that) I would do it merely as the humble instrument to avenge the wrongs of my poor, oppressed country. Little peace should he find by day or night: thorns should be planted in his couch; his dreams should be of Holofernes, and my dry goods bill as long as the internal revenue law.

> P.S.4.—Come home, brother, Tom and take the amnesty oath for two months, or thereabouts. I want to tell you a secret. On due consideration I have come to the determination to make a martyr of myself. Yes, brother Tom, I am going to marry the captain on patriotic principles.[22]

Occupying troops, young and lonely, were also quick to overlook politics for romance. Some used every available avenue to courtship, including personal ads: "A Young, intelligent and well-meaning 'boy in blue,' desires to open a correspondence with some of the fair daughters of Montgomery. All letters strictly confidential."[23]

And this message from a young soldier in Danville: "LAURA—I saw you for the first time yesterday! And I adore you! Dinner time passed unnoticed, breakfast ditto. Say you will be mine!!! Answer through personal and relieve your admiring BLUE COAT."[24]

Had occupation been only confined to such minor matters as socializing or the temporary displacement from homes, it would have been easy enough. Southerners quickly learned, however, that occupation was, indeed, an end to their liberties, especially with respect to property. In Tuscaloosa, the first terrifying night of occupation brought looting and burning and the destruction of the university, including its library with more than thirty thousand volumes. The campus also boasted one of the finest refracting telescopes in the country. Yankees smashed the priceless instrument to pieces. Black children were observed carrying off precious lenses given them by Federal soldiers.[25]

While honorable officers struggled to keep their men in line, many soldiers took advantage of their position to prey upon the defeated. Maj. Gen. George Thomas arrested an entire regiment in Nashville for depredations committed at Stevenson, Alabama.[26] Thievery among occupation troops was rampant, but most citizens were reluctant to take action. When a Yankee captain in Texas ordered his soldiers to tear down the family's cow sheds, Eudora Inez Moore's father reminded him that the war was over and he had no right to disturb private property.

"He [the captain] ordered them to shoot the d——d old rebel," recorded Eudora. More prudent troops arrived in time to intervene, and the old man was spared.[27]

Another man who attempted to defend his property was tried before a military tribunal and sentenced to five years in the penitentiary.[28]

Twenty-one-year-old Pauline De Caradeuc of Aiken, South Carolina, describes an event that became all too common in the occupied South:

> While we were at dinner, two Yankee soldiers walked in and asked father for some brandy, he told them he had none to spare; they insisted, father persisted, until they said they would go down to the wine cellar & look for themselves, Father went with them, they were both armed with muskets & revolvers, and when they found that there was none there, they said they would search the house, father told them that would be an outrage upon his family that he would not allow, and he would resist any such act. When he said that the one behind him struck him over the head with his musket, which being so wholly unexpected, knocked him down, then they fell on him and kicked him and knocked him with their guns until he was insensible, the negroes all ran to his assistance, but they shot at them, and threatened to kill them, if they dared render any aid.

When Pauline attempted to go for help, one of the marauders cocked his pistol and threatened to kill anyone who moved. After stripping the house of liquor and tobacco, the intruders finally left.[29]

In addition to accounts such as this, numerous reports of citizens being "accidentally" shot by troops also spread terror of the enemy in their midst. From Montgomery, this story appeared:

> Mrs. Goodwin, a highly esteemed lady of this city, was shot yesterday under the following circumstances: Mrs. Goodwin, with some other ladies and children, was sitting in the gallery at her residence on the Jackson road, when a squad of colored soldiers fired on a soldier who was galloping up the street, whom they had ordered to halt. The soldier either did not hear or did not obey the order, when three of the colored soldiers fired at him, one of the balls striking Mrs. Goodwin in the left breast, inflicting a dangerous, if not mortal wound.[30]

In Selma, a greater tragedy occurred when a ten-year-old girl was shot by a soldier who thought his gun unloaded.[31] Elsewhere, recklessness and sometimes criminal abuse of weapons placed occupied populations in great peril. The editor of the *Montgomery Daily Mail* complained that drunken soldiers were brawling in the streets each night, shooting up signs, shattering windows, and threatening the lives of citizens. The troops "make night hideous with their pistols and indecent yelling . . . ," wrote the newspaperman, "as they are privileged characters."[32]

Eudora Inez Moore recalled that the Federals in south Texas were especially reckless. "Often we could hear shots rattling through the tree tops around our house, a bullet made a hole in the kitchen window; mother stooped to bring in some wood when a ball whistled over her head and lodged in a shed nearby, my little brother Baxter came very near being shot by one of them."[33]

"It seems that a portion of our soldiers are determined that bloodshed shall not end with the coming of peace," wrote a Louisiana editor, describing the situation in Alexandria:

> If they cannot have the excitement of battles and perilous marches, they will seek it in street brawls, in murder, assassination and robbery. We live in almost a "reign of terror." No man can walk the streets at night without danger to his life. The reports of fire arms are heard throughout the whole night and assaults upon peaceable citizens are of such frequent occurrence that they have nearly ceased to be thought of as outrages. . . . We do not see what good is effected by having our city thronged by drunken men with guns in their hands or pistols in their belts, ready, at the least provocation, and anxious, upon the least pretext, to take the lives of her citizens.[34]

This volatile situation was made even more so by the fact that many of the occupying troops were black. For a majority of Southerners, this was nearly unbearable. To see former slaves in uniform with the power to now harass and arrest was the final insult. "They were the first black troops I ever saw," said Pauline De Caradeuc. "I felt every imaginable emotion upon seeing them, they, who two or three months ago were our respectful slaves, were there as impertinent as possible, pushing & jostling us about." Also, some white officers encouraged their black troops to drive home the fact that the South was a conquered land. "Black heels should stand on white necks," sniffed one officer's wife in Augusta. Given the explosive situation, hostilities were inevitable. In Columbus, Georgia, a veritable battle broke out when black troops knocked whites off the sidewalk. One citizen pulled a pistol and shot a soldier, beginning a bloody free-for-all.[35]

Reports grew more frightening with each tale of black troops preying on helpless populations. From the Federal capital, William Owner wrote:

> All the roads leading into the City are guarded by squads of nigger troops, they stop all persons on horseback or in carriages[.] a nig sergeant is called by the sentry and he emerges from his tent

> or guardhouse at his leisure with a squad of nigs at his heels and proceeds [to examine] the horse or horses to see if they have not been stolen. . . . The nigs meantime indulge in insolent and insulting remarks towards the whites. . . .[36]

A company of black soldiers drove off the family's hogs, Eudora Inez Moore reported from Texas, and when her father tried to stop them, the troops picked up sticks and threatened to "beat his brains out" if he came any closer. The family was forced to hire a guard to protect their property. Complaints against black troops alleged not only mistreatment of whites but harassment of fellow blacks as well. A freedwoman in Norfolk, considered to be a violent and "bitter Rebel" was put to work sweeping streets, more for humiliation than for legitimate punishment.[37]

"We were soon all engaged in a fight," recalled an ex-Confederate after encountering a squad of black soldiers. "I killed one of the negroes in self defense." Fearing his story would not be believed, or matter, the young man fled into the woods and eventually made it to Texas, a thousand miles away.[38]

"On looking out," reported a man from Vicksburg, Mississippi, concerning another incident, "I discovered a negro mob, together with a few infuriated negro soldiers, hurrying along a white prisoner. He moved along without a murmur or resistance, yet the guard continued to strike him over the head with their guns and to thrust him with bayonets."[39]

One of the most horrific encounters between black soldiers and white citizens also occurred near Vicksburg. Just as word of Appomattox was reaching many parts of the beleaguered South, so was the news of the murder of Minerva Cook.

Maj. J. R. Cook and his family lived about seven miles from Vicksburg, not far from the railroad line. Despite numerous murders in their community, the Cooks felt some sense of security. General Grant himself had guaranteed that Hardtimes Plantation would not be subject to further searches or depredations. The family had retired for the evening when a party of twenty-five black soldiers, armed with muskets and carbines, burst into the house. During the confrontation, gunfire erupted and Minerva was struck in the chest. When the major rushed to her aid, he too was shot. Before leaving, the intruders plundered the house and grounds, taking not only valuables, but also every chicken on the farm. Believing his wife dead, the wounded husband fled with one of his children to a brother's home. When help finally arrived at the Cook home, Minerva was found alive, "weltering in her own blood, surrounded by her little children." She was conscious, remembered a neighbor, and clear enough to describe the men who shot her.

The commanding Yankee officer posted a five-hundred-dollar reward for the capture of the culprits. Early that summer, nine black soldiers were hanged for the murder of Mrs. Cook.[40]

While some Northern officers struggled against almost overwhelming odds to maintain order, and others simply turned their backs on the anarchy at their doors, there could be no mistaking the intentions of the Federal government in Washington. Of all the many harsh acts committed by the conqueror against the conquered, nothing said it so well or more clearly illustrated the vindictive mood of the victors than the show trial and legal lynching of Henry Wirz. Long before the Andersonville prison commander was set before a military tribunal, his fate was sealed.

The inhuman wretch . . . the Andersonville savage . . . the most bloodthirsty monster which this or any other age has produced—hundreds of Northern editorials and articles fed the ravenous public a steady diet of truths, half-truths, and outright lies.[41] Not content with merely reporting the already grim facts of death by starvation, abuse, and neglect, excited writers embellished each outrage with hair-raising hyperbole. Even the celebrated poet Walt Whitman joined the national lynch mob:

> There are deeds, crimes, that may be forgiven, but this is not among them. It steeps its perpetrators in the blackest, escapeless, endless damnation. Over fifty thousand have been compelled to die the death of starvation—reader, did you ever try to realize what *starvation* actually is?—in those prisons—and in a land of plenty![42]

Henry Wirz was acccused of conspiring "with others unknown" to commit mass murder, and his trial, according to William Owner, who followed the case closely, was "a mere farce."

> Of all the rascally trials . . . this takes precedence. Every scoundrel that it was certain would swear falsely has been brought before it and his testimony taken as Gospel. Yesterday a rascal . . . gave his evidence that he had seen a man who had seen another [who said] that he saw Wirtz [*sic*] bayonet to the ground prisoners who were crawling on their hands and knees, that he had seen Wirtz shoot prisoners with his own pistol by dozens. To clinch the testimony the Judge Advocate ordered Wirtz to stand up and face the witness. Wirtz made an attempt

> to contradict the rascal but was dragged down on the sofa by the officer of the Guard and not allowed to open his mouth after the first few words.[43]

Despite an abundance of evidence proving that Wirz, far from exacerbating an already desperate prison situation, had on numerous occasions actually tried hard to alleviate it, the Confederate officer was sentenced to death.[44]

On November 6, only four days before his scheduled execution, Wirz addressed an appeal to President Johnson for clemency:

> For six weary months I have been a prisoner. . . . By thousands I am considered a monster of cruelty, a wretch that ought not to pollute the earth any longer. Truly, when I pass in my mind over the testimony given, I sometimes almost doubt my own existence. I doubt that I am the Captain Wirz spoken of. I am inclined to call on the mountains to fall upon and bury me and my shame. But . . . a small but unmistakable voice within me . . . says: "Console thyself, thou knowest thy innocence. . . ." The pangs of death are short, and therefore I humbly pray that you will pass on your sentence without delay. Give me death or liberty. The one I do not fear; the other I crave.

Curiously, but a short time later, several men entered the prisoner's cell. As representatives of "a high Cabinet officer," the men were prepared to offer the condemned man his life—for one small consideration. If Wirz would implicate Jefferson Davis in the Andersonville horror, his sentence would be commuted. Although he longed passionately for life and family, Henry Wirz nevertheless refused. "I would not become a traitor to him or anyone else to save my life," he said.[45]

On the morning of November 10, 1865, Wirz was roused by guards in his cell at the Old Capitol Prison. "As they were leaving the room," wrote a witness, "Wirz turned to the mantel, and with as much nonchalance as if he had been in a bar-room, took up a bottle of whisky, and pouring out a liberal draught, drank it down with apparent relish. Then taking a chew of tobacco, he took his place in the procession."[46]

As the prisoner, his wounded arm in a sling, was marched outside to the gallows, soldiers along the wall jeered and shouted.[47] In the neighboring trees, on rooftops, even above on the nearby Capitol dome, those who had been perched for hours strained for a better view with full expectations of witnessing Wirz die a dog's death. On this score, however, hopes were dashed.

Execution of Henry Wirz U.S. MILITARY HISTORY INSTITUTE, CARLISLE BARRACKS

"He disappointed all those who expected to see him quiver at the brink of death . . . ," wrote a reporter for the *New York Times,* only one of a flock of correspondents scribbling away. "His step was steady, his demeanor calm, his tongue silent. . . . He met his fate with unblanched eye, unmoving feature, and a calm, deliberate prayer for all those whom he has deemed his persecutors."[48]

Standing on the scaffold, a Federal officer read to the condemned the order of execution, then asked if he understood.

"I know what orders are, Major," the victim replied. "And I am being hanged for obeying them."[49]

Continued the *Times* reporter:

> During these few moments shouts could be heard from the soldiers in the tree tops of "Hang Him," "Andersonville," "Remember Andersonville," and others not calculated to increase his calm demeanor, but he paid no attention to them. . . . At thirty minutes past ten, his hands and legs having been pinioned by straps, the noose was adjusted . . . and the doomed

> man shook hands with the priests and officers. At exactly thirty-two minutes past ten, the executioner . . . put his foot upon the fatal spring; the trap fell with a heavy noise, and the Andersonville jailor was dangling in the air. There were a few spasmodic convulsions of the chest, a slight movement of the extremities, and all was over. When it was known in the street that Wirz was hung, the soldiers sent up a loud ringing cheer, just such as I have heard scores of times on the battle-field after a successful charge.[50]

"We believe," said the *St. Louis Press* in a postmortem, "that he was a monster whose breathings were a disgrace to humanity and the sacred and martyred names of departed heroes, starved and tortured to death."[51]

"Wirz may deserve the death punishment," countered a Southern editor, "but not more than scores of brutes for cruelty to Confederate prisoners."[52]

From the Natchez, Mississippi, *Daily Courier:*

> Starving prisoners, keeping their money, keeping them from having their clothing; driving them into the snow and ice unclad, and keeping them there; presided over in ranks, with pistol and bayonet, to keep any one from stamping his feet to keep them from freezing . . . beating them over the head with sticks to drive them from their stoves. . . . All these things have been the habit in Northern Prisons, besides from four to fifteen murders per week, in most of them, just added on.[53]

According to one Alabamian, "All of this here talk about Andersonville atrocities is just darned nonsense. I knowed a heap of fellars what was in *thar* prisons, and they said rats was a luckshury, and a little dog was a big thing. . . . *They* didn't shoot no prisoners, and didn't starve em—Oh! No! They is all christchuns, and we is kanibels."[54]

The execution of Henry Wirz was only one indicator of a growing enmity between the South and North that would soon eclipse the animosity that had existed before and during the war. Eliza Frances Andrews acknowledged that she was not the only moderate whom circumstance had transformed into a zealot. Her brother had become equally resolute. "If they had shown one spark of magnanimity towards us since we gave up the fight," he said, he would have eagerly entered their service the first time the United States entered a foreign war. But after experiencing the vindictive peace, he concluded that now he would fight in the ranks of any army marshaled *against* them.[55] When a Yankee soldier suggested to another Rebel that in a possible war with France, the U.S. would need the South's aid, the response was to the point: "If the Devil was fighting you, I would help him."[56]

"Now we are slaves," wrote one woman as occupation tightened its grip, "slaves to the vilest race that ever disgraced humanity."[57]

Increasingly, for these people and millions more, "peace" revealed itself for what it really was—war by other means.

CHAPTER 17

Death by Peace

ABRAM DAVID REYNOLDS CAME HOME TO PATRICK COUNTY MUCH older and wiser than his eighteen years might suggest. Now a tested veteran, the major sought to put the war behind him. Along with his fifteen-year-old brother, Richard Joshua, the Virginian went to work trying to salvage the crops and restore the family's lost fortunes.

These plans came to a grinding halt one day when a local burst into the Reynolds home with news that guerrillas flying the U.S. flag had murdered a neighboring woman, recently widowed by the war. "She had given birth to twins," recalled Reynolds, "& Some of Scotts men had Come & rob[b]ed her Crib & Commenced to take her bed Clothes." When the poor woman protested, she was killed.

Outraged by the news, the ex-Rebel walked to the door, "If I have Surrendered to a government who will tolerate Such treatment as that I will sell my life as dear as I Can and die."

And again Reynolds went to war. Immediately Reynolds set about the difficult task of raising a posse. Since most of the men in the area were paroled soldiers, there was great concern about violating their terms by firing on men who were nominally, at least, Federal soldiers. When they finally reached the marauders' camp, it was the major who went under a flag of truce to demand their surrender. Instead, he was met by a hail of bullets.[1]

As many as five hundred raiders ran unchecked across Patrick County.[2] Eventually, military authorities in Richmond granted permission to form a militia. Reynolds was appointed a first lieutenant in his unit and was wounded while rounding up the brigands. Although struggling by day and by night to ensure his community's safety, the Virginian couldn't forget that the corn and tobacco crops needed attention. He sometimes worked all night with young "R. J." plowing, chopping, and handling other hard

Abram David Reynolds

REYNOLDS HOMESTEAD, CRITZ, VIRGINIA

chores. The former Confederate and other veterans had fully expected to begin the arduous task of rebuilding once they returned home; they had not, however, expected to keep on fighting.

At the very least, Federal authorities occupying Virginia, much to the relief of Reynolds and others, recognized the need for local militias to safeguard society in such perilous times. George Cary Eggleston also commented on the willingness of the occupation troops in his area to "protect all quiet citizens, to restore order." As proof, Eggleston reported to the commanding officer eighteen miles away that a group of marauders was threatening his rural Virginia neighborhood. "They were captured," said Eggleston, "marched at a double-quick to the camp, and shot forthwith."[3]

Unfortunately, not every Federal commander stationed in the South was so diligent in his duty. Many Union officials, still harboring grudges from the war, seemed content to watch while freebooters preyed upon former Rebels. Consequently, outlaw gangs formed by the flotsam of both armies—deserters, draft dodgers, common criminals—seized upon the chaos at war's end and roamed the countryside virtually unhindered. "They were," Eggleston revealed,

> simply the offscourings of the two armies and of the suddenly freed Negro population . . . who found common ground upon which to fraternize in their common depravity. They moved about in bands, from two to ten strong, cutting horses out of plows, plundering helpless people, and wantonly destroying valuables which they could not carry away. At the house of one of my friends where only ladies lived, a body of these men demanded dinner, which was given them. They then required the mistress of the mansion to fill their canteens from sorghum molasses, which they immediately proceeded to pour over the carpets and furniture of the parlor. . . . We had no courts, no justices of the peace, no sheriffs, no officers of any kind.[4]

And thus it fell largely to the people to protect themselves.

Because of its size and western location, Texas had its own peculiar set of circumstances following the war. When news of the surrender of the Trans-Mississippi army reached the Frontier Districts, it found a body of men who could not simply lay down their arms and head home. Many of these men were already home, guarding it against the lawlessness that enveloped the Texas frontier. Unlike their comrades farther east, however, Texans were faced with the additional challenge of Indian raids. Leaving their posts at war's end would have invited wholesale slaughter of white settlers. Thus, volunteering their services, and encouraged by dedicated officers, the men of Texas remained in place, guarding their borders and homes, until they could be relieved by Federal troops.[5]

Even with these thinly spread patrols in place, the fear of Indian incursions was omnipresent. During the summer of 1865, a series of events occurred that sent shivers racing along the western settlements. One such incident took place in central Texas. Together with his adult children and their families, Matthew Taylor had built a home near the headwaters of the Perdinales River. A chronicler describes what happened:

> During the absence of Matthew and his son . . . a band of twenty Kiowa Indians approached the house and secreted themselves in a thicket near the spring. Mrs. Gilead Taylor [Matthew's daughter-in-law] . . . went to the spring for some water. Just as she approached the spring she was shot in the breast with an arrow by an Indian lying in ambuscade. She turned and fled towards the house, but as she ran she was shot with an arrow in the back. She continued running until she

> reached the house, but in endeavoring to enter, she tripped and fell backwards, driving the arrow which was sticking in her back entirely through her body, killing her instantly. The Indians followed her and attacked the house but Mr. McDonald [a son-in-law] . . . saw them approaching, and alone and unaided, he fought them for two hours, and prevented them from entering. At length, finding it would be a hard matter to take the house, the Indians resorted to strategy. . . . McDonald, supposing they had abandoned the idea of making another attempt to take the house, was standing outside of his yard near the gate, when they suddenly showed themselves again. They rushed upon him, shot him several times, stabbed him repeatedly with their butcher knives, and then scalped him. They also scalped Mrs. Gilead Taylor. . . . They then stripped her and McDonald of all their clothing and entering the house they took all they wanted and destroyed what remained.[6]

After the Indians had plundered the home, Matthew's daughter and her five young children were seized, tied to horses, then carried off into the wilderness. His wife was found the next day, lost, wandering aimlessly, almost insane.[7]

In addition to the savagery on its frontier, Texas was also unique among the Southern states in that it had suffered far less from war. Thus, the Lone Star State was viewed by many in the former Confederacy—those who wanted to "get shet of the Yankees"—as a land of opportunity.[8]

Turning the wheels of progress required hands, and with slavery at an end, a labor crisis ensued. Thomas Affleck was one proponent of bringing white workers to the South. Affleck visited Europe, singing the praises of Texas and painting a rosy picture to lure labor across the ocean. His job was made more difficult, however, by conflicting reports coming from America. An article written by a *New York Times* correspondent in Galveston was picked up by a London newspaper, much to Affleck's chagrin:

> This is the commercial capital of the Lone Star dominions, and the city where they shoot cross-eyed men and red-headed women at sight, where they used to draw and quarter a Dutchman, scheme for emigration, and eat pork until you can feel the bristles. The real old Galvestonians wear long hair like crazy poets, soap their greazy locks and the ends of their dismally thin mustaches, and look daggers at intellectual people. They drink whiskey that will [kill] at twelve paces, go home blind drunk

> every night and get up ditto every morning. The full programme of a high toned ranger is to get full of bad whisky, lick some small boy, fire off his revolver three or four times, kill a Mexican, and beat his wife. . . . Not a night has passed for a month but what some poor fellow has been found murdered the next morning. Before the war, Galveston had about nine thousand inhabitants; now it has full fourteen thousand, of which at least two thousand are murderers, vagabonds, and thieves. The state of society is most unhealthy I can assure you, and no person who has any knowledge of these things, and respect for his own life, ventures out after dark.[9]

Not surprisingly, following reports like the above, Affleck's success in luring to Texas shepherds from Scotland and clockmakers from Germany was marginal. But many of the wild and reckless young Southerners adrift after the war found the violence and mayhem of Texas much to their liking. From the chaos were born the origins of the Wild West.

Before stagecoach and train robberies made the headlines, steamboats were the targets. Navigating the tributaries of the Mississippi and other Southern rivers was an incredibly risky business after the war. Whether the actions were true partisan activity exhibiting the refusal to surrender or pure piracy, they made traveling by river a perilous undertaking. Wrote one Mississippian:

> On Sunday afternoon while lying at a landing on Yazoo river . . . the st[eame]r *Dove* was boarded by a party of robbers and robbed of about thirty thousand dollars and such other valuables as they could carry away, they opened fire upon passengers and crew, severely wounding the mate and [a] passenger . . . trunks, baggage and safes all broken, pocket books, and watches of passengers taken.[10]

And only weeks later, the *Keoto,* while docked on the Sunflower River in the same state, was robbed by guerrillas claiming to be the same group that had stopped the *Dove.*[11]

In what may have been the last skirmish of the war, a large band of bushwhackers attacked the steamer *Lilly* in January 1866, as it navigated the Bigbee River in Alabama. When Federal soldiers on board returned fire, the boat became a floating battleground. After gaining control of the craft, the Rebels set off for a landing where they intended to confiscate the *Lilly*'s shipment of government cotton.

While unloading the cargo, a black deckhand managed to escape and alert the local military, who surprised the guerrillas and ran them into the brush. Although no one was seriously injured in the fight, the bullet-riddled hull of the boat was testimony to the fury of the contest. While prisoners, some passengers overheard the guerrillas declare that they were going up the Red River "to make war on all the boats that navigated that stream."[12]

In late spring 1865, a slim young man, seemingly too slight and fresh-faced to have been a guerrilla, rode toward a Federal picket line just outside of Lexington, Missouri. With him were several others. Above them, waving on the point of a saber, was a white flag. As soon as the Yankees spotted the riders, they opened fire. Bleeding from a hole in his chest, the young man wheeled his horse and fled, vowing through the pain that he would never again attempt to surrender.[13]

Less than a year later, in Liberty, Missouri, the eighteen-year-old returned. Reported a local newspaper:

> Our usually quiet city was startled last Tuesday by one of the most cold-blooded murders and heavy robberies on record. It appears that in the afternoon some ten or twelve persons rode into town, and two of them went into the Clay County Savings Bank, and asked the clerk . . . to change a ten dollar bill, and as he started to do so, they drew their revolvers on him and. . . . [14]

Jesse James and his brother, Frank, along with Cole and Bob Younger, remained Rebels, not because they loved war or wanted to die, but because there was no other option. Retaliation was in the Missouri air, not forgiveness. Four years of war had forged an enmity there and elsewhere that would not go quietly. From Texas to Nebraska, the defeated, the dispossessed, the discontented set new standards of warfare.

Whatever the West would become, it was born of war, especially that war where neighbors truly had turned on neighbors. In the borderlands of Maryland, West Virginia, Kentucky, Missouri, Kansas, and Indian Territory, in the swamps of Louisiana and Florida, in the Appalachian Mountains, a ferocious war within a war had been waged between guerrillas on both sides. Nowhere had that war been more bitter, and nowhere was peace more unattainable than in these regions. Although some leaders—William Quantrill in Missouri, John S. Mosby in Virginia—tried to maintain a level of civility in their areas, the irregular war was, for the most part,

Jesse James
B. L. WILLIAMS COLLECTION

a merciless, no quarter contest in which winners lived and losers died. Beastly atrocities were committed by both sides with sadistic abandon. But while the Unionist winners of this war—Redlegs, Jayhawkers, White Rags, antibushwhacking leagues, groups whose crimes were every bit as bad as those of their counterparts—returned home as heroes and saw their leaders elected to high public office, there was no such homecoming for the losers.

When Rebels returned to these parts of the Confederacy, they found boundaries as real as stone fences blocking their way. Such was the case in East Tennessee.

With William G. "Parson" Brownlow controlling the *Knoxville Whig,* as well as serving as "radical Republican" governor of Tennessee, the state lay under almost dictatorial power. Thus, the "cleansing" in the mountainous part of the state occurred, if not with Brownlow's outright urging, at least with his covert blessing. "This war," wrote Brownlow earlier, "ought to be pursued with fury and vengeance until men[,] women and children South of Masons & Dixons line are exterminated from the face of God Almighty's earth."[15] The Governor and his cohorts, homegrown "scalawags," proved the greatest obstacle to returning Confederates trying to rebuild their lives. The endless harassment made it nearly impossible.

"When it came time to commence plowing," recalled John Carroll, "I plowed a mule, kept my horse bridled and saddled near the center of the field. At night I slept in the woods where I might be safe." The "reign of terror" continued, said Carroll, until he could no longer remain without "either killing a lot of them or being killed."[16]

His fears were justified. At first Unionists tried terror tactics to scare people out of East Tennessee, as in this posting:

> Spetial Order No 1
> In the Woods near NewMarket Tenn
> July the 24th 65
>
> All damned Rebels are hereby notified to lieve at wonce, if found her at the expiration of ten days from the date of this order and no preparation to lieve Thrashing mashiens will sit at wonce enough to thrash all crops wit the usal tole hickry withs and cowhides or anything els that may be required on the occasion. We are working by the order that you theving God forsaken helldeserving Rebels issued four years ago Union men and Rebels cannot live together which we find not altogether bogus
>
> We are vary
> Respectively
> Old Soldier[17]

At Strawberry Plain, two men, a townsman and traveler, observed a man dashing into the village on horseback. "There's a dog-goned Rebel now!" nudged the local. "He's a Rebel colonel, just come back. . . . He'll get warned; and then if he don't leave, he must look out!"[18]

Many men, did indeed "get warned," then packed their belongings and fled. "Scarcely a day passes but what our streets are filled with wagons moving through our place towards the far west," one Tennessean observed. "The exodus of population from all parts of East Tennessee, is now said to be very great."[19]

"A number of our best citizens are seeking other homes," penned one diarist, "and even conservative union men are thinking of leaving."[20]

When words and icy stares weren't enough, the threats were carried out with a deadly vengeance. "Not a day passes but what some 'rebel' receives his 400 lashes or its equivalent—the contents of a minnie rifle," observed a resident of East Tennessee.[21] One gang of Unionists visited the home of a returned soldier, marched him to a tree in the yard, and in front of his aged father and mother, shot him to death. They then burned the house and contents.[22]

"No man's life is safe," wrote Ellen Renshaw House in Knoxville. "Scarcely a days passes [that] some one is not killed. Yesterday two were." The woman described an incident in a local store in which an ex-Confederate was shot in the back without provocation. Southern sympathizers called it cold-blooded murder; Unionists said the man was such an unrepentant Rebel that his life should have been taken "ten times over."[23]

When a drunken Unionist in Knoxville shouted to his friends, "Now I'll go knock some damned Rebel down," House described what followed:

> The first one he met chanced to be Ab Baker. He struck him three times with a stick, broke his stick, when Ab finding that he would not stop, drew his pistol and shot him dead. He was arrested and put in jail.
>
> The Union men said they would take him out and hang him. I did not for a moment suppose it would be allowed. But the first thing we heard this morning was that over a hundred . . . went to the jail last night about ten o'clock, tied the jailer and took the poor boy out. They told him they were going to hang him. He told them if there was only one he could hold his own, but against so many he could do nothing, but he added I will show you how a brave man can die, and he did. He never flinched. They left him hanging four or five hours then threw him in an ambulance on some shavings, with not even a sheet and drove him [into] town. . . .
>
> I have just come from the funeral. . . . and I can see his grave from where I sit writing. . . . There was a Yankee at the funeral. He looked at all the boys there as if he could kill them. . . . When they brought his coffin there were some Yankee officers standing near, and they were laughing and going on about putting a d——d rebel in such a fine one. . . . They say they intend to hang nine more.[24]

"Not a day passes but some man of family is either beaten almost to death, or driven from the county," wrote Sam Milligan, prominent Unionist and member of the Tennessee Supreme Court, "and all it would seem, under the Governor's organ under his sanction."[25]

Chasing and murdering Rebels already in East Tennessee was not enough. "There are several other rebels coming home to Tennessee," exhorted Governor Brownlow's *Knoxville Whig*. "Can't some Union soldiers or citizens dispose of them before they get here?"[26]

For those who stubbornly held their ground in East Tennessee, other methods were employed. Mobs would not allow the children of former secessionists to go to school.[27] Legal actions were brought against their parents, suing for damages that had occurred during the war. Of one such case, Brownlow boasted: "This is only the beginning of the end. Other suits are on the docket, and others are to come. Let them be impoverished, and made bankrupt. Let them be made beggars, going from door to door for their bread. They brought on this rebellion—they caused all this suffering and trouble—let them be made odious."[28]

Those who questioned Brownlow's tactics grew more and more vocal as the governor's tyrannical grip on the state tightened. Wrote one Memphis editor regarding the powers controlling Tennessee:

> The boiling cauldron of war has cast into power in this State a race of small men—a filthy scum which the people will skim off with the big ladle of the ballot box in due course of time. As the rattlesnake becomes more poisonous and blind with rage when the dogdays approach, so do these little men grow more venomous and vindictive.[29]

The situation in East Tennessee gained such national notoriety that even some Yankees were compelled to speak up. "We have had great sympathy for the people of Tennessee," began Horace Greeley of the *New York Tribune*, "but if this brutality continues, we shall feel that all our sympathy has been misplaced."[30] Other Northern papers, like the Alton, Illinois, *Democrat*, targeted Brownlow through his newspaper:

> It [the *Knoxville Whig*] is not content with having the poor rebels of the neighborhood shut up in a loathesome prison, but busys itself in pointing out those who may merely arrive under the protection of the amnesty proclamation, and advises their murder.[31]

Such actions, added the editor, have earned the governor the title "Bloody Brownlow."[32]

Brownlow denied that the situation was as bad as reported, informing President Johnson that accounts had been exaggerated.[33] At the same time, however, the governor's own newspaper was bragging that "old Rebels and

William G. "Parson" Brownlow
UNIVERSITY OF NORTH CAROLINA AT CHAPEL HILL

young ones have been spotted and . . . are being held fearfully responsible for their disloyalty. Some of the most prominent are being killed every week. . . . While we regret the occurrences, society will suffer but little by dispatching such characters."[34]

"There has been only four men killed here today," Ellen House wrote on August 16, 1865, as if matters were finally returning to normal in Knoxville.[35]

The bloody purge was not confined to East Tennessee. A traveler in the western counties of North Carolina was appalled that Unionists were not laying aside their differences and welcoming back Rebel brothers with open arms. "There's six or seven creeturs up in my deestric' as can't live there a gret while," a wiry mountaineer informed a visitor. "Now I tell ye, our deestric' 'll git shet of 'em putty soon. Ef they's fellers as can't take a wink, we'll jest haf ter giv' 'em a nod." As the man spoke, his raised his arms and lowered his head as if to aim a gun.

Shocked, the guest questioned the use of violence. The old man reaffirmed his stand: "Thar's jest six God damned infernal sneakin' Rebels . . . as can't no how at all live thar six weeks longer. That thing's settled, Mister, and thar ain't no use talkin'!"[36]

Hoping to find this man's sentiments an aberration in the Tarheel State, the traveler was soon disappointed. Every inquiry led to the revelation of yet another murder. Near Morganton, a Rebel lieutenant was found slain, shot from behind by an unknown assassin. A returned Confederate in Salisbury met the same fate.[37]

One former Rebel soldier refused to be cowed. Branding those white Unionists who did not go to war as cowards or "nigger Yankees," when he returned home the unrepentant Rebel announced that no "stay-at-home-cuss" would "lord it over him."[38]

In West Virginia, citizens took measures to ensure that Rebels would not return at all. Ordinances were passed making it illegal for those who had served in the Confederate army to again reside in the state and instructing those already returned to leave at once.[39] In the nation's capital, a similar law was passed.[40] A Maryland newspaper echoed the unforgiving spirit: "Do the Government or State authorities intend to allow the sneaking Maryland rebels, who when darkness covered the earth, stealthily made their way into Virginia, and there assisted to murder, starve and destroy her soldiers, to be again reinstated in our loyal community? We opine not."[41]

One of those soldiers coming home to Maryland found the state fully as divided after the war as during it. "The Union population . . . were afflicted . . . with a species of loyal rabies," he observed, "and their passion and this malignant malady expended itself even on the children." The situation was so dangerous for returning Rebels that Maj. Gen. Lew Wallace found it necessary to arrest Confederates "to avoid collisions and bloodshed." Why Wallace did not arrest those who were threatening the returning Rebels is not mentioned. At the very least, the above soldiers were offered some protection. Confederate veterans arriving at Martinsburg, West Virginia, were mobbed and beaten in the streets.[42]

After the "notorious guerrilla," Champ Ferguson of Tennessee, returned to his home at war's end, he was quickly arrested, tried, convicted, and hanged. In the same state, another forty men were rounded up in Giles County, declared "outlaws," then shot or hanged.[43] Ten more guerrillas were lynched by a group of citizens in Georgia.[44]

In Kentucky, the purge of former guerrillas was especially vindictive. Perhaps hundreds died following the war. In August 1865, at the trotting grounds in Lexington, one ex-partisan stood on the gallows with a black federal soldier convicted of murdering a white man. Had he a thousand lives, the Rebel declared defiantly, he would "willingly give them all for the same cause."

"When the drop was sprung," wrote a horrified witness, "both of the ropes broke, and the two men fell to the ground."

Despite superstition that a broken rope signified innocence, both men were lugged back up to the scaffold.[45]

Also in Lexington, two more guerrillas, Samuel Robinson and Thomas Evans, prepared to meet their fate. As the ropes were being adjusted, a horseman was seen approaching madly waving a handkerchief. When the rider pulled up he announced that there had been a reprieve. Evans would go free. The order of execution for Robinson stood. Among the spectators was Capt. John W. Tuttle:

> Each of the culprits received the announcement unmoved and with apparent indifference. Their hands being pinioned behind them they turned back to back and took each other by the hand. They stood thus a moment in perfect silence when Evans was untied and conducted from the scaffold to the wagon in which he came which was near by. Robinson said a few words to the crowd but I was not near enough to understand what he said. The noose was then adjusted about his neck, the black cap pulled over his face[,] the word given, the prop pulled from under him and he dangled in the air. The rope was not well adjusted. It caught under his jaw bone on one side. . . . The fall did not break his neck so he hung an hour and a quarter before life was pronounced extinct.[46]

Remarked one hard-pressed Rebel from Texas:

> I suffered more hardships and trials and experienced more dangers after the war had ended and peace had been declared than I had ever encountered during the four years in the field. . . . I have slept on high eminences in order that I might watch for scouring search parties who were shooting down in cold blood every man that wore the Southern uniform, and for no other reason. I have seen the horizon at night lit up with the burning houses of my friends whose only offense was that they had been soldiers in the Confederate army.[47]

In the minds of many Missourians, four years of fierce partisan warfare had settled nothing. Hatreds became more savage with each loss incurred, and with peace, formerly outnumbered and cornered Unionists and "infidel Germans" were quick to seize the advantage.[48]

> Mr. Frean, take our advice and seek that peace which you now appear so much to desire—the loyal men don't want you here; you are not safe in remaining. If you want peace and protection you had better go and join Claib. Jackson [and] Bill Anderson: Both in that world where Claib. was going to take Missouri to—but didn't. There may be some kind of peace for such as you down there.[49]

A Missouri newspaper described a typical incident that occurred in August 1865:

> A squad of Miller County Militia, some nine in number, under command of Colonel Babcocke . . . arrested Judge [Lewis] Wright and five of his sons—some sort of investigation was made into accusations brought against the parties, either fancied or real, when it was determined to take them to Rolla. . . . Mrs. Wright . . . at first implored Colonel Babcocke not to take her family away. Finding that her entreaties were unavailing she then besought him to permit her to accompany them. This also was refused. But upon her imploring him to do something for her protection, as she was fearful of being murdered if left alone, the youngest son, a mere stripling, was released.
>
> The judge was then mounted on a horse by himself, and his four sons upon two other horses . . . ostensibly to be taken to Rolla. Before reaching that point . . . they were all inhumanly butchered and their bodies left lying in the brush by the roadside. No less than twenty-six shots were fired into the persons of the five! Twelve of them took effect in their heads. Before the bodies were reached by the frantic wife and mother and her remaining son, four of the five were dead, and the fifth insensible and dying.[50]

As the death of Judge Wright and his sons made clear, the families of Missouri soldiers were fair game. Waiting for her brothers to come home after the war, a sixteen-year-old girl answered the door one night to find a squad of soldiers wishing to warm themselves by the fire. Strangely, only the leader entered. The man asked if there were bushwhackers in the house. When the girl replied that only she and her father were at home, the soldier then inquired, "Your two brothers are in the Rebel army, eh?" Answering in the affirmative, the girl was startled when the intruder pointed a gun to her father's head and said, "Old man, I have come to kill you." During the scuffle over the gun, the daughter ran to the kitchen, grabbed a corn knife, and began hacking her father's assailant. Severely injured, the soldier stumbled out the door and muttered, "I am a dead man." Hauling their leader's corpse away, the raiders troubled the little family no more this night.[51]

When paroled soldiers did finally return to their Missouri homes, even those with safety vouchers or promises of amnesty were sometimes dragged out in the middle of the night by Unionist neighbors and lynched.[52]

"I . . . fought for things I thought was right," said one former Rebel guerrilla. "When the war was over and I wanted to settle down they would not let me, but pursued me with a malignant hatred."[53]

As a consequence, many of these wild young men either slipped away to the wilderness of the Far West or, like Jesse James, held fast to their familiar woodlands to begin a new life of outlawry and crime.

PART 3

Mr. Lincoln naturally longed for the glory and repose of a second term to be spent in peace. At the time it occurred, his death, even by natural causes, would have been a serious injury to the prospects of the South. But the manner of his death, frenzying the northern mind, was the last crowning calamity of a despairing and defeated . . . cause.

Jefferson Davis

CHAPTER 18

Through a Glass Darkly

> It was not the same Texas I had left. . . . I was not the same Rebel.

THUS WROTE FRANCIS LUBBOCK, RETURNING HOME AFTER MONTHS OF imprisonment. The observations of the former governor of the Lone Star State were generally true of every Rebel soldier, high or low.

It was as if the world had been picked up and shaken, then the broken parts scattered down on top of each other in chaos. The men were broken, the homes were broken, even the landscape had the appearance of jagged parts, no longer seeming to fit.

The whole of the South had been maimed and the impact upon the spirit and emotions of such a crippled society cannot be overstated. How could people cling to hope when all that met their gaze was a ruin? "Everything in nature wears a funeral aspect," Mary Rives wrote from Louisiana on May 12, 1865. "The bright sunshine, the woods and fields, the song of birds. All to me is mockery."[1] Traveling through South Carolina, Mary Chesnut also noted how sad and surreal spring flowers seemed among the deathlike stillness: "From Chester to Winnsboro we did not see one living thing—man, woman, or animal."[2]

Lizzie Hardin, once familiar with the streets of Atlanta, now wandered the half-fallen walls searching for landmarks. Instead, the woman found herself again and again "amid unbroken ruins as much lost as though I were on a prairie or the ocean."[3]

A correspondent in Mississippi noted only "four or five houses standing and inhabited on the whole route from Vicksburg to Jackson." Arriving in Jackson, the reporter found the State House, the governor's mansion, city hall, and the asylum to be the only public buildings left standing—all else were ashes and ruin. So total was the destruction in Jackson that many began calling it "chimneyville."[4]

Three months after the fall of the capital, the ruins of Richmond continued to smolder, its acrid scent clinging to the broken buildings.[5] Florida had managed to repel most Yankee invasions during the war, but not the ravages of neglect. Grass grew in the streets of Apalachicola, and one visitor commented that it was "only a wreck of its former beauty."[6] At Pensacola, where most of the residents had long since left, the railroad was broken up for forty miles.[7]

Hundreds of miles of levees had been destroyed in Louisiana and Mississippi.[8] Wharves rotted in Alabama, decaying into the streams and bays. Steamboats were wrecked, their sunken shells blocking navigation on rivers in Arkansas. Locomotives in Georgia and South Carolina were burned-out and broken hulks among the twisted tracks. Elsewhere, the picture was the same: bridges burned, roads destroyed, towns leveled.

"Desolation met our gaze," said one soldier returning through Arkansas. "Abandoned and burned homes, uncultivated land overgrown with bushes; half starved women and children; gaunt, ragged men, stumbling along the road . . . trying to find their families, and wondering if they had a home left."

"It is scarcely possible to exaggerate," said another viewer. "The march of hostile armies, the deadly carnage of fiercely contested battles, and all the horrors and devastations of ruthless war may be traced in ruins, blood, and new-made graves."[9]

Nowhere was this more evident than war-ravaged Missouri. George Hedges of Warrensburg wrote to his daughter describing the death and destruction he observed as he surveyed the landscape:

> We are well and surprising to tell, have lived through without any particular personal harm; we have been robbed and plundered in the house and out of it, by . . . both friends and foes of the government party, and the country has been full of [those] who have gone about robbing and plundering . . . and in a great many instances, murdering men for mere opinion's sake. . . . Then the Federals would in the night generally turn out and kill as many more or perhaps twice or thrice as many by the way of retaliation and so it went until half our people were either killed or run away to avoid death.
>
> Mr. Shaw our neighbor was killed, Joseph Matthew of Blackwater town was killed, Baldwin Fine, Mr. Rogers, Mr. Shaffer, Mr. Dean, Mr. Kean, Offutt, Cockerel, Sanders,

> Fitzgerald, Stephens, Andrews, and a host of others I could mention. . . .
>
> Columbus and a large part of our county toward the West has been burned, part by Federals and part by Rebels; nearly all of . . . the counties South along the Kansas border are consumed. . . .
>
> [My son], James, reached home a few days ago, well and hearty and greatly grown, a man of fine size and good appearance. He is still crippled in his hand, but not so badly as I feared it would prove to be; he received no other wound. He came into Missouri last fall with General [Sterling] Price, and was captured near Fort Scott. . . . His horse was shot under him on the open prairie, his command routed, and he and about 600 others were captured. . . .
>
> James and Sallie Stone, Ellis Stone and family and Dick Ellis . . . left here the second year of the war and have not returned. Joseph Stone left his farm and moved to Warrensburg, where his daughter Anna married a Federal soldier. Caleb Stone, his oldest son, was killed at Springfield the first year of the war. One of the Ramsey boys was killed and another crippled for life. Mr. Kelly's son had his leg shot off; Robert Renick also a cripple for life, and many others I could mention.
>
> I have sold my land, and shall leave this country; it was all I had left.[10]

Even if one had been able to close his eyes to the picture of devastation, the smell was inescapable. "The road was lined with carcasses of hogs, horses, and cattle that the invaders had wantonly shot down," remembered a young woman. "The stench in some places was unbearable." Another lady observed that the "blood-soaked soil and the dead animals emitted sickening odors until the frosts came to chain them up." Upon returning to her home near Petersburg, Sara Rice Pryor wrote:

> The earth was ploughed and trampled, the grass and flowers were gone, the carcasses of six dead cows lay in the yard, and filth unspeakable had gathered in the corners of the house. The very air was heavy with the sickening odor of decaying flesh. As the front door opened, millions of flies swarmed forth. . . . Within was dirt and desolation. Pieces of fat pork lay on the floors, molasses trickled from the library shelves, where bottles lay uncorked. Filthy, malodorous tin cans were scattered on the floors.[11]

Kate Stone
LOUISIANA STATE UNIVERSITY, SPECIAL COLLECTIONS, HILL MEMORIAL LIBRARY

Attracted by the carrion, great numbers of dogs, dislocated by the war, now roamed the Southern landscape, killing what little livestock remained and adding yet another menace to movement on the roads.[12] Unfortunately, the increase in feral canines did little to stem a similar increase in the rodent population. "A great army of large, light brown Norway rats now overran the farm," said the much-assailed Sara Pryor:

> They would walk to the corner before our eyes and help themselves to the army rations. We never moved a finger to drive them away. After awhile Aleck appeared with an enormous black-and-white cat. "Dis' jest a little mo' n I can stand," said Aleck. "De Yankees has stole ev'rything, and dug up de whole face o' the earth . . . but I ain' obleedged to stan' sassyness fum dese outlandish rats." Aleck had to surrender. The very first night after the arrival of his valiant cat there was a scuffle in the room where the crackers were kept, a chair was overturned, and a flying cat burst through the hall, pursued by three or four huge rats. The cat took refuge in a tree . . . and left the field to the enemy.[13]

"With God Against Them" U.S. MILITARY HISTORY INSTITUTE, CARLISLE BARRACKS

Unlike many who returned to find their homes in ashes, in disarray, or vermin-infested, Kate Stone was more fortunate. Reaching her Louisiana plantation, she found it merely empty. "At home again," she said with relief, "but so many, many changes in two years. It does not seem the same place. The bare echoing rooms, the neglect and defacement of all. . . . How still and lifeless everything seems."[14]

Rachel Sanders had struggled to keep the family farm in Texas operable and ready for her sons' homecoming, only to be met by tragedy at every turn. Unable any longer to deal with the situation, the mother fled.

"Oh my dear son, I have seen more trouble since we parted than I ever had in all my life before," Rachel wrote. "The death of your dear father was one of the greatest afflictions on earth. We were left without a protector and we were robbed and cheated out of everything almost. . . . [Then] there came this awful high water and destroyed everything. I could not stand it. I believe I should have died if I had not got away from such a scene of distress."[15]

Most vulnerable to the ravages of war had been the churches; the marching armies had found them deserted and left them defiled. "The doors were thrown open, benches were removed . . . and sometimes broken up for fuel," wrote one observer. "The audience chamber is strewn with fragments of hard tack, beef and whatever other rations the soldier may chance have had—The sight of these Churches, desolate and desecrated, make a Christian's heart almost bleed. It is by far the saddest scene in the ruin."[16]

For many devout Southerners, the abomination of their churches was the final evidence that God had turned against them. So sure had Southerners been of God's blessing that the scene spread before them caused many to doubt His presence. In her misery, Lizzie Hardin felt forced to admit that "through four long years of blackness, of horror, and bloodshed we have fought the whole world and it seems Heaven itself. The world we expected to fight, but, My God! my God! why hast Thou forsaken us?"[17]

So sweeping was the destruction and so total the defeat, that even the strongest of rocks were shaken. "Can all . . . be in vain?" questioned Rev. William Watt in his diary.

> Why so much blood shed? So many wounds inflicted, so many noble lives lost, so many hearts crushed, so much devastation & ruin in the land? is it all for nought, Oh! God have all of our prayers, faith, hope & love of liberty and privations & sacrifices been in vain, Oh! God? has God closed His ears to our cries & His eyes to our sufferings and is His heart unfeeling toward us? will God, can God forget his people?[18]

If the devout expressed such doubts, the disillusionment among simple believers might well be imagined. Sgt. Edwin Fay struggled to maintain his faith but admitted, "I fear the subjugation of the South will make an infidel of me."[19] Reflected one Kentuckian: "It has been a terrible rebellion and a fearful revolution; possibly a chastisement for our sins."[20] "The South has sinned in her pride, her prosperity, her confidence," said Cornelia Phillips Spencer simply, "and God has humbled her."[21]

Looking upon the ruined South, abolitionist preacher Henry Ward Beecher was "glad that God hath set a mark upon treason, that all ages shall dread and abhor it."[22]

Some likeminded Northerners were more than willing to impose similar beliefs on Southerners. One such minister, a "smug little man,—sleek, unctuous, and trim, with Pecksniffian self-esteem oozing out of every pore of his face" visited a family near Petersburg. His hostess recalled the conversation.

"Well, Madam," began the clergyman, "I trust I find you lying meekly under the chastening rod of the Lord. I trust you can say 'it is good I was afflicted.'"

"Are there none on the other side who need the rod?" the indignant lady inquired.

"Oh—well, now—my dear lady!" he replied. "You must consider! You were in the wrong in this unhappy contest, or I should say, this most righteous war."[23]

At a church in Richmond, the pastor sought to comfort his congregation in the face of their growing guilt and doubt:

> And does it not seem to you, my brethren, that during the last terrible four years the prayers of God's people in these Southern States, because they have not been answered in just the way you had chosen, have not been heard at all? Be not cast down. Do we not know that the fervent prayers of the saints cannot fail of an answer? But now we see through a glass darkly, By-and bye, if we will but wait, in God's good time we shall see, and know, and understand.[24]

Sometimes, Providence did indeed favor those who had lost so much, and little pieces were given back. When Yankee troops occupied Baton Rouge, a raiding party plundered a nearby home and a young soldier took two French vases and two books from the library. He sent them to an uncle in Indiana, who was not appreciative.

"I never wanted them," he said. "I felt like a thief every time I looked at them." Determined to return the belongings, the uncle finally located the owner through the Masonic Temple. Coincidentally, when the stolen items eventually arrived, the owner had just been raking through the ashes of his home, thinking all was gone. The vases and books were his only link between the past and future, and he was overwhelmed by the kindness of the stranger who had returned them.[25]

"It is curious to consider what has become of all the jewels and finery of which our armies robbed the people of the South," mused Northern correspondent John Trowbridge. "On two or three occasions gentlemen of respectability have shown me, with considerably more pride than I could have felt under the circumstances, vases and trinkets which they 'picked up when they were in the army.'" Sometimes stolen articles were recovered seemingly by chance, as Trowbridge related of this young woman visiting New York:

> One Sunday morning [at church]. . . she saw, upon the shoulders of a lady kneeling before her, a shawl which had been lost when her plantation, between Charleston and Savannah, was plundered by the Federals. Her attention being thus attracted, she next observed on the lady's arm a bracelet which was taken from her at the same time. This was to her a very precious souvenir, for it had been presented to her by her father, and it contained his picture.
>
> The services ended, she followed the lady home and rang at the door. She was shown into the parlor, and presently the lady appeared with the shawl upon her shoulders and the bracelet on her arm. Frankly the visitor related the story of the bracelet, and at once the wearer restored it to her with apologies and regrets. The visitor, quite overcome by this generosity and delighted at the recovery of the bracelet, had not the heart to say a word about the shawl, but left it in the possession of the innocent wearer.[26]

Appreciative as these individuals were to recover the smallest tokens of their former lives, they realized that these items were but a pathetic remnant of what could never be replaced—the only photograph of a child who had died, a crib built by an expectant father, blankets knitted by loving hands—the cherished mementos of life. When Sara Pryor returned to her home, her heart leaped when she saw picture frames piled in the corner, but sank again when she realized that the faces had been torn out and destroyed. All the sundry nothings that gather dust and warm the heart, the trinkets that young girls hide in bureau drawers, the watches passed from fathers to sons—all were gone, and they would never be recovered. These were just drops in a vast sea of destruction.

The Richmond *Republic* estimated the total loss to the South caused by the war to be nearly six billion dollars.[27] Contrasted with the burgeoning economy enjoyed by the North during the same time, the destitution of the South seemed even more acute.[28] Said one man from Mongtomery:

> Hard times are upon us and there is a fearful looking for of worse times to come. Let no man suppose that he can repair in one year, or in two, the losses of the war. Industry, economy—living within our means whatever they may be, discarding luxu-

> ries from our table—adopting reasonable plainness in our dress and disposing of everything we can spare for the necessaries of existence—these are the duties of the present time.[29]

"Poverty reigned king," recalled a woman from North Carolina, "and was a cruel tyrant to his subjects, and they were legion."[30]

"I don't mind being poor myself," said a woman in Virginia. "I know I am ready and willing to give up all self-indulgences."[31]

Soon after the destruction had been surveyed and the damage assessed, many Southerners quickly accepted their new situation. For most, this was a necessary first step to rebuilding. And their courage was remarkable.

"The plucky way in which our men keep up is beyond praise," Mary Chesnut recounted with pride. "There is no howling, and our poverty is a matter of laughing."[32]

"Absolute poverty, cheerfully borne, was the badge of respectability," wrote George Cary Eggleston. "The want of means became a jest, and nobody mourned over it."[33]

Even one of the harshest critics of the former Confederacy, the *New York Times,* felt moved to note the remarkable resilience of the Southern people in the face of the terrible scourge they had suffered: "They have lost property, population, pride, hope—all that great communities hold dear—but they have not lost their manliness. . . . They do not moan for pity like defeated Hungarians, nor conspire like conquered Frenchmen, nor swear like the beaten Irish. They accept their fate with self-reliant resignation, and at once proceed with firmness and sagacity, to make the best of their new condition."[34]

One Floridian, left penniless, his treasured library destroyed, but realizing the plight of many others was worse, reflected: "I have a good profession which is worth more than a cotton plantation—have good health, a cheerful and hopeful spirit, and with the blessings of providence on my labours, I do not fear."[35]

Even before their men returned, it had fallen to the females of the South to persevere. A Georgia woman, forced to leave her home during the war, returned to toiling in the house and the field as she put their farm in order. Because of her efforts, when the husband finally arrived, he found "the nucleus of a new start in life . . . under the most trying ordeal."[36]

Three young ladies in Hanover, Virginia, from a formerly wealthy family and unaccustomed to field work, managed to plant a larger crop of corn than had been grown during the war.[37]

"Taking stock of our possessions, I found that we had one horse left, a little corn, and a cow, and two small children," recalled a returned soldier.

"I would rise up early in the morning and go to plowing. My wife would get breakfast and churn, bringing milk, hot corn bread and butter for me, so we began to retrieve our broken fortunes.[38]

Another veteran found to his chagrin that the only tableware left at his home were tin plates. Desperate for drinking cups and lacking tools, the family fashioned tumblers from old bottles by sawing them in two with the rapid back-and-forth motion of a yarn string, which heated and severed the glass.[39]

Retrieving lost fortunes was no easy matter for returning Rebels. With an estimated forty-five thousand amputees alone coming home, many were too sick or crippled to work, at least in the beginning. "I could not work at that time, as my left hand were badlye mangled," John Bishop of Tennessee explained. "Three fingers gone at the palm."[40] Another soldier admitted that he tried to farm but was too weak from chronic diarrhea.[41] Some were lucky merely to be alive. Henry Barksdale reached home without his right arm, a leg badly mauled, and a wound in the side.[42]

For those able to work, new realities had to be faced. In many cases, jobs they had left before the war no longer existed; in other cases, the money to pay them was not available. "Men went to work at new and strange occupations," reminisced a man in Richmond, "doing not what they would, but what they could, in the bitter struggle with want for their daily bread."[43]

It seemed strange, said one lady, to see a once lordly planter, formerly worth thousands, now "working as a deck-hand on a dirty little river steamer, hardly fit to ship cotton on." Another considered it odd to witness an aristocratic blueblood struggling as "a porter of a dry goods store."[44]

These menial jobs provided the most meager of wages. "Every month," one observer noted, "it seemed to grow harder and harder to make the bare means of life."[45]

For some, the problem seemed insurmountable. An unemployed man in Charleston who had not eaten in three days slit his throat.[46] Near Huntsville, Alabama, families of dead Rebel soldiers were dying of starvation.[47] In the Ozarks of Missouri and Arkansas, much of the scattered and decimated population was surviving on "greens, slippery elm bark, and roots."[48]

"We had nothing to eat but musty meal and hardtack," a man from Georgia recalled. "We just kept from starving and that was all."[49] Another Georgian acknowledged, "We did not starve; but, like thousands of others, we 'most starved.'"[50] And elsewhere, the wolf of starvation mercilessly stalked Southern footsteps. In North Carolina, a reporter for the *New York Herald* watched as "wasted women" lurked around train stations, "moving like clothed skeletons around the cars to gather up any corn which . . . may escape from the sack." In neighboring Virginia, "here a tired woman, with a babe in one arm and a little toddler clinging to her skirts. . . . There a twelve-year-old boy, dragging a wooden cart. . . . Aged women, hobbling along . . . shy young girls, with basket and bag, blushing under the impudent leers and coarse jests of the loafing soldiery."[51]

A Texas cavalryman along the Red River in Louisiana reported that women and children were living in the woods without shelter or adequate clothing. "There are many," said the soldier, "that have been in easy circumstances who are actually living on blackberries."[52]

Not surprisingly, food of any sort in the ravaged Red River Valley was a delicacy, and Yankee soldiers sailing to Shreveport soon found sport in the situation:

> In front of every farm-house would be a large assemblage of whites and blacks, of all ages and assorted sizes. Our boys amused themselves by throwing "hard-tack" at them, and then what running and tumbling and scrambling would ensue! little nigs and little whites, little dogs and big dogs, all joined in the race, and by the time the "hard-tack" was secured it was difficult to determine what were the original ingredients.[53]

There seemed no limit to the privation; an estimated thirty-five thousand people in and around Atlanta had to be fed by government rations or starve.[54] In South Carolina, "hundreds of mortal beings are perishing around us each day for want of food and raiment . . . ," the *Charleston Courier* reported. "There are numbers of white families who know not where to get their next meal."[55]

In addition to a myriad of miseries, including starvation, his wife's poor health added to this minister's already heavy burdens:

> Alas, our future is dark—and grows darker! . . . and the health of my dear wife is wretched. She is no better; she is reduced sadly, and those exhausting hemorrhages still continue. . . . I am often very miserable. No prospect of a church before me, and no school for our boys. . . . My crop is not a third-crop. My having to plant so late exposed the crop to the drought, and there was no recovery. It is impossible for me to keep all of our people, even if they should stay. And to turn them off—although they seem so indifferent to me—will be painful.[56]

Former Rebel officers fared not much better. At age twenty-nine, Gen. M. C. Butler had, at the war's end, "one leg gone, a wife and three children to support, seventy emancipated slaves, a debt of $15,000, and in his pocket $1.75."[57]

Like their countrymen, these returned soldiers were forced into unfamiliar and poorly paying positions. "My poor brother Edgeworth," wrote a lady in Augusta, "lays aside the captaincy with a sigh as he opens an up-country store."[58]

Richard Anderson was compelled to work as a day laborer in the yards of the South Carolina Railroad, even though as a general during the war he had commanded thousands of men.[59] "It was not uncommon," observed a veteran, "to see a private and a colonel in their old uniforms, working side by side!"[60] Such was the case of a farm near Appomattox, whose owner employed many disbanded soldiers. The farmer divided his hands into work details according to their military rank. A neighbor asked how the arrangement was working:

> "Who are those men working over there?"
>
> "Them is privates, sir, of Lee's army."
>
> "Well, how do they work?"
>
> "Very fine, sir; first-rate workers."
>
> "Who are those in the second group?"
>
> "Them is lieutenants and captains, and they works fairly well, but not as good as the privates."
>
> "I see you have a third squad: who are they?"
>
> "Them is colonels."
>
> "Well, what about the colonels? How do they work?"
>
> "Now, neighbor, you'll never hear me say one word ag'in' any man who fit in the Southern army; but I ain't a-gwine to hire no generals."[61]

Because of the scarcity of jobs, many were forced to seize any opportunity that presented itself. Henry Clay Thruston, stepping in at well over seven feet tall, capitalized on his unusual appearance by working with a circus after the war. Thruston accented his size by wearing a tall beaver hat, high top boots, and a long frock coat. The Southern giant marched at the front of parades, carrying the Rebel flag in the South or, dressed as Uncle Sam, bearing both flags in the North.[62]

Many professional men, such as attorney Roger Pryor, left their homeland. His wife, Sara, recalled the situation:

> He would sit for days in hopeless despair, looking out on the desolate landscape. . . . A difficult task lay before him. Ruined in fortune, his occupation gone, his friends dead or impoverished, his health impaired, his heart broken, he had yet to win support for a wife and seven children, and that in a hostile community. Only two things were left to him—the ability to work and the willingness to work.[63]

Sara took her watch and a cherished cameo to a banker as collateral for a loan. She used the money to buy her husband a new suit of clothes to replace his threadbare Confederate gray, and quinine to treat chills suffered since the war. A career was not the only reason Pryor chose to leave Virginia. Having served as a general in the Confederate army, he had never been pardoned, and rumors of punishment and imprisonment persisted. Pryor felt it was in his best interest to leave, and leave he did. He was not alone.[64]

The *Richmond Whig* estimated that as many as fifty thousand young men moved north for jobs.[65] "It is lamentable to note the steady influx of Southern 'refugees' into the North," said a New Yorker. "These poor people come here absolutely begging their bread."[66]

Among those least likely to find financial success in the South after the war were writers and artists. Many migrated to the artistic colonies of the North. Among those was William Rudolph O'Donovan. An aspiring sculptor, O'Donovan went first to Baltimore, then New York. The competition was keen. The Virginian reminisced, "[I was] an unexperienced young man, ambitious to make a name as an artist, knowing nothing of art, and in a great city where there were over forty sculptors, most of whom had been educated in the schools of Europe, all older than myself and in possession of connections formed by years of residence in the Metropolis."[67]

Despite his inauspicious arrival, O'Donovan found opportunities and eventual success in the burgeoning Northern city, as did many other former Rebels. For some Confederates, however, moving north to live among Yankees was fully as odious as living among them in the South.

They instead looked farther south—to Mexico, Latin America, and South America. This self-imposed exile was led by former military and government officials, who justly feared the retribution of the Federal government: Sterling Price, Joseph Shelby, E. Kirby Smith, Jubal Early, former Texas governor Pendleton Murrah, former Louisiana governor Henry W. Allen, to name just a few. These and thousands of former Rebels and their families who followed them hoped to recreate the lost land of their past.

In his farewell address to Louisiana, Governor Allen poignantly expressed the desire to someday return to his home:

> Perhaps in better days when the storms of passion and prejudice shall have passed away we may meet again; I may then be permitted to return—to mingle with my friends, to take them by the hand and "forget my own griefs to be happy with you." If this should be denied me, I humbly trust we may all meet in Heaven at last to part no more.[68]

Henry Allen died in Mexico a short time after.

Pauline De Caradeuc of South Carolina, with legions of others, wished to join the exiles. The young woman wrote in her diary about a friend who visited her family while en route to South America. "We *all* want to go . . . ," Pauline lamented. "All I want to do is leave this vile place, to go to some other country. I hate everything here."[69]

Most stayed and faced the consequences, though, however painful. Former Confederate general P. G. T. Beauregard, courted by foreign military powers, proclaimed from New Orleans, "I prefer to live here, poor and forgotten, than to be endowed with honor and riches in a foreign country."[70]

Likewise, the indomitable Nathan Bedford Forrest declared, "I certainly do not intend to leave the country, for my destiny is now with the great American Union."[71] In his farewell to his men, he urged them to stay as well.

Even with some of the South's old leadership still alive and capable, however, the best and brightest of a generation had been drained away, first by war, then by peace.

CHAPTER 19

The Best Blood

SARA RICE PRYOR RETURNED TO HER VIRGINIA HOME WITH APPREHENSION. She was afraid to sleep, even though a Yankee guard was posted at her door. She knew he could easily be overpowered by whatever lay out there in the darkness. All night Sara kept her vigil by the shuttered window, her faced pressed against the glass to see through the slats. The doors were bolted against some unknown menace, her ears keen for warnings. Occasionally her nervous fingers brushed the hair from the faces of her children, who slept on a quilt laid across the floor. She watched it rain—endlessly, it seemed. And then a sliver of moon appeared, just a hint of light, but in that light she could see the fresh-made grave of a soldier on her lawn. The rain had washed away the soil. From the damp earth, a stiff arm rose.

Of all the horrors, real and imagined, that lay beyond the walls of her home, this scene, somehow, was the least frightening. The sight held her eyes. Transfixed, fascinated, she was saddened beyond words, but not fearful:

> I thought of the tens of thousands, of the hundreds of thousands, of upturned faces beneath the green sod of old Virginia. Strong in early manhood, brave, high-spirited men of genius, men whom their country had educated for her own defence in time of peril,—they had died because that country could devise in her wisdom no better means of settling a family quarrel than the wholesale slaughter of her sons.

"Tomorrow," Sara told herself, she "would reverently cover the appealing arm, be it clad in blue or gray, and mark the spot."[1]

So many hastily dug graves covered the Southern landscape that for a while, the legions of the dead had been ignored as the living struggled to

Hastily dug graves covered the Southern landscape U.S. MILITARY HISTORY INSTITUTE, CARLISLE BARRACKS

survive. Buried so shallowly, many bodies became exposed as the elements swept away their cover.

"Upon the two fields of Shiloh and Corinth there are not less than twelve thousand Confederate dead, whose bones for the most part lie bleaching above ground," penned a witness to the scene.[2]

At Chickamauga, months after the war was over, details of Federal soldiers were assigned the task of exhuming bodies and gathering up the unburied from both sides for interment. "A desolate, dreary scene," said a viewer. "The day was cold and wet; dead leaves strewed the ground; the wind whistled in the trees. . . . Shovels and picks were ready on the ground; and beside the long, low trenches of the dead waited piles of yellow pine coffins spattered with rain."[3]

In Charleston, a wanderer found the churchyard there symbolic of the city itself—sunken graves, broken headstones, a "mangy cur . . . slinking" amid the markers. Then he noted a particular grave: "All around the little plat is a border of myrtle, sweet in its rich greenness, but untrimmed and broken and goat-eaten. It is the grave of the father of the Rebellion, and on the marble slab there is cut the one word,—'CALHOUN.' . . . Time was when South Carolina guarded this grave as a holy spot. Now it lies in ruin."[4]

These hallowed grounds were only temporarily forgotten. A visitor to Hollywood Cemetery in Richmond observed a "solitary man" lost in thought at the grave of J. E. B. Stuart. "Finally he plucked a wild flower, dropped it upon the grave, and with tears in his eyes, left the spot. This lonely mourner at the grave of Stuart was [John Singleton] Mosby."[5]

Later that year, an estimated eight hundred veterans came to the same cemetery armed with gardening tools and began restoring the ground to its former dignity and beauty. Curiously enough, two Federal soldiers pitched in to help.[6] Reading accounts of how ancient Greeks adorned their heroes with olive and ribbon wreaths, a young woman in Mississippi called upon "the daughters of Southland" to gather at the Jackson cemetery "to garland the graves of our fallen braves." The custom was imitated across the South and became an annual event.[7]

Slowly, slowly, the vanquished began putting their lives in order: their homes, their farms, their towns. Just as they devoted time and effort to caring for the dead, so too were Southerners mindful of the living.

> The sounding hammer, the grating saw, the metal clang of the trowel, the "aye" of the hod carrier, the screaming locomotive, the moving cars, the rattling wagons, the busy, moving, jostling crowd, the tumbling down of old walls to be replaced by new, is a fair picture of Atlanta to-day. Those who saw the city a month since would be astonished to see it now. Houses are built in 30 days and opened for trade with a large stock of goods.[8]

No city so symbolized the resurrection of the South as Atlanta. Hardly had the embers cooled from the fires that nearly destroyed it than like a phoenix it rose from the ashes. When Sidney Andrews of the *Boston Daily Advertiser* stopped at the city in late 1865, he was astonished by what he saw:

> Chicago in her busiest days could scarcely show such a sight as clamors for observation here. Every horse and mule and wagon is in active use. The four railroads centering here groan with the freight and passenger traffic, and yet are unable to meet the demand of the nervous and palpitating city. Men rush about the streets with little regard for comfort or pleasure, and yet find the days all too short and too few for the work in hand. . . . The one sole idea first in every man's mind is to make money.[9]

Across the South, the material picture was the same—rebuilding, rejuvenation, rebirth. For the most part, the sounds of progress were welcome. And yet, many Southerners who remembered and revered the Old South were troubled. One such man was Edward Pollard:

> It is to be feared that in the present condition of the Southern States, losses will be experienced greater than the immediate inflictions of fire and sword. The danger is that they will lose their literature, their former habits of thought, their intellectual self-assertion, while they are too intent upon recovering the mere material prosperity, ravaged and impaired by the war. . . . In the life of nations . . . there is something better than pelf, and the prosperity of dollars and cents. . . . It would be immeasurably the worst consequence of defeat in this war that the South should lose its moral and intellectual distinctiveness as a people, and cease to assert its well-known superiority in civilization.[10]

"We have just emerged from the ruins of the most gigantic and terrible war recorded in history," said an equally concerned Alabamian. "And while we have spilled the best blood of our land, and lost our liberties and property, who can say that we have escaped the next greatest calamity of war—the demoralization of society?"[11]

The voids left in Southern society by so many deaths and exiles were incomprehensible—the void of leadership, the void of ideas, the void of energy, the void of values. Despite all the best efforts to maintain some semblance of civilization, chaos swiftly filled the vacuum.

Although the crumbling of values began long before Appomattox, following the Confederacy's final collapse the moral climate plummeted. High and low, young and old—no one, it seemed, was totally impervious to the crisis of convictions that swept the South at war's end. "The props that held society up are broken," sadly noted Eliza Andrews of Georgia. "Everything is in a state of disorganization and tumult."[12] "All is chaos and confusion . . . ," recorded a troubled John Dooley from Georgia. "Murder, rapine, and other foul crimes are rife in the land."[13]

"Murders in our city are of such frequent occurrence now," wailed a Lexington, Kentucky, editor in the fall of 1865, "that they seem to come as regular as night approaches."[14]

As restraints slipped, many white Southerners on the lower rung of the economic ladder were quick to seize the moment. "Our danger now is more from the poor people around us than from the Yankees, as they are going about stealing what they please . . . ," Clarissa Bowen of South Carolina jotted in her journal. "The country is in a wretched state—the only law seeming to be the old one that 'he should take who has the power and they should keep who can.'"[15]

"It is a fact," noted a Montgomery man, "that scarcely a decent house in Middle Alabama has escaped the ravages of the negro and the robber, from the finger ring to the household provisions."[16]

"If things go on this way," wrote a Louisiana editor, "people will take their belongings to bed with them to keep them from being stolen from over their heads."[17]

While murder and robbery posed the greatest threats, vice and immorality were ubiquitous as well. "A perfect saturnalia of debauchery and misrule seems to have set in," said a man from Alabama. "Masked balls for officers and citizens are advertisied. Drinking shops are numerous, and the city is full of idle negroes and white men. The influence of the army of occupation is decidedly unfavorable." As noted, the proximity of young soldiers in the occupation army greatly exacerbated the situation. Gambling, prostitution, and licentiousness were plagues that soon engulfed many Southern communities, with gaming "hells," "miscegenation halls" and "infernal orgies" running day and night. Public drunkenness, frowned upon and ridiculed in antebellum days, now became too common to note, as thousands of Southerners tried to drown their woes in drink.[18] Not surprisingly, "self-destruction" or suicide often followed closely in alcohol's wake. Observing the high incidence of suicide, one Kentuckian cynically wrote:

> We would advise [those] . . . contemplating suicide to visit Louisville. They wouldn't be there more than two days before they would get out of the world, and would not be answerable for self-murder. They'll find it there ready-made. . . . It would only be necessary for a citizen of that city to look out of his door at any hour of any day in the week to see a funeral passing the streets.[19]

Additionally, pathetically, with thousands of orphans created by the war running loose in the land, many became voluntary victims of the great moral disaster. At Fort Smith, Arkansas, an editor was aghast at the "youthful depravity" he saw so rampant all around him.[20] In Memphis, a gang of Jewish and Irish children, ages eight through twelve, pilfered, robbed, and terrorized their community.[21] Another man noticed "mere children" staggering through the streets of another Southern city "in a beastly state of intoxication."[22] Elsewhere throughout the defeated nation, crime, drunkenness, and debauchery had become pandemic.

Citizens tried mightily to grapple with the lawlessness and moral decay, as evidenced by the proceedings at one county courthouse: "Judging from the number of indictments found, for murder, robbery, horse stealing, shooting with intent to kill, etc, they [the grand jury] faithfully performed their duty. There seems to be a resolution to bring all offenders to justice, and have order and quiet once again."[23]

Order. Quiet. They did not come to pass. The social structure of the South had been turned inside out, ripped apart, leaving Southerners reeling. Despite the terrifying trends, there were a few left who believed that Southern civilization could, and someday would, overcome its current degradation. Although hundreds of thousands of the South's finest were in the ground, abroad, or imprisoned, the nucleus was left, as evidenced by Pollard, Ravenel, Affleck, and others; a nucleus of a better day ahead.

Few more personified the hope of the South than Kate Cumming, a spirited girl from Mobile, Alabama. Despite her own lack of knowledge and experience, the Scottish-born woman had seen the need for nurses during the war and decided to become one. Unusually bright and articulate, she wrote a book of her wartime experiences, a graphic account of life and death in Confederate hospitals. Kate thereupon began industriously peddling her title, traveling throughout the South. While in Louisville, she had the chance to join her father, who was also there conducting business. Quite by coincidence, President Johnson was in the city, and Kate and her father joined the throngs watching the official parade through town.

"We had a good view. . . . I think the President quite fine looking," remarked the young woman, but "I could scarcely keep from shedding tears, when I looked on at the parade, and thought of Davis in his lonely prison. A man so very much the superior . . . to any man that we saw today, but such is the world."[24]

As was the case with Kate, for all those rebuilding their fortunes and future, and for all those reburying and remembering their past, the imprisonment of President Davis forced all Southerners to pause and reconsider not only who they were and who they would be, but who they had been as well.

Despite a smattering of creature comforts now allowed in his cell—books, table, chairs—the maddening monotony and petty annoyances persisted in the personal hell of Jefferson Davis.[25] In spite of the pain and irritation it caused his throbbing eyes—or because of it—the lamp in the prisoner's cell continued to burn night and day.[26] And Davis's appointed keeper, Nelson

Jefferson Davis in his cell KANSAS STATE HISTORICAL SOCIETY, TOPEKA

Miles, seemed determined to daily play the petty bureaucrat and interpret his instructions "to the letter."

When the general noticed a long piece of "contraband" tape in the prisoner's room one day, he quickly found an officer and ordered it removed. "When I asked Mr. Davis if he had any use for the tape, which I was directed by General Miles to remove," said the officer, "he replied: 'The ass! Tell the damned ass that it was used to keep up the mosquito net on my bed. I had it in the casemate and he knew it. The miserable ass!'"[27]

Because of such harassments, as well as poor diet and minimal exercise, Davis's physical condition continued to slip. "His pulse is somewhat more rapid than it has been . . . ," noted a physician. "The skin of his hands is cold and clammy. His face gives indication of more mental anxiety."[28]

Added to his tortures from within were the tortures from without. Although the clamor had lessened somewhat, the howl to hang the "unhung traitor" continued.

"I believe that Mr. Davis . . . will be hung," Rev. Henry Ward Beecher told his New York congregation one Sunday in September 1865. "Already the scene rises before me. He is tried; he is convicted; he stands on the scaffold. . . . And I claim that such a scene and spectacle as that will do more for the stability of the country, and for the cause of public order, than almost anything else."[29]

More and more, however, Beecher's wishful vision was becoming less and less likely. To the great disappointment of radicals throughout the North, prosecutors at both the assassination trial and that of Henry Wirz failed to find firm links between Davis and the murder of Lincoln or the mistreatment of Union prisoners. When angry men argued that all the same, Davis was more than guilty since the rebellion he had led spawned such crimes, one writer retorted that such shallow reasoning "was like attributing the measles to the creation of man."[30]

Adding their weight to the matter was the British press. Already angered and horrified by the "infamous cruelty" visited upon Davis and reports of how the victors had "chained the fallen statesman in manacles as a felon," English newspapers warned that Great Britain would sever diplomatic relations with the United States should the prisoner be executed.[31]

As months passed and tempers cooled, the likelihood of Davis's trial and execution for murder waned. Many, like the editor of the New York *Evening Post,* who had hoped for a showy tribunal and ignominious death on the gallows, now rued that the Confederate president had not been murdered the moment he was captured.[32]

Increasingly, pressure was brought to bear on the new U.S. president to hang his old foe and have an end of it—"without," added a man in Delaware, "the benefit of breeches or clergy."[33]

"Not until Jefferson Davis is hung will the American people be content," assured the governor of Wisconsin.[34]

"We would very respectfully request you to have Mr. President Davis hung because we want him hung," ran a petition signed by "many Kansans" to Andrew Johnson. "If you don't hang him there must be a few from Kansas to do it for you. Please let us know what you will do about it."[35]

According to hard-line radicals like Thaddeus Stevens, the Kansans might have saved their postage. "Johnson," said the Republican congressman, "had only pluck enough to hang those two poor devils Wirz and Mrs. Surratt."[36]

As Stevens intimated, a growing discontent with Johnson and his policies was rising within the ranks of radical Republicans. Despite his wild and angry statements earlier, the responsibility of high office soon began to shape the new president. Increasingly, and ironically, a transformation took place in the hearts of Southerners as well. Once called a "vulgar renegade" and "drunken demagogue," Andrew Johnson was seen more and more as the last and only champion of the vanquished South.[37] With the proposed civil-rights bill and the perceived Northern attempt to elevate blacks up to and even over Southern Unionists and common whites, Johnson discovered that, after all, he was a Southerner first and a politician second. His opposition to the Republican-sponsored bill, his sweeping amnesty for nearly all former Rebels save the wealthiest, his well-known refusal to extend the vote to blacks, and his revulsion of "New England fanaticism" endeared him to those who had formerly despised him.[38]

"I am of the Southern people, and I love them and will do all in my power to restore them," announced Johnson, who was hoping to build a coalition of former adversaries to fend off a radical takeover.[40]

"He was born in North Carolina and raised in Tennessee . . . ," proclaimed the *New Orleans Times.* "He does not pass his time in singing psalms through his nose . . . he has never peddled a clock or palmed off a wooden nutmeg."[40]

Although radicals persisted in their efforts to win Johnson over to the "hard peace" treatment of the South, the president all but drew the battle lines during a private exchange with leading radical Charles Sumner.

"You and I might as well understand each other now as any other time," Johnson said, staring at the Massachusetts senator. "You are aware, Sir, I have no respect for a secessionist; I still have a greater detestation and contempt for a fanatic!"[41]

Because of such statements and his opposition to radical reconstruction of the South, Johnson would face increasing opposition in Congress during the coming months. But though his greatest battles—including an impeachment trial—lay just ahead and would be played out on the world stage for Andrew Johnson, his former foe was merely trying to maintain his sanity.

* * *

One of the few moments of pleasure granted the former Confederate president was his daily exercise. "It was my duty to take Mr. Davis for walks around the fort," recalled Lt. J. W. Kaye.

> One night late Mr. Davis was very restless and unable to sleep, and he and I went for a walk around the fortress. It was my custom to rattle my sword as loudly as possible so as not to catch a sentry asleep at his post; but this night even my rattling sword did not serve to arouse a man whom we found asleep fully ten feet from his gun. The man sprang to his feet and saluted, and as we passed on Mr. Davis said that the war was over and enough blood had been shed, and that if the man was reported most possibly he would lose his life, and as a great favor to him he would beg me not to report the sentry, to forget that I had seen him.
>
> Of course I knew that I should have reported him; but I could not find it in my heart to do so after Mr. Davis's earnest appeal.[42]

CHAPTER 20

On Bloodless Battlefields

YANKEES HAD MONEY.

If there was a silver lining to the blue cloud that enveloped the South, it was the silver jingling in the pockets of Northerners. Yankees brought badly needed goods to Southern doors; in return, they bought property, rented rooms, hired services, ate at restaurants. Their money pumped life back into the dead economy of the South. Whether buying a haircut and shave or bargaining for lettuce from a local garden, the soldiers' dollars, if not their presence, were welcome in a land virtually stripped of wealth.

Contemplating the family's financial circumstances after the war, Eliza Andrews commented, "I have serious notions of trying to sell cigarettes to the Yankees in order to get a little pocket money,—only I could not bear the humiliation."[1]

It was indeed humiliating for Southerners to solicit business among Yankees, but many swallowed their pride yet again and did exactly that. John B. Jones noted that among formerly wealthy families, "the ladies are daily engaged making pies and cakes for the Yankee soldiers of all colors, that they may obtain enough 'greenbacks' to purchase such articles as are daily required."[2]

"We knit gloves and socks and sold them," recalled Myrta Lockett Avary. "Miss Beth Sampson had some old pieces of ante-bellum silk that she made into neckties and sold."[3]

With her father and brothers killed in the war, and her mother and sister sewing to support the family, Laura Elizabeth Lee, though only a child, saw opportunity in the family's garden. She carried a basket of plums to the Yankee camp and returned with such delicacies as canned meat and sugar, to the outrage of her mother and even their servant. "I never specks to git over you a little chile sellin' dem nice plums and lettuce to de ole lazy Yankees," the black woman berated her, "and I'll be seized by cats if I ain't scandalized."[4]

Not all those willing to do business with Yankees profited from their labors. Joseph Waddell of Augusta County, Virginia, recorded an episode in which a local black servant, Betty, sold pastries to the occupying troops. Waddell suspected that the girl's mistress was a silent partner but too proud to visit the camps herself. Betty returned from the Yankee encampment, thrilled with her success and carrying a "handful of notes."

"But alas!" Waddell continued, "The rascality of the Yankees, and, alas! Betty's ignorance of United States currency. Upon examination, it turned out that the papers for which she had exchanged her pies were bottle labels, advertising cards, etc., without a cent of money among them."[5]

A writer in Marietta, Georgia, recalled that one day the local commandant sent his shoes to a cobbler for mending. When the shoemaker had finished and asked to be paid, the outraged general ordered him to appear at headquarters. Persisting in his efforts to be compensated, the craftsman was seized by two soldiers and kicked down the steps and into the street. Above, noted the writer, "the stars and stripes were floating on the breeze all around the square."[6]

Every encounter seemed to be a match of wills, with Southerners holding no bargaining chips. Thus was the experience of Sara Pryor. The young Virginian presented Federal authorities with a list of items taken from her family during the war, in hopes of recovering at least some of them. This was the only response:

> To Mr. Pryor:
>
> Dear Sir: A very fine mare belonging to you came into my camp near Richmond and is now with me. It would add much to her value if I could get her pedigree. Kindly send it at your earliest convenience, and oblige.
>
> Yours Truly,
>
> _______ ______________
>
> P. S. The mare is in good health, as you will doubtless be glad to know.[7]

"This was a little too much!" said Sara. "The pedigree was not sent."[8]

Another irksome aspect of occupation was the deluge of anti-Southern literature. "The South is now full of bookagents, peddling their trash without license from the State . . . ," observed one outraged Southerner. "Our children are taught from Readers which contain matter, not only offensive to our politics but injurious to the morals." He suggested heavily taxing "all books and magazines which bear a Northern trade-mark."[9]

Particularly offensive were textbooks. Wrote one Kentucky editor:

> There is scarcely a school book to be found in any store or school in the United States, which does not contain some base and cowardly stab or slur at the people of the South. The most open and causeless insults are offered to the parents of the children in whose hands these text books are placed—glaring and cruel falsehoods for which there never was the slightest foundation of truth.[10]

The journalist also encouraged Southerners not to rely on Northern publishers, but to begin printing books themselves. "If they [Southerners] do not wish to be rendered infamous in the eyes of their children, let them at once abolish all the Yankee text books and periodicals."[11]

Parents, stated another man, "would let their children grow up uneducated before they would have them taught by these enemies of our rights and interests."[12]

"All news," complained Henry Ravenel, "comes to us through the sieve of Yankee eyes." As Ravenel made note, Southern editors found the columns of their newspapers closely monitored and daily walked the razor's edge between news and "treason."[13] Many papers were suppressed. In the case of the Augusta *Transcript,* the offense was publishing an obituary of a soldier who had died from a "disease contracted in the icy prisons of the North." "Disloyal discharge" was the reason for closing the Salisbury, North Carolina, *Banner.* Even black newspapers like *The Loyal Georgian* were shut down with no explanation given by the Freedman's Bureau.[14]

Tired of mincing words, the angry editor of a Charlotte, North Carolina newspaper decided that if his journal were to be throttled, it would at least go out in a blaze: "The South is now under a more grinding despotism than had heretofore found a place upon the face of the earth. . . . We have fallen from our high estate. . . . [T]he proud Southron . . . once roamed his field a free man, and sat under his own vine and fig tree, and none dared make him afraid. He was equal if not the superior of the mercenary race which now dominates over him."[15]

Because of harsh commentary and bias in reporting, correspondents to Northern papers were considered by many Southerners to be the lowest form of Yankee:

> He is writing villainous lies to some radical sheet. He was not a fighter in the army, but a newspaper correspondent. . . . He is a nuisance from the crown of his head to the sole of his foot. . . . In the early Grecian days, such despicable mortals would have been exposed, when infants, upon some bleak hill, and left to perish from the fury of wild beasts. In the days of our Republic they become editors, and hound the rabble to demand the blood of men whose shoe-latchets they are unworthy to loose.[16]

J. M. Taylor, a Baton Rouge newspaper editor, expressed similar sentiments: "There is a brood of persons prowling through the South busily engaged in misrepresenting and slandering our people . . . whose only object seems to be to incense and prejudice the people of the North and the National authorities against us."[17]

Copies of Northern newspapers occasionally found their way into Southern hands, often infuriating the readers. In Mobile, a reader became so incensed that he publicly flogged a correspondent for the St. Louis *Press,* then dropped the whip and surrendered to authorities.[18] "I get in such a rage when I look at them," confessed Eliza Frances Andrews, "that I sometimes take off my slipper and beat the senseless paper with it. No words can express the wrath of a Southerner on beholding pictures of President Davis in woman's dress; and Lee, that star of light before which even Washington's glory pales, crouching on his knees before a beetle-browed image of 'Columbia' suing for pardon."19

As Eliza makes clear, those articles most likely to incense Southerners were vitriolic attacks against Confederate leaders, especially Robert E. Lee. Upon Lee's acceptance of the presidency of Washington College in Lexington, Virginia, one Northern minister protested:

> We would as soon send our son to a pest-house for health or to a gambler's den for education, as to send him to this villainous college—Altogether he stands out the most inexcusable, vilest traitor of the whole crowd of criminals whom he headed—Every student who receives a diploma at his hands should be hissed through life—A more flagrant, indecent, unspeakable outrage than his election has never been perpetrated in the name of education.[20]

In a speech before a Northern audience, abolitionist Wendell Phillips blasted the Southern hero: "If Lee is fit to be President of a college, then for Heaven's sake [take] Henry Wirz and make him professor of what the Scots call the Humanities."[21]

Robert E. Lee
LIBRARY OF CONGRESS

An Ohio newspaper editor called Lee "the greatest criminal in Christendom. . . . It is difficult to decide whether hanging or banishment be his doom. We can only suggest that he be hung first and then banished."[22]

No one was more revered in the South than Lee. Thus nothing could have so provoked Southerners than the gross insults hurled at the old Virginian and the persistent cries to hang him. Rumors of Lee's arrest swirled, though many, including Thomas Affleck, dismissed the possibility outright, since nothing would so inflame the South. "The arrest of General Lee, or any disrespect to him, would be a lasting disgrace to the parties concerned in it, and certainly there is nothing which would implant such ineradicable resentment in the Southern breast."[23]

"His word is law for us," one Southern woman plainly stated.[24]

Evidence of this love was illustrated one day while the general was on his way to assume the position at Washington College. He was spotted by an old black man in Staunton, Virginia. "Why that's our great old general," shouted the surprised man, "That's Massa Robert E. Lee." A local editor described the scene: "If a thousand mortars had suddenly let loose upon the town, a greater excitement could scarcely have been created. The news spread like wild-fire; crowds from town and country rushed in to get a sight of the great and good man."[25]

Well aware of the affection felt by Southerners for Lee and other former leaders, one New York editor advised his countrymen to at least allow the defeated their heroes to cling to: "No punishment can convince the Southern people that they were wrong in principle. . . . They will believe, and their children and children's children will believe, that . . . those that sought to maintain that cause will for ever and ever, in despite of scaffolds, prisons, confiscations, and whatever penalties, be honored by the South as patriots and heroes."[26]

As chronicles of the late war began to appear, ex-Rebels were concerned over their portrayal and how the struggle would be presented to subsequent generations. When Lee informed his friend and former comrade Jubal Early that he was writing a history of the Army of Northern Virginia, Early beseeched Lee to complete the task. "The most that is left to us is the history of our struggle, and I think that ought to be accurately written. We lost nearly everything else but honor, and that should be religiously guarded."[27]

That Southerners felt this legacy threatened, there can be no doubt. With each vindictive attack on their "traitorous" heroes, with each disparagement of their "ragamuffin" soldiers, with each slur of their "so-called" Confederate nation, Southerners felt their identity slipping away.

A woman in Virginia keenly felt the loss. "We have no country, our very name is lost to us."[28] Challenged one writer: "Do they think the Southerners more or less than human? Do they think they have shorter memories, or more obtuse feelings than other men? Do they think it possible for them to forget their glorious four year's Epic? Their dead and living heroes? Their martyrs and their exiles?"[29]

Fading, assailed memories of the war needed champions who would write histories and raise monuments so that none might forget. The recollections were too precious to be lost. From Savannah, a writer reminded his countrymen of one very telling moment of the war: "When the Catholic cemetery of this city was ordered to be leveled for useless breast works, our ladies, widows, and orphans carried the bones of their dead in *baskets, sheets* and *boxes* two miles, and kept them in their *houses* until places of interment, secure from violation could be found."[30]

Obviously moved, the writer drew a lesson from the story:

> What an incident! . . . Imagine groups of women, young and old, learned and unlearned, high and low . . . anxious to secure from desecration the relics of those they loved, and then back again, bending under the weight of their precious burdens. . . . We say that a people whose memories are stored with such inci-

> dents should be protected from cruelty or oppression as carefully as a magazine of gunpowder would be from a spark of fire.[31]

The mere term *Rebel,* which Northerners rarely uttered without a sneer, suddenly became a word of pride for Southerners, a thing to be treasured. Virginians, explained a Petersburg man, would always take pride in being called a Rebel:

> Her annals are the biographies of rebels. She cherishes few memories save those of rebels. She has never raised a monument except to a rebel. . . . A rebel lies in the hallowed bounds of Mt. Vernon. A rebel looks down on her noblest work from Monticello. A rebel in enduring bronze keeps watch and ward over her capital, and none but rebels are thought worthy to line the pedestals of the rebels statue.[32]

It was also a Virginian, Innes Randolph, who penned the words that spoke to many hearts:

> Oh, I'm a good old Rebel,
> Now that's just what I am . . . ;
> And I don't want no pardon
> For what I was and am. . . .[33]

"Last night," Ella Clanton Thomas of Augusta scribbled in her journal, "three men all intoxicated passed by, one of them gloriously tight—said he 'I told him I was a rebel. . . . I am a rebel now, will be for twenty years, will be for fifty years, will be forever, hip hurra'—'Bully for you' cried the other and with shouts they proceeded up the street. I felt my face flush, my eyes filled with tears and in my heart I echoed the sentiment."[34] Like Ella, there were others who voiced their true feelings only in private. "One of the girls tells me," related Constance Cary, "she finds great comfort in singing 'Dixie' with her head buried in a feather pillow."[35]

Had the battle for identity been merely one of words, it would have been taxing enough for the prostrate South. But to the chagrin of the defeated, war's end brought more than Yankee books and newspapers to the region. Thousands of Northerners flooded the South, some to get rich and change society, others simply to satisfy their curiosity. The presence of the latter was an especial annoyance to the conquered.

"Pleasure parties to Richmond were of constant occurrence," it was observed, "and for the time quite eclipsed in popularity, with the Washington idlers, the inevitable pilgrimage to Mt. Vernon."[36] Finely dressed, conversing festively, many visited Virginia to gape in awe at the destruction. Others called on their antebellum friends and in hushed tones commiserated on their failed attempts at independence. Such well-meaning but empty gestures rang hollow for those "sitting in desolation by the ashes of their household goods."[37]

The Pryor home lay in the path of these tourists, and a family servant earned tips drawing water and playing the gracious host. "Sometimes the tourists would ask permission to call on us, claiming some common acquaintance," said Sara.

> My husband was inclined to resent this. Their sympathetic attitude was offensive to him. . . . We were perfectly aware that they wished to see *us,* and not to gain, as they affected, information about the historic localities on the farm. Still less did they desire ignobly to triumph over us. A boy, when he tears off the wings of a fly, is much interested in observing its actions, not that he is cruel—far from it! He is only curious to see how the creature will behave under very disadvantageous circumstances.[38]

Northerners also swarmed to the battlefields where their countrymen had fallen, and some impoverished Southerners were quick to capitalize:

> The "Crater" and the mine are now partly surrounded by a fence; and are shown at twenty-five cents a head, by one Griffiths, who farmed the land before the siege, and now makes a living as showman. Take the showman for what he is worth. He said, "Twice during the siege I have seen my farm nearly covered with dead men. It is calculated that upon the forty acres just round the 'Crater' 48,000 men were killed."[39]

Like adventuresome tourists themselves, itinerant gangs of Northern troublemakers with names like "Plug uglies," "Blood tubs," and "Stunners" also swooped down on Southern cities, drinking, brawling, and bullying the "damn secesh."[40] Groups of pickpockets slipped into new fields of plunder as well.[41] "Sharpers" and "confidence men," not above preying upon freedmen as well as whites, scoured the countryside for gullible victims. One swindle involved individuals posing as agents of the newly formed Freedman's Savings Bank and taking deposits from the unsuspecting. In another ruse, a man accepted donations for a monument to President Lincoln, then quietly skipped town.[42]

Even Horace Greeley advised blacks to beware of that class of Yankee that pours from New England and then "wander[s] all over the earth shuffling and swindling."

> Now let it be generally presumed by the ignorant blacks of the South that a Yankee, because a Yankee, is necessarily their friend, and this unclean brood will overspread the South like locusts, starting schools and prayer meetings at every cross roads, getting hold of abandoned or confiscated plantations and hiring laborers right and left, cutting timber here, trying out tar and turpentine there, and growing corn, cotton, rice and sugar, which they will have sold at the errliest [*sic*] day and run away with the proceeds, leaving the negroes in rags and foodless, with the winter just coming on.[43]

Most egregious of all to Southerners were the flocks of speculators, opportunists, and office seekers descending from the North, each seeking to turn the misfortunes of the South into their profit. As early as the fall of Richmond, recalled one Virginian, "sutlers, peddlers and hucksters swarmed in like locusts, on the very first steamers up the river. They crowded Broad street, the unburned stores on Main, and even the alleyways, with great piles of every known thing that could be put in tin."[44]

The "carpet-baggers," proclaimed a Southerner, were "worse than Attila, scourge of God. He could only destroy existing fruits, while, by the modern invention of public credit, these caterans stole the labor of unborn generations."[45]

A Louisianan felt the same way: "They crowd the public conveyances, and are running to and fro in every direction, in quest of a fortune. But they propose to shave very close to all their transactions; they all want to get the land of the Southerner for a song, and if he declines to be cheated out of his inheritance they at once accuse him of disloyalty."[46]

"There is an atmosphere of greed and vulgar shopkeeper prosperity about the whole Yankee nation that makes the very poverty and desolation of the South seem dignified in comparison," observed Eliza Frances Andrews.[47]

And yet, some Southerners were reluctantly forced to admit that there was a positive side to the economic invasion. Showing journalist Sidney Andrews through the renewed streets of Charleston, a resident indicated the shops owned by Northern merchants. "The presence of these men was at first very distasteful to our people," he admitted, "and they are not liked any too well now; but we know they are doing a good work for the city."[48]

Henry Ravenel
SOUTH CAROLINIANA LIBRARY,
UNIVERSITY OF SOUTH CAROLINA,
COLUMBIA

"Resident merchants are mostly at the bottom of the ladder of prosperity," noted Andrews. "They have idled away the summer in vain regrets for vanquished hopes, and most of them are only just now beginning to wake to the new life. . . . While they vacillate with laggard time, Northern men are springing in with hands swift to catch opportunity."[49]

When a magazine exploded in Mobile, leveling eight city blocks and shattering windows throughout the city, a Northern merchant dining nearby was severely cut by flying glass. Despite the injury, the man rushed to the telegraph office and wired his partner to ship "nothing but glass and putty." His mission complete, the Yankee thereupon fainted from blood loss.[50]

Although they brought much-needed goods to the South and some recognized their contributions, Yankees prospered, many thought, at the great expense of their hosts. Resentment grew as the toll taken by the war became more painfully clear each day. When plantations, cotton mills, and cotton itself went on the auction block, it was Northern money that was exchanged, and Southerners were slow to reap the rewards. People who had managed to hold on to cotton throughout the war, knowing prices would skyrocket when the hostilities ceased, saw their hopes dashed again when treasury agents confiscated the staple.

"A swarm of thieves in the shape of officials and officers" had invaded the South, said William Owner. "It has been no uncommon occurrence for a military officer with a train of wagons to go to a planters house, place a guard around it with orders to shoot him if he attempts to leave and [have] his cotton hauled to steamboats . . . and shipped off."[51]

While traveling in Mississippi, a Northern correspondent found Southerners particularly angered over Yankee cotton speculators: "One shrill-voiced dagger-tongued elderly young woman in the cars, 'wished that not another boll of cotton would ever grow.' She 'would rather wear woolen the hottest day of August' than contribute anything to Yankee manufacture!" In South Carolina, Henry Ravenel heard troubling accounts from other counties. "Robberies are of daily occurrence. Ebaugh, Markly & Easterling & others are buying all the cotton the negroes can steal & carry to them. Every body is losing cotton. . . . William had his cotton removed into his dwelling house at Woodlawn, & it has been stolen."[52]

It was the cotton-buying New England middlemen, derisively referred to as "Cottontots," who encouraged blacks to steal and who garnered the lion's share of profit and the lion's share of blame for Southern suffering.[53] A Montgomery resident was livid in his characterization of such "miscreants": "Before the war he toadied Southern people, and used every wile and art to be introduced into Southern families; but during the war he delighted in calling Southern women 'vipers' and 'vixens,' and Southern men 'cowards' and 'odious traitors.' Since the war he has come South to 'play develish [*sic*] fine' on cotton."[54]

Another invasion of the South involved religion and education. Missionary efforts and the Freedman's Bureau brought well-intentioned but unwanted "fanatics" to the very doorsteps of the South. Even though reports indicate that they issued twice as many rations to destitute whites as blacks, generally such organizations were not welcome.[55]

"Mississippi," said the *Vicksburg Herald,* "needs no more of those self-appointed emissaries who come down here to teach the negroes their rights, and inflame their minds against their former masters, and against the race who are to employ them, and benefit them."[56]

"The friends of the negro are determined to fight for the equality of the blackman," another Mississippian explained. "With them the negro is of first importance. His right to vote, his right to hold office, his right to enter our homes and hearts, his right to marry our daughters and, in fact, his right to do everything . . . is demanded by the admirers of amelioration, regeneration and miscegenation."[57]

"They have a miserable, crack-brained fanatic here now, named French," wrote Eliza Andrews, "who has been sent out from somewhere in

New England to 'elevate' the negroes and stuff their poor woolly heads full of all sorts of impossible nonsense." When word arrived that French would be performing marriage ceremonies for blacks who, under slavery, had not had the benefit, locals refused him the use of their buildings. Not, explained Eliza, because they objected to the marrying of blacks, but because they did not want their property "polluted by the spoutings of such a creature." "His very presence in a town where his first footfall would have once been his death warrant," she added, "is a sufficient disgrace."[58]

The use of the term "death warrant" is not apocryphal. In Georgia, a representative of the Freedman's Bureau was shot to death in his front yard. At Pontotoc, Mississippi, another agent met a similar fate.[59] Southern whites saw organizations such as the Freedman's Bureau as perpetuating, if not instigating, problems with blacks. If slaves had behaved in an orderly and deferential manner all these years, it was the meddling of Yankees that made them act otherwise now. Similarly, Northern missionaires were viewed as the long arm of radical Republicans whose "object . . . is simply to debase the whites of this section by exalting the blacks."[60]

"Now children," began the daily chant of a Yankee teacher in Louisville to a class of black students, "you don't think white people are any better than you because they have straight hair and white faces?"

"No, sir."

"No, they are no better, but they are different," the instructor continued. "They possess great power. They control this vast country. Now, what makes them different from you?"

"MONEY."

"Yes, but how did they get money?"

"Got it off us. Stole it off we all!"[61]

With catechisms like the above being repeated across the South, whites became understandably concerned for the future of race relations. "They pretend to teach them letters," growled a North Carolinian, "but they teach them ideas and implant within their bosoms feelings that, if unchecked, will ripen into a harvest of blood and murder."[62]

The hypocrisy of some invaders became patently clear to many Southern blacks, as well. Sara Rice Pryor described an incident in which a group of tourists observed her former bondsman named Aleck tying up a rose-bush. Assuming that the Pryors were still holding him in servitude, one of them addressed the old man, "Recollect, boy . . . the white woman in that house is now your slave!"

"Aleck was standing beneath my window . . . ," said Sara. "He looked up, simply advising me, 'Let 'em go 'long,' and resumed his work in training the rose bush."[63]

"Now, white folks," announced a Louisiana black, "I'se a gwine to tell you de difference 'between a Southern man and de Yankee":

> Well, de Southern man he stop at de hotel, he ax for a room, he get de key; he say, "Here Jim, take my valise." When he git de room, he say, "Jim, you black rascal, brush my coat and boots, and be in a hurry." While I'se doing dat he wash hissef, comb his hair, and take a drink, and when I gives him de boots he hands me a dollar. When de Yankee stops at de hotel, he say, "Mr. Johnson, please brush my boots—Mr. Johnson, please carry dis note to Mr. Smith at de railroad depot—Mr. Johnson, please carry dis message to de telegraph office—Mr. Johnson, guess I'll have to trouble you to bring me a pitcher of water—Mr. Johnson, I guess I ought to have a cigar—run down and get me a five cent one." I cum back, and spec, of course he give me 'bout two dollars, but stead of given me de money, he ax me to take a seat, and tell him 'bout my grandfader, my grand modder, my brudder, and my sister, and my cousin, and my ole massa, and how much I'se making, and how I is, and all such nonsense, and arter a while he say, "Well, Mr. Johnson, I guess I'll have to give you a dime afore I leave here." Now, white folks dats de difference 'tween de Southern man and de Yankee, and it's every word truf.[64]

After centuries of life together, many white Southerners felt that they knew the characters of black Southerners better than that of their own race from the North.

No matter how outrageous an act committed by a black, many Southerners felt the root cause lay in the North. "The poor negroes don't do us any harm except when they are put up to it," rationalized one Southern woman. "Even when they murdered that white man and quartered him, I believe pernicious teachings were responsible."[65]

Likewise, Henry Ravenel was dismayed by the downward spiral of society and placed the blame squarely on the interlopers. "Neither the negro slave nor his master is responsible," the South Carolinian asserted. "It has been done by those, who having political power, are determined to carry into practice the sentimental philanthropy they have so long and & angrily advocated."[66]

In many ways, this second invasion of the South following the war, the invasion of words, thoughts, and ideas, worked to accomplish what armies never could. As one editor phrased it:

It shows us that a more remorseless war can be carried on under the white banner of peace than under the black flag of extermination. It shows us the anomalous "magnanimity" that spares life and crushes out hope. . . ; that leaves unscathed the bodies of its victims, and with a refinement of cruelty fastens upon the mind and wrings the sensitive spirit with a torture so exquisite that extinction would be welcome as a boon. It shows us a fierce and furious conflict raging in the midst of an apparent peace; it shows us on bloodless battlefields, opposing ideas and principles striving for mastery; it shows us the commencement of a struggle in which Force is not an element, which numbers cannot decide, and which material resources are of no avail. A struggle in which soul, not sinew, will be of account, keen wits, not sharp swords, ultimately triumphant.

This is the second phase of the war, this the form it has now assumed, these are the forces that now come into play. Intellect, Character, Will, the three great powers, will determine the issue.[67]

CHAPTER 21

The Second Snakebite

IN JULY 1865, AMOS BLACK, A HARDEMAN COUNTY, TENNESSEE, PLANTER, shot one of his fieldhands and told the others, "You have been fooled by the damned Yankee lies till you thought you were free, and you got so you could not obey your master. There is no law against killing niggers and I will kill every damned one I have if they do not obey me and work just as they did before the war."[1]

The end of the war marked no clear end of slavery. With the institution still legal in some states, many masters believed emancipation would be declared unconstitutional by the courts; or, at the very least, most felt that they would be compensated for their property.[2] "I 'low the gov'ment won't take away all our niggers fur nothin'. . . ," one South Carolina planter reasoned. "The Cons'tution makes niggers prop'ty, and gov'ment is bound to pay for 'em."[3] Rather than freeing their slaves, many, like this man, held on, waiting.[4]

"When we all got free, they were a long time letting us know. They wanted to get through with the corn and cotton," explained freedwoman Isabella Boyd. "When people from other plantations came by and asked why they were working when they had been freed, they replied, 'The government will tell us when we're free.'"[5]

As the above examples illustrate, there was confusion among both blacks and whites. "Slavery [is] in such a condition that neither masters nor Negroes know whether it exists or not," observed Lizzie Hardin.[6]

Freedom for all came not in a moment; freedom came in waves, rocking society's foundations each time. While some of their brethren had been celebrating for weeks, "prime field hands" and other slaves, including a seven-year-old girl, were auctioned to the highest bidder in Augusta as late as April 19. Macon held auctions as well.[7]

Kentucky continued to allow slavery, though bondsmen gambled for freedom by the thousands, fleeing to neighboring free states. One individual estimated that more than sixty thousand fugitives crossed the Ohio River between May 1 and September 15, 1865.[8] Nevertheless, a Kentucky newspaper continued to print advertisements for runaway slaves: "I will prosecute to the full extent of the law . . . [anyone] for hiring or harboring one of my negroes."[9]

In August 1865, on the steps of a Delaware courthouse, a black was sold into servitude for seven years when he could not pay a debt. Another man in the same state had been brought from Maryland and was sold to a farmer in Dover.[10]

Some planters tried to ignore emancipation, counting on the ignorance of their slaves and the distance of the Federals. Others used the letter of the law to their advantage, forcing freedmen into legal labor contracts—agreements that many blacks considered little better than bondage itself.

William Cameron, a planter in Gainesville, Alabama, drew up the following contract with five of his former slaves:

> Any of them who fails to work faithfully or behave properly or shall take or injure any of my property shall leave my plantation and not return and any of them who fails to observe this agreement or leaves the plantation before the 1st day of January next shall forfeit all right, support, clothing, Medical attentions and compensation for services. All of said colored persons are to obey my orders in regard to their conduct, and duties on said plantation . . . and none of them are to leave said plantation without my written permission.[11]

Some contracts contained clauses allowing those who hired to administer punishment for misbehavior—flogging, bucking and gagging, and suspending by the thumbs were favored methods.[12] Understandably, most freedmen viewed such contracts as slavery, pure and simple, and many did not enter or fulfill them voluntarily.

Lewis and Green Rhodes, along with their wives, contracted to work for John Spinks of Warren County, Georgia. After a month's service, some "difficulty" arose, and the planter reportedly punished one of the women by giving her a hundred lashes. When an agent from the Freedman's Bureau did nothing, the four were forced to return to the farm. Following another disagreement, Spinks chained the two men and padlocked them to the floors of the kitchen and smokehouse. Working themselves free, and with the chains still clanking around their necks, the blacks managed to slip

Black Shantytown KANSAS STATE HISTORICAL SOCIETY, TOPEKA

outdoors and race toward safety. Spinks shot at them as they fled, wounding one severely. In retaliation for the escape, another hundred lashes were administered to one of the women. Again receiving no justice from the local Freedman's Bureau, the men, with the chains still upon them, related the incident to the bureau office in Augusta.[13]

"Is it surprising," asked a black editor, "that freedmen dread to go into the country to work, and lounge around our cities? We know that many stay in the cities, who would rather live in the country, because they are afraid."[14]

Simply being called a freedman did not necessarily make it so. In some areas of the South, the old "patrol-and-pass" continued as if no war had been fought and no Emancipation Proclamation issued.[15]

While en route to Shreveport, former bondsman Henry Adams met several white men on the road who stopped him and asked to whom he belonged. When Adams replied that he was free and belonged to no one, three of the men began beating him with sticks. "[They] told me they were going to kill me and every other Negro who told them that they did not belong to anyone," said Adams. "One of them who knew me told the others, 'Let Henry alone for he is a hard-working nigger and a good nigger.'"[16]

Near Wetumpka, Alabama, a black educator was stopped for the same purpose. "The government of the United States has made me free," the teacher said. "I have no owner." "Shoot the damned son of a bitch!" shouted one of the white men. The man was hustled away to jail, although he was shortly released.[17]

When a dozen men and boys determined to leave their plantation, a posse of whites pursued and fired on them. "Said they were going to kill every nigger they found leaving their masters," explained one of those who escaped.[18]

"God never did intend to free niggers," raged Anthony Edwards's master, and, said Edwards, "he cussed till he died."[19]

When the fact of freedom could no longer be denied, some slave owners, in their poverty and anger, simply forced freedmen off the land with no food, clothing, or money. "We was jus' turned out like a lot of cattle. You know how they turn cattle out in a pasture?" recalled Fountain Hughes. "Well after freedom . . . colored people didn' have nothing."[20]

One black recalled how his irate master ordered all hands from the property, even though they were penniless. As they left, the master warned that should he arise the next morning to find that any had returned, "he'd horsewhip him."[21]

At another home, when word reached the family that only one of their sons would be returning and that the Confederate cause was lost, the mother was devastated, but the father became uncontrollably angry. Only a child at the time, Annie Row described the scene:

> Missy started crying and marster jumped up and started cursing . . . and he picked up the hot poker and said, "Free the nigger will they, I'll free them." And he hit my mammy on the neck, and she started moaning and crying and dropped to the floor. There they were, the missy a-moaning, my mammy a-moaning, and the marster cussing as loud as he could. He took the gun off the rack and started for the field where the niggers were working. My sister and I saw that, and we started running and screaming, because we had brothers and sisters in the field. . . . The marster hadn't gone far in the field when he dropped all of a sudden. . . . He couldn't talk or move, and they toted him in the house. The doctor came, and the next day marster died.[22]

When the surviving son returned and took over the plantation, he was forced to let many of the workers go. A short time afterward, the mother found her son with his throat cut; a suicide note stated that he did not care to live "because the niggers were free and they were all broken up."[23]

Like the man above, some slaveholders were so furious at freeing their chattel that they became crazed. Citizens of Montgomery were appalled to see blacks entering town with "their ears cut off and large pieces torn from their heads."[24]

"You could see lots of niggers hanging to trees in Sabine bottom," said a former Texas bondswoman, "cause they caught them swimming across the Sabine River and shot them."[25] In the Indian Territory, slave-holding Choctaws and Chickasaws, resentful over the loss of their property, hunted and killed blacks like wild game.[26]

Although many owners wished to be rid of people they no longer controlled, some would not succeed. In many military districts, Southerners were compelled by Federal bayonets to provide for their former slaves. Placed in command of the Columbia-Orangeburg section of South Carolina, Gen. Alfred Hartwell issued a typical edict:

> The colored people will not be turned off the places on which they have lived in any case whatever without orders from these headquarters. Whites [will not] throw off those who have been their slaves. Where the former owners refuse or neglect to make or offer fair contracts with the colored people, it will be necessary to use strict measures.[27]

Some Northern newspaper correspondents commiserated with the planters of the South. "The freedom of the negro there is freedom from work," proclaimed the Cincinnati *Enquirer,* "and the freedom of the master is to support him in his idleness."[28]

"One of the negroes had reported me to the Yankee in command of this department for not feeding them," stated an impoverished Georgian. "I had a note from the officer saying that unless I issued rations regularly he would have me brought before him. This order I ignored, as it was impossible to obey."[29]

It was not only the financial support of freed blacks that rankled former slaveholders; it was also the juxtaposition of familiar roles. "On my own plantation I can give no order unless approved by an insolent negro . . . ," wrote an indignant South Carolina planter. "The ferocious and licentious negro is encouraged to insult us, and no atrocity which he may commit meets with punishment. I am disarmed while every negro on my plantation has a gun, they are allowed to rob and plunder at discretion."[30]

This world of contradictions was just too much, too quickly. Whites were sick of the issue, of all it had cost them, and the quagmire into which slavery and freedom had cast them. If blacks were no longer to be property, many whites wanted them out of their midst.

"The mass of the people," a Northerner commented on Virginia, "including alike the well-educated and the illiterate . . . generally detested the Negroes, and wished every one of them driven out of the State. The black man was well enough as a slave; but even those who rejoiced that slavery was no more, desired to get rid of him along with it."[31]

"I wish they were all hung around the necks of the Abolitionists," vehemently wrote one widow, abandoned by her servants.[32]

Mary Chesnut reflected: "The negroes would be a good riddance. A hired man is far cheaper than a man whose father and mother, his wife and twelve children have to be fed, clothed, housed, nursed, taxes paid, and doctors' bills—all for his half-done, slovenly, lazy work. So for years we have thought—negroes a nuisance that did not pay."[33]

"I tell you we get along a good deal better and get more done," said Sallie Bateman of Mississippi, "than when all the negroes was here."[34]

"I never was free until my slaves were free," recalled one Tennessean. "They were a constant 'thorn in my side,' and the increasing responsibility which rested upon me was well nigh intolerable."[35] Observed Henry Grider from neighboring Kentucky, "We . . . are doing pretty well [without them] and rejoice in the peace we have."[36]

Rather than turn out her slaves, one Louisiana woman decided it would be easier just to leave herself. "I am getting very anxious to leave my home," the widowed mother of two wrote. "There is no pleasure in living where no one seems to be willing to do their part. My horses are not fed and watered as they used to be. The corn is pulled and left on the ground for four or five days. My fine mare was stolen last night by a freed man." When she finally moved weeks later, she commented, "I could not stay with negroes."[37]

Whether abandoned deliberately or turned out due to the poverty of their former masters, blacks were left with few options. In desperation, most looked to their liberators. Unfortunately, many of these turned their backs. Perhaps nothing was more disheartening to the former slaves than the treatment they received from Federal soldiers. For some freedmen, it must have seemed that with the death of "Father Abraham," goodwill had died as well.

"It reaches us from many quarters that the Negroes are bitterly disappointed in the results of emancipation," one observer reported, "and by the change in the tone of the Yankees to them *before* the overthrow of the South and *since*."[38]

On a plantation in Georgia, some blacks who reportedly refused to work according to their contracts were suspended by their thumbs and "unmercifully" lashed by Federal troops. "Negroes are astounded at the idea of being whipped by Yankees," noted one witness wryly.[39]

So intent were some occupation commanders on controlling the black population in North Carolina that the Freedman's Bureau in Salisbury established a chain gang for their punishment. "We think it is a good idea," hailed a citizen of Raleigh, "and would like to see it established here, provided they were carefully guarded."[40]

The chain gang was, in the words of one freedman, "not one ace above a condition of slavery." Writing to a black newspaper on conditions in Selma, Alabama, he continued:

> Here we have the rebel overseer, with his club in his hand, driving a gang of negro men, in this, our day of *freedom,* foreshadowing a future to us . . . which has its counterpart only in the horrors of our past slavery. I was told that many of the men of this same chain-gang have been arrested upon the most trivial charges, and condemned to work in this degraded manner from thirty to sixty days, while white scoundrels go unpunished for much greater crimes.[41]

A black writer was appalled at how quickly the chain gang was filled. "All are in danger—the innocent almost as much so as the guilty. Even a female chain-gang is being organized."[42]

Chain gangs were not the only form of corporal punishment the Federals employed. "In South-West Georgia . . . they keep great straps to beat them with," wrote Eliza Andrews. "Mrs. Stowe need not come South for the Legree of her next novel." A woman living in North Carolina agreed: "The whip with which the Yankee vice-provost has armed himself is one which no Southern overseer ever dared use—even own."[43]

Many blacks, no doubt, had viewed the Northern nation as being of one mind on the issue of race. If "massa Linkum" had taken a benign approach to blacks, then it stood to reason that his soldiers would as well. Thus the shock of these people might well be imagined when they first witnessed the brutal behavior of many Yankees who came South.

Anne Frobel watched from her Virginia bedroom one day as several occupying troops tormented a "half witted" black boy. They dragged him by the hair, then raced him into the yard, where one would give him a kick, then another. The girl described the scene that followed:

> Another man with an immense sword gave him three or four severe blows across the back with it, and while he was writhing and howling with pain, another ran out of the kitchen with a handful of pepper, or something else, and dashed it into his eyes. Then they all set up such a shouting and hurrah, as if it was something very witty. I thought if such cruelties had been seen by them, practiced by Southern people, what volumes would have been written to the yankee papers about it.[44]

There were even more horrid accounts of the victors preying on blacks. As the following words reveal, not all their "fun" was limited to boyish pranks or stunts: "They dug up at Minnie Frierson's eighteen negro women with bayonet stabs in the breast. The Yankees were done with them!"[45]

CHAPTER 22

Standing on a Volcano

"PERHAPS THERE IS NO PROBLEM OF GREATER GRAVITY BEFORE THE American people than the just and wise solution of the race question . . . ," wrote Southern educator Jabez Lamar Monroe Curry. "It needs the calm, patient, thoughtful, intelligent foreseeing and forecasting study of our best men and women."[1]

Curry was a brilliant, idealistic man . . . but no one had time for idealism. There was no calm, no patience among the war-ravaged white Southerners and the newly freed black Southerners. The one longed for normalcy, for a return to a more stable, more civilized time; the other prayed for a new order, a new world of hope and happiness.

Both would be bitterly disappointed.

The greatest fear of whites had come to pass. The slaves had been freed, and whites saw them running wild, raping, looting, plundering, and murdering almost at will. If one read of crimes occurring a town or two away, the surliness of blacks at home gave credence to the possibility that the reader's community would be next.

The greatest hopes of blacks had been dashed. They were free—but to what end? The South was devastated financially and physically, and ironically, the reversal of Southern fortunes had left as many blacks homeless and destitute as whites. For most freed people, the "promised land" was a phantasm.

Both peoples were struggling for survival in a land without the resources to support either. Neither felt safe. Each feared the other. Each viewed the other as responsible, at least in part, for their current condition. Into this volatile mix was added suspicion, anger, and above all, hatred.

Newspaper articles such as the following were copied throughout the South and struck at the core of white fear: "Fifteen hundred dollars reward is offered for the apprehension of Frank, Picayune and Calup, the negroes who waylaid and murdered . . ."[2]

Other newspaper articles sparked fear among blacks. "A negro man, Lewis, formerly belonging to the Jordan plantation . . . was found dead in the woods . . . his throat cut."[3]

White Southerners were overwhelmed by the black crime wave spreading across their homeland. In a moment, Freedmen were everywhere. Defeated whites felt out of place in this new world and, for the first time in their lives, vulnerable. It was probably this phenomenon that skewed their perceptions. They were seeing blacks in new locations, filling the cities and towns, wandering aimlessly along the roads and over the countryside . . . and it was unnerving. But it was also nonetheless true that the majority of freedmen were not committing crimes, and that every crime committed was an exception to the rule.

Henry Ravenel observed that most blacks, including his former slaves, had handled freedom well and did not pose a threat to society. "I think that the negroes generally as a race, have withstood the temptations to lawlessness & violence which might have been expected from 3 or 4 millions suddenly passing from slavery to freedom."[4]

The truth of Ravenel's assertion did little to allay fear that stemmed from acts of violence that were indeed committed. For those touched by black crime, the exception *was* the rule.

In North Carolina, a former slave attacked her erstwhile mistress with a rock and "beat out her brains."[5] In Kentucky, a freedman slew his former master with an ax, then went to town and enlisted in the army. The military refused to turn the man over for trial.[6] "Only one more white man" was the ominous phrase heard throughout murder-plagued Kentucky.[7]

In another incident:

> Mr. W. B. Wilkinson, an old and highly respected citizen of Lauderdale county, was most brutally murdered on Sunday night last by a party of his former slaves, at his plantation. . . . They supposed that he had a large sum of money and to secure it fell upon the old gentleman first beating him severely and afterwards hanging him and stabbing him in different parts of the body.[8]

Near Anderson, South Carolina, young Albert Geer happened upon two freedmen butchering a hog belonging to his father. At his insistence, the men threw the animal onto the son's horse, but rather than letting Geer ride away, they pulled him from the saddle and killed him.[9]

Near Chattanooga, black troops entered the home of an old man, robbed him, beat him "nearly to death," then raped his wife and daughter.[10] Horribly, rape often went hand in hand with murder, and it was this aspect of the anarchy rocking the South that gripped whites with perhaps their greatest terror. "There seems to be an epidemic of this blackest and most detestable of crimes," observed the *Nashville Press*.[11]

In another case, near Gallatin, Tennessee, a black "laid in wait" for a white girl he had been watching in the neighborhood. Sensing his opportunity, he seized and "violated" the young woman. When another black man approached, the criminal fled. Helping the terrified girl to a nearby home, the rescuer sounded the alarm.[12]

An enraged father near Bridgeport, Alabama, set out in search of the freedman who had brutally raped his daughter. Overtaking a black on the road, the frenzied father asked his name. "None of your damned business," was the reply. Without a second thought, the father shot the man on the spot. Later, it was determined that he had killed an innocent man.[13]

In Richmond, two black soldiers raped a white girl. . . . In New Orleans, a Freedman ravished a nine-year-old. . . .[14] In Salisbury, a white woman was raped by a black.[15] Scores of reports such as these as well as numerous "attempted" assaults (it was usually put that way, said one woman; "'consummated' nails the victim to the stake") fueled fear and widened the gulf between blacks and whites. But this was only the beginning.[16] The anticipated new year plunged the South into a maelstrom of violence.

In Augusta, a regular battle ensued when black soldiers were chased from a woman's home by her son, who wielded a pistol. More troops returned, broke down the door, and stormed upstairs. When it was over and an officer had finally forced them out, four blacks were dead.[17] In Beaufort, North Carolina, a squad of black soldiers entered a home near the fort and, reported a Charlotte editor, "while the man of the house and his wife were held, they ravished their daughter, a girl fifteen years of age. Another squad went to another house, and attempted a rape on a child ten years of age." At almost the same time, four black troops from Fort Macon were brought to Raleigh in chains on charges of raping a thirteen-year-old.[18] In Texas, a band of several hundred black soldiers went on a rampage, raiding, robbing, and raping.[19]

Retribution for such heinous acts as homicide and rape was often swift and certain, albeit at times overzealous. Upon her arrest, a freedwoman who confessed to the murder of her former mistress was seized by neighbors and, without trial, hanged from a nearby tree.[20] Near Forrestville, North Carolina, a black man caught raping a white woman was riddled by fifteen bullets, "each ball giving a mortal wound."[21]

After he had beaten his wife severely and stabbed to death a white man who tried to intervene, Fortune Wright indeed found that justice was sure, if not always swift. At the gallows, Wright began "a long, rambling and disconnected explanation of his crime." Wrote a witness:

> As the doomed man concluded, a white cap was drawn over his face, and the rope adjusted. He began shouting "farewell friends," and was still repeating these words when the supporting ropes of the drop were cut. He fell some six or eight feet; but the rope, not being properly greased, the knot failed to slip, so that when the body rebounded the knot twisted around to his forehead. . . . The body was lowered, taken from the rope, and carried up a second time to the drop. The knot was re-tied, and the rope placed about his neck, the body propped up and the stay ropes again cut. The noose again failed to slip, the rope being new and stiff and not soaped, and the knot came around to the back of his head. The rope remained under the chin, however, immediately strangling the . . . unconscious man.[22]

No matter how rapidly turned the wheels of justice, it was not enough to mollify white Southerners. Black crime was so endemic that many in the South were kept watching over their shoulders by day and tossing and turning by night. Frances Butler Leigh of Georgia, who while alone on her plantation during the war never worried, now began retiring at night with a pistol under her pillow.[23]

"They do not care, the men and women of the North, if we are raped," one terrified girl burst out. "They do not care that we are prisoners of fear, that we fear to take a ramble in the woods alone, fear to go about the farms on necessary duties, fear to sit in our houses alone; fear, if we live in cities, to go alone on the streets. . . ."[24]

"I am always so frightened and uneasy in the streets after dark that it greatly detracts from the pleasure of going out," wrote Eliza Andrews, echoing the sentiments of her peers. "We can generally avoid the Yankees by taking the back streets, but the Negroes swarm in every by-way." She continued: "We had a dancing party at Dr. Robertson's in the evening. Most of the young men go to parties fully armed. The parlor mantelpiece at the back was covered with pistols brought there by our escorts."[25]

"I wouldn't think of walking two blocks at night without my revolver," commented a man from Norfolk.[26]

Not only did people have to travel in these circumstances, but farmers and plantation owners were forced to work in them as well.

Eliza Frances Andrews
UNIVERSITY OF NORTH CAROLINA LIBRARY, CHAPEL HILL

When it was learned that her former slaves had obtained the keys to her storage barns on the plantations, Elizabeth Allston's mother set out to retrieve them. Though she had requested a guard from Federal authorities, none was forthcoming. With a note from the local Union officer instructing the blacks to turn over the keys, and only her teenage daughter as company, Mrs. Allston stopped at the first plantation.

"Negroes assembled in great numbers," Elizabeth wrote of their arrival. When her mother stated their mission, "there rose up a sullen murmur from the crowd."[27] Aware that the Freedmen had already measured out rations for themselves to last the coming year, Mrs. Allston announced that if there remained any need among them, she would come and apportion it herself. There were dark rumblings and a mood of menace in the group. With a firm face, Mrs. Allston stepped from her carriage and walked among the people, calling each by name and inquiring after their children. She displayed "no sense that they could possibly be enemies," Elizabeth observed. The keys were soon surrendered.

Later that week, at a plantation owned by her absent son, the reception was quite different. Since the onset of war in 1861, no white person had set foot on the estate. Daddy Aleck, a black servant, drove the women's carriage, and Elizabeth described what transpired:

As we neared the place the road was lined on either side by angry, sullen black faces; instead of the pleasant smile and courtesy [curtsy] or bow to which we were accustomed, not a sign of recognition or welcome, only an ominous silence. As the carriage passed on they formed an irregular line and followed. This would be a test case, as it were. If the keys were given up, it would mean that the former owners still had some rights. We drove into the barnyard and stopped in front of the barn. Several hundred Negroes were there . . . armed with pitchforks and hickory sticks, and some had guns. . . . They crowded closer and closer around the carriage, and mamma got out into the midst of them. . . . She called for the head man and told him she wished to see the crop, and he cleared the way before us to the rice barn and then to the corn barn. Mamma complimented him on the crops. As she was about to leave the corn barn a woman stretched her arms across the wide door so as to hold up the passageway.

Mamma said, "Sukey, let me pass," but Sukey did not budge. Then mamma turned to Jacob. "This woman has lost her hearing; you must make her move from the doorway." Very gently Jacob pushed her aside and we went out and Jacob locked the door. Then mamma said: "And now, Jacob, I want the keys."

"No, ma'am, I kyant gie yu de key. De officer gen me de key, en I kyant gie um to nobody but de officer."

"I have the officer's written order to you to give me the keys—here it is"— and she drew from her reticule the paper and handed it to Jacob. He examined it carefully and returned it to her, and proceeded slowly to draw the keys from his pocket and was about to hand them to mamma, when a young man who had stood near, with a threatening expression sprang forward and shouted, "Ef yu gie up de key, blood'll flow," shaking his fist at Jacob. Then the crowd took up the shout, "Yes, blood'll flow for true," and a deafening clamor followed. Jacob returned the keys to the depths of his pocket. The crowd, yelling, talking, gesticulating, pressed closer and closer upon us, until there was scarcely room to stand.

Daddy Aleck had followed with the carriage as closely as the crowd would allow without trampling some one, and now said to mamma: "Miss, yu better git een de carriage." Mamma answered by saying: "Aleck, go and bring Mas' Charles here."

Most reluctantly the old man obeyed, and drove off, leaving us alone in the midst of this raging crowd. I must say my heart sank as I saw the carriage with the faithful old man disappear down the avenue—for there was no white person within five miles and in this crowd there was certainly not one friendly Negro. Jacob, the head man, was the most so, but evidently he was in great fear of the others and incapable of showing his good feeling openly. . . . The crowd continued to clamor and yell, first one thing and then another, but the predominant cry was: "Go for de officer—fetch de Yankee." Mamma said, "By all means bring the officer; I wish to see him quite as much as you do."

The much-desired and talked-of officer was fourteen miles away. In the midst of the uproar a new man came running and shouting out that the officers were at a plantation three miles away, so six men started at a run to fetch him. Mamma and I walked slowly down the avenue to the public road, with a yelling mob of men, women, and children around us. They sang sometimes in unison, sometimes in parts, strange words which we did not understand, followed by a much-repeated chorus:

I free, I free!
I free as a frog!
I free till I fool!
Glory Alleluia!

They revolved around us, holding out their skirts and dancing—now with slow, swinging movements, now with rapid jig-motions, but always with weird chant and wild gestures.

When the men sent for the officer reached the gate they turned and shouted, "don't let no white man een dat gate," which was answered by many voices, "No, no we won't let no white pusson een, we'll chop um to pieces sho"—and they brandished their large, sharp, gleaming rice-field hoes, which looked most formidable weapons truly. . . .

It was a strange situation: Two women, one fifty, the other eighteen, pacing up and down the road between two dense hedges of angry blacks, while a little way off in the woods was a company of men, drawn up in something like military order—guns held behind them—solemn, silent, gloomy, a contrast to the noisy mob around us. There we paced for hours while the autumn day wore on.

> In the afternoon Daddy Aleck returned without Charley, having failed to find him. It was a great relief to me, for though I have been often laughed at for the opinion, I hold that there is a certain kind of chivalry in the Negroes—they wanted blood, they wanted to kill some one, but they couldn't make up their minds to kill two defenseless ladies; but if Charley had been found and brought, I firmly believe it would have kindled the flame. When the carriage came, I said to mamma in a low tone: "Let us go now."
>
> She answered with emphasis, but equally low, "Say not one word about going; we must stay until the officers come"—so we paced on, listening to blasphemous mutterings and threats, but appearing not to hear at all. . . . I heard the little children say to each other: "Luk a dem buckra 'oman, ain't 'fraid."
>
> The sun sank in a blaze of glory, and I began to wonder if we would spend the night there, when there was a cry, "Dey comin'!" We thought it was the officers, and how I did wish they could come and see us there, but it turned out to be four of the runners, who had returned, saying they had not found the officers, and that Jacob and one of the men had gone on to Georgetown to see them.
>
> Then we got into the carriage and drove home. We were hungry and exhausted, having tasted no morsel of food or drop of water through the long day. We went to bed in our log castle, which had no lock of any kind on the door, and slept soundly.
>
> In the early dawn of the next morning there was a knock at the door, and before we could reach the hallway the door was opened, and a black hand thrust through, with the keys. No word was spoken—it was Jacob; he gave them in silence, and mamma received them with the same solemnity.
>
> The bloodless battle had been won.[28]

Feeding the fear of whites was the onset of blacks gathering. Previously confined to farms and plantations, their newfound freedom brought them together in numbers like never before. As emancipation had swept the South, entire communities of blacks sprang up outside the cities. Understandably, many Freedmen expected to find work in the urban areas, and most wisely banded together both for social reasons and for safety. Their numbers and their behavior, however, frightened the white citizenry. Incidents of theft, robbery, and violence increased dramatically, and there were nightly displays of drunkenness and debauchery. In Mississippi, Gov. W. L. Sharkey, with permission from Federal authorities, called out the state militia to deal with the lawlessness.[29] The threat of crime and riots was so great in Texas that the military allowed some communities to form home guards.[30]

Maj. Gen. John Schofield, commanding the Department of North Carolina, issued a proclamation removing any doubt as to the end of slavery. In the same statement, however, Schofield ordered blacks that chose to leave former masters to "immediately seek employment elsewhere."

"It is not well for them to congregate about towns or military camps," said Schofield. "They will not be supported in their idleness."[31]

It was not simply their idleness that was frightening to whites, but what blacks were planning. So pervasive were the reports of black crimes against whites that many came to infer a more sinister plan at work—that these were not isolated incidents, but evidence of an insidious and far-reaching plot. "JC finds his Negro men all have Enfield rifles," commented Mary Chesnut. "The next move will be on pretense of hunting public arms to disarm all white men. Then we will have the long desired Negro insurrection."[32]

An agent of the Freedman's Bureau near Columbia, South Carolina, was compelled to investigate, upon receiving so many reports of blacks forming military companies. He secreted himself on a plantation, near enough to observe the "whole parade." Wrote the official:

> Negroes to the number of thirty or forty men, women and children had gathered themselves together near their cabins and were drawn up in line. Some shouldered sticks, some had gun-stocks, some gun-barrels, some guns, and some were empty-handed. They marched and counter-marched and halted, and marched again in straight lines and curves for nearly half an hour, their evolutions being interspersed with dancing and rough play, and accompanied by much laughter and noise.

When the agent walked over and asked what they were doing, the blacks informed him that they were having a "frolic" and imitating soldiers. Since none of their guns were serviceable, he found this explanation plausible. Likewise, the agent found nothing suspicious in the "several other instances" that were reported to him. Thus, he determined, further concerns of armed blacks were not "worthy of consideration."[33]

Among local whites, however, the bureau agent's report confirmed rather than dispelled fears. Throughout the South reports arrived of "secret meetings" in the woods attended by hundreds and thousands of blacks.[34] In Macon, an editor urged authorities to defuse the situation before the "scenes of bloodshed and massacre of St. Domingo [are] reenacted in our midst."

"We speak advisedly," proclaimed the excited editor. "We have authentic information of speeches and conversations among blacks, which sufficiently convinces us of their purpose. They make no secret of their movements."[35]

Many freedmen were incredulous at the reports and rumors of plots. Referring to the "utter groundlessness" of such stories, one black newspaper editor responded:

> A race that has remained quiet and inoffensive for upwards of two hundred years under the most oppressive system of tyranny the world has ever known, will not now, under the smiles of liberty, attempt the destruction of the planters. . . . Gen. Beecher was ordered there [Edisto Island] to put down the insurrectionists. He found a large number assembled quietly together enjoying the perusal of the *Leader* and other loyal newspapers. The General was as much surprised not to find an insurrection as the people were to know that they had been suspected of such a thing.
>
> The person who originated these foolish and absurd stories should remember the fable of the shepherd boy who cried "wolf."[36]

Far from plotting conspiracies, argued blacks, they were much more concerned with surviving the more ominous parts of freedom. As the *Mobile Nationalist* reported, there were just as many reasons for blacks to fear whites:

> In one town . . . an old negro man was horsewhipped at noonday, on the public street, for asking a white man for money due him for services rendered. In another, a Negro boy was threatened with shooting if he did not quietly accept a dollar as the price of a summer's work in a blacksmith's shop. In another, a girl was hung up by the thumbs for twelve hours, because she failed to accomplish a certain task in spinning. In another, a woman was severely whipped about the head for asserting that she was a free person. In still another, a woman was almost murdered by the cowhide—one white man whipping her, while two others held her.[37]

At Griffin, Georgia, Rhoda Ann Childs walked into the local Freedman's Bureau and spoke with the agent. One night while her husband was out, said the black woman, eight white men came to her door.

> They then Seized me and took me Some distance from the house, where they "bucked" me down across a log. Stripped my clothes over my head, one of the men Standing astride my neck, and beat me across my posterior, two men holding my legs. In this manner I was beaten until they were tired. Then they turned me parallel with the log, laying my neck on a limb which projected from the log, and one man placing his foot upon my neck, beat me again on hip and thigh. Then I was thrown upon the ground on my back, one of the men Stood upon my breast, while two others took hold of my feet and stretched My limbs as far apart as they could, while the man Standing upon my breast applied the Strap to my private parts until fatigued into stopping, and I was more dead than alive. Then a man . . . fell upon me and ravished me. During the whipping one of the men ran his pistol into me, and Said he had a hell of a mind to pull the trigger, and Swore they ought to Shoot me, as my husband had been in the "God damned Yankee Army," and Swore they meant to kill every black Son-of-a-bitch they could find that had ever fought against them. They then went back to the house, Seized my two daughters and beat them. . . .[38]

Near Talladega, Alabama, a fisherman drawing a seine in the Coosa River was horrified by what he brought up—fifteen bodies of blacks, among them "a woman with a child in her arms."[39] In Georgia, a white man reported that twenty "big buck niggers" had been dredged from a river near Atlanta. The same man added, with a laugh, that a "right smart chance of niggers" had been found recently with bullet holes in their heads around Columbus.[40]

"I think it would not be exaggeration to say that as many as one thousand colored persons have been killed in the city and county of Mobile, within the last nine months, by citizens and federal soldiers," one black man revealed to the *Nationalist*.[41] Wrote the outraged editor of another black newspaper:

> Any time that a poor black man is shot in the woods, or hanged to a tree, no village paper mentions it. The most absolute silence is kept upon these vengeances. No coroner is called for to hold an inquest on the corpse; no jury will inquire about the assassin; and no sheriff or constable will do anything to detect the murderer.[42]

For understandable reasons, in much of the Northern press, it was just such accounts of white assaults on blacks that made news. Although many articles accurately reported the truth, others were sensational at best, and fictitious at worst. The much-maligned Nathan Bedford Forrest, whose command had perpetrated the Fort Pillow massacre, made startling headlines again when he killed a freedman near Mobile. To most Northern readers, this seemed added evidence of the general's innate ferocity. In the rush to press, though, many details of this killing were omitted. Forrest had ordered blacks to clean up their premises to prevent the spread of cholera. A friend explained what happened:

> A Freedman named Thos. Edwards went to his quarters with a knife and began cursing and abusing his wife. Forrest ordered him to stop; he told the man he would flail him with a broom if he did not stop, and he hit him with the broom. The man turned his knife to Forrest and cut his hand. The General grabbed an axe and hit him on the head with the handle, killing him. A crowd of Freedmen gathered outside and the General made a speech, explaining what happened, and submitting to legal authority.[43]

"That is most unfortunate is felt by all, and by none so deeply as the General himself," said the friend.[44]

Other accounts, based on outlandish rumors, were contrived by correspondents for the appetites of their Northern subscribers. Much to the disgust of Southerners who considered the story patently false, the *New York Tribune* printed an article on an eighty-year-old freedman who was robbed and kicked to death. The white murderers then reportedly raked coals over his body, roasted one side, then the other, and burned two other blacks nearly to death. "Why not add," responded an angry Alabama editor, "that these white men were cannibals, and ate the negro, and this would make the story complete?"[45]

"The people of the South have subsisted on nigger meat during the whole continuance of the war," said William Owner cynically after reading such reports. "The Fed prisoners had no other kind of meat served to them as rations." Owner also wryly noted the Northern accounts of terrified blacks fleeing to cities for protection "with their throats cut."[46]

No one, black or white, wanted to believe such barbarous tales. No one of either race wanted to live in fear or believe that his own people were capable of such despicable atrocities. But whether or not these accounts were true mattered little. People read them, they generally believed them, and their actions were guided by them. A grim prospect for the future began to shape the perceptions of both races.

"The colored man and the white man cannot live together in this country," concluded one black editor despairingly. "They must and will have to separate."[47]

Eliza Andrews, along with many other Southern whites, agreed that there was no solution in sight. "I know that I am standing on a volcano that may burst forth any day," wrote the frightened woman in her journal.[48]

CHAPTER 23

Some Fine Morning

IN WASHINGTON, D.C., WILLIAM OWNER TOOK UP HIS PEN, OPENED HIS diary, then wrote:

> A nig preacher stated to a large meeting held at Brooklyn. . . . "In the South there will be another revolution, there is a deep under current feeling among the Colored people, there will yet come one of the darkest periods in our history in the Southern States. The whites down there will rise up some fine morning and find———I was going to say it (laughter)———you know what I mean! (continued laughter)."

"To be sure," Owner concluded grimly, "they knew what the rascal meant."[1]

The waning months of 1865 were ones of high expectation and deep trepidation. Rumors and half-truths concerning the confiscation and redistribution of Rebel-owned lands at Christmas 1865 agitated the whole of the South. Believing they were to receive their own farms—"forty acres and a mule"—blacks had even less incentive to toil for others than ever. Near Gordonsville, Virginia, a Yankee officer and his men were dispatched to a plantation to deal with the "insubordination" of former slaves contracted to work. The exasperated soldier summoned the blacks together and plainly stated that they were to work and "behave themselves." A spokesman for the group demanded to know what sort of freedom this was and inquired of the land the freedmen were to receive. "The officer turned to the overseer and asked where the graveyard was; it was pointed out. Turning to the Negro he said, 'The only land you will get, or any of you, will be 6 x 3 feet in that lot, and if you do not behave yourselves properly you will get your share very quickly.'"[2]

"The Government has given you your freedom, and you must not expect anything further from it," explained an agent of the Freedman's Bureau in North Carolina. "The Government expects you to labor and work out your own salvation, and unless you do you go back to slavery or a condition far worse. . . . Many of you are under the impression that the Government will feed you. This is not so."[3]

Even Henry Ravenel, who earlier felt blacks were handling their freedom remarkably well, noted the changes in their behavior. "The Negroes positively refuse to engage to work on the plantations," he observed with alarm. "There seems to be a general agreement & concert of action among them . . . in the expectation that Govt. is to provide them with lands in January. I think it is probable they have been told this by enemies from the North."[4]

"Every one expects trouble about Xmas," noted another South Carolinian.

"Where do they get all their ideas. . . ?" a troubled Louisiana editor asked.

> "Why this sullen refusal to work at any price. . . ? Why this increasing hatred to the land holders and the white man. . . .[?] Why, since they have their liberty, are they so unhappy and dissatisfied? The negroes in this country were never so unhappy, so dissatisfied and miserable as they now are. Why these combinations among negroes? . . . Why these midnight assemblages of negroes . . . by the hundreds in one assemblage, nearly a thousand in one instance, with renegade white men for advisers? There is deep secret, damnable rascality somewhere in connection with this unfortunate and misguided race.[5]

"All think the negroes intend something," said a frightened woman in Virginia. "The yankees have all the time been promising them the whole country, and they think the land should be theirs." Continued the distraught woman:

> The way to get it will be to exterminate the whites, and from their manner and talk and every thing it is believed some such attempt will be made about Christmas time—and every thing we see and hear makes us believe it too—and O what a dreadful—dreadful state we live in, night after night we sit up until almost daylight, watching and listening for every sound, and if a rat or a mouse moves, or a dog barks we are up and at the doors

> or window in a moment. There is no sleep, or rest for us, we start up at every little noise.[6]

In Georgia, blacks "engaged in insurrectionary movements" were arrested. Also in Georgia, a white man and his sisters were horrified when they received a death threat addressed in blood.[7]

"If providence does not interfere our history yet will be written in blood . . . ," said a frightened South Carolina physician. "I'm no alarmist, but it seems to me that . . . [the] massacre of white or black must soon come."[8]

The restlessness of the black population was due not only to the anticipation of owning land, but also the fear of being returned to bondage. "Our negroes are told that when the soldiers are withdrawn, that the whites will endeavor to enslave them again," wrote one Mississippi planter, "and they are urged to begin at an early day, perhaps about Christmas, a massacre of the whites."[9]

Rumors of reenslavement were not altogether idle. Published in the *Chicago Tribune* was a letter concerning the actions of the Freedman's Bureau at Memphis, and its use of Illinois soldiers to "go about the town and kidnap . . . all likely looking negroes they could find, and report them to the pen." The prisoners were then hustled off to nearby plantations "and there put into involuntary servitude . . . and so forced back into slavery." The letter continued:

> But the worst feature of this business is, that these planters pay so much per head for the capture and delivery to them of these people. . . . By and with his [the bureau agent's] knowledge the officers have been induced to take money for this wicked work. . . . I will cite a few facts. Our men say that they have had to lay around houses until late in the night and then make a descent upon them and seize and bear off the inmates. They have also been employed to patrol the streets and seize all who had no pass and bear them off under what is called a vagrant order. . . . I am informed that a young girl but a day or two since [was] set upon while going to school, with her books in hand, and the attempt made to carry her off but she tore herself free.[10]

Freedmen were not long in learning of yet another outrage. Hired ostensibly to work in the Gulf states at good wages, blacks were actually being shipped off to Cuba and sold back into slavery. "For many weeks," wrote one witness, "parties from the North, as well as parties from the

South, have been engaged along the coast and inland rivers in employing blacks for the pretended purpose of laboring at a distance, but really to be forced into Cuban bondage."[11]

"The attention of the Government authorities has been called to the matter," said the angry editor of a black newspaper, "but they have thus far taken no steps."[12]

Christmas Day came . . . and went. There were no long-awaited gifts, nor were there any massacres. Then people looked to New Year's Day. It would happen, some said, at the first of the year. Again there was nothing—nothing but frustration and fear to add to the tinderbox the South had become. Blacks were met with only disappointment and unfulfilled promises. Whites saw their growing sullenness and dissension as further evidence that there still might be a day of reckoning ahead.

Long before the beginning of 1866, however, there had been terrible omens of things to come. Whether or not there had been actual conspiracies, there had indeed been clashes, terrible portents, and Southerners suspected that Northern radicals were behind the constant outbreaks of violence. And whether or not there was a conscious, concerted conspiracy, there was without doubt a mood, as if a fog had descended upon the South, obscuring the view but magnifying the sounds.

Moreover, if there was not an all-encompassing plot, some reasoned, perhaps there did exist small, homegrown conspiracies, independent of one another. One such example occurred in New Madrid, Missouri, when a Federal soldier killed a black man, resulting in a "conspiracy" to kill all the whites in the community. At least thirty-five individuals were part of the plot, one report said. When the blacks did indeed fire upon the citizenry, riddling their houses, a melee erupted. Although no whites were killed, many blacks were shot outright or hanged. Had a single white death occurred, declared the citizens, "not a Negro should have been left alive."[13]

At Chapel Hill, North Carolina, blacks were discovered holding a "secret meeting." Determined to break up the gathering, white college students attacked. "A general fight ensued . . . ," said the *Raleigh Standard,* "some of the students were pretty badly injured and the Negroes roughly handled, pistols and sticks being freely used." Following the confrontation, university buildings were vandalized. "[They] will not allow a negro to show his head in the campus," concluded the *Standard.*[14] Another reported plot was uncovered in Virginia, where blacks were preparing to massacre white railroad workers at Aquia Creek.[15]

In Charleston—where one takeover plan had already been crushed earlier—an incident between black and white soldiers resulted in a volley of bullets, bricks, and stones raining on the crowd. The confrontation incited two weeks of violence, during which "robbing, clubbing, stabbing, and shooting were freely indulged in."[16]

At Concord, North Carolina, heavy drinking by both races resulted in a bloody altercation.[17] In Grenada, Mississippi, white militiamen attempted to disarm some freedmen. Black soldiers stepped in and fired, wounding several severely.[18] In Lewisburg, Arkansas, black and white soldiers squared off and fired volleys into one another, leaving a number dead.[19]

Near Louisville, outside an "outrageous" saloon, blacks took over the street, brandishing guns and threatening to kill any white foolish enough to pass.[20] At a fair in Danville, Kentucky, when black soldiers were told to go to the "Nig" section, one of the soldiers drew a pistol and shot a white man. Fearing a mob, the black soldiers rode for help. When they returned with their entire company, they began sniping and shooting randomly into the crowd.[21]

Sparks flew from the Ohio to the Gulf, from the Brazos to Chesapeake Bay. It was Memphis, however, that became the lightning rod of violence, and it was this city that was struck over and over during the storm rocking the South.

For a number of reasons, freedmen flocked to Memphis following the war. Varying reports placed the black population as high as sixteen thousand—in a city of less than thirty thousand residents. Whatever the figures, the number of blacks had at least quadrupled since the war began, fueling white fears of takeover.

"Can you wonder . . . that I was uneasy?" asked Elizabeth Merriweather, aghast at the changes that had occurred in Memphis during her exile. Perhaps the greatest shock to Elizabeth was the presence of armed black troops. "During my walks from one shop to another I sometimes had to get off the sidewalk into the street in order to make way for these Negro soldiers. . . . Sometimes one of them would say: 'We's all ekal now. Git out o' our way, white woman.'"[22]

Elizabeth was equally appalled to find black squatters on her front lawn. When she contacted military authorities and asked to have the intruders removed, black soldiers informed the outraged woman that freedmen had a right to "abandoned lands," including hers.[23]

Into this unstable situation was added a significant Irish population, whose ranks composed almost the entirety of the police and fire departments. With every element struggling for economic survival, there were constant clashes.

Headquartered in Memphis, Maj. Gen. George Stoneman, Department of Tennessee commander, reported that many whites, including some of the policemen, had been apprehended by blacks in their military capacity and were treated with a harshness "altogether unnecessary."[24] On one occasion, two white men were stopped by black soldiers. When one of the whites tried to escape, he was shot and bayoneted.[25] Similarly, black soldiers and civilians were arrested and roughed up on a regular basis by white policemen. Reported one black sergeant stationed in Memphis:

> I was sitting in the door with this man Tom talking quitly [*sic*], and a policeman . . . said to me I wish I could get a chance to kill all the Damned Nigger Soldiers. and I said you cant kill me—he then stepped back a few paces and ran up and struck me with his *club,* on the head—at that time another Policeman came up and he struck me several times. and they thru me down and stamped me in the back while lying on the ground. My shirt was torn off and I was badly bruised.[26]

"There were no less than three negro disturbances yesterday," reported the *Memphis Ledger* soon after the above altercation. The editor went on to describe minor incidents that escalated rapidly into riotous situations. When a white boy was intentionally tripped by a black who called him "a white-livered son of a bitch," a witness standing nearby rushed over and struck the assailant with a brick. At that, "about 100 negroes gathered," soon followed by armed black soldiers. When the white man fled to a barn, a crowd of angry blacks pursued, clamoring for his life. The scene ended with several injuries but, miraculously, no deaths. "One Negro," the *Ledger* continued, "made the remark that the colored people would yet rule Memphis, or they would kill every white man in the place." This, said the editor in a great understatement, "bodes no good to the peace of the community."[27]

By springtime 1866, everyone could see that Memphis had become a tinderbox.

At 4 P.M. on Monday, April 30, four policemen walking on a Memphis sidewalk encountered several black soldiers going in the opposite direction. Words were exchanged. Said a witness to the scene:

> They all used some strong language to each other, the police to the negroes, and the negroes to the police. Finally, the negroes started down the street. One of the policeman ran after this negro . . . and struck him on the head with a pistol. While he was doing that, another negro ran and struck the policeman with a stick. Then the negro stood up and dared the policeman to fight him. The policeman stepped back, and then another policeman threw something at the negroes, I presume a brickbat

> or stone. They continued talking to each other, and the negroes passed on down the street, while the policeman went back up in the city.[28]

"The colored man who was struck with a pistol appeared to be considerably hurt," remarked another viewer. "The blood ran from his nostrils and from the side of his head. The blood ran from the back of the head of the one struck with the brick."[29]

The following day, May 1, scores of angry and armed blacks, including recently discharged soldiers, stood on a street corner drinking. Two white policemen appeared. According to a bystander, Dr. S. J. Quimby, the police, "in a perfectly orderly manner," arrested two of the more "boisterous" blacks. Quimby continued:

> As the police officers took the men along, the soldiers began to gather around them from all over the street, and began to call out, "Stone them, club them, shoot them. . . ." The officers took the men and started down [the] . . . street; the other four officers joined in a little distance behind and attempted to keep the crowd off. . . . The soldiers began to fire their revolvers in the air; from what I saw I should judge there were about forty of them armed with revolvers, and the rest had stones, clubs, and whatever else they could get hold of. As they began firing in the air the officers seemed to think that they were firing at them, turned round and began firing at the crowd. Then, at once, I saw the crowd firing at them, and heard one of the crowd sing out, "One of them . . . was shot." I saw him carried into a grocery. . . . I heard one of the colored soldiers speak back to the crowd, making the remark, "They have killed one of our men." At that all this crowd . . . reloaded their revolvers, or took whatever they could get in their hands to fight with, and ran back towards the police, very much excited. . . . I saw about one hundred and fifty colored soldiers; they were chasing officers in all directions . . . they were calling out to the policemen, "Halt," and firing after them all the time. . . . I saw a black man come up, armed with a Spencer rifle, who called out to the officers, "Halt, you white son of a bitch," and fired at him.[30]

"The negroes have risen, and are going to take Memphis," citizens shouted as they ran through the streets.[31]

"I was in my office," said the startled Memphis sheriff, "when word came up that the negroes had come out of the fort and were killing everybody."[32]

What transpired over the next several days, when whites and blacks met, was war—race war. Residents grabbed the latest editions of the newspapers, where gruesome details filled the pages:

> There were three white men killed . . . who were not found until daylight. . . .
> He had been shot through the head. . . . The brain was oozing out. . . .
> Those negroes killed . . . were still lying in the street at 1:30 yesterday.
> She was dead . . . and the blood running out of her mouth . . .
> Nothing now but the walls are standing.
> Bloody Carnival . . . War of Races!

"Colored men, women & children were shot in open day light as if they were mad dogs . . . ," raged a Northern missionary in the city. "The sick were murdered in their beds. . . . [We] came upon a man who had been set upon by four men & most shockingly beaten, & shot twice, once through the body & once through the head, & then left to breath[e] out his last moments upon the side walk. . . . This poor dying man was old & infirm. . . ."[33]

Discharged black soldiers who had given up their weapons when they left the army were now determined to retrieve them. Said the *Memphis Daily Argus:*

> Before daylight . . . some two or three hundred of these unrestrained villains, after they held a consultation of war, went to Fort Pickering and demanded their arms. . . . This request was . . . refused. . . . About sunrise [they] returned and threatened to charge the fort if they were not furnished with arms. The regulars . . . threatened to bring out six pieces of artillery and "turn loose" on them. This caused them to fall back to the ravine near the . . . RR depot. With what arms they could collect, such as Enfield rifles, Springfield muskets and Colt's pistols, the negroes scattered all over South Memphis, determined, it is presumed, to make an attack upon the city.[34]

The Memphis Riot KANSAS STATE HISTORICAL SOCIETY, TOPEKA

As shots were exchanged at the railroad depot, someone shouted, "*Look at the black flag!*"[35]

"Sure enough," wrote the correspondent, "on the eminence near the depot, and in the midst of the black rascals, was a regular black flag upon a staff, supported and waved by a Negro boy. . . . This tended a great deal to inflame the already too much incensed [white] populace."[36]

When twenty-five white regulars appeared, a wholesale battle ensued. Eventually, the blacks were forced into the fort at the point of bayonets. The correspondent, who was caught in the middle of the action, continued: "At 11:15 a.m., the city was all in an uproar. The alarm bells were rung, and the most frightful stories were told of the wholesale slaughter. Attorney-General Wallace raised a company, armed them at Folsum's gun store and proceeded to the scene of the action."[37]

"We are not prepared," thundered another city official, "but let us . . . clean out every negro son of a bitch out of town."[38]

Blacks turned their attention to the magazine, just outside town, taking "as much powder as they wanted."[39] The local sheriff swore in nearly fifty men, armed them with shotguns, then ordered the posse to scout the area where rioting had been concentrated. Despite such armed patrols, flames shot up around the city. Fire alarms rang, but buildings burned before the brigades could reach them.

"Negro Shanties Burned by the Infuriated White Men in the Afternoon and Night," read next day's headline.[40]

As the paper was about to be printed, the editor hastily set the type to add one more bit of information: "FIRE AGAIN.—1:30 a.m., just as we go to press, the whole south is lurid with flames and the alarm bells are ringing."[41]

Convinced the bloodshed and destruction would not end otherwise, General Stoneman eventually ordered enough troops into Memphis to overwhelm the rioters. After three days, quiet finally returned to the city.

A local editor at last felt safe enough to walk through the silent, charred streets. "We saw some very appalling things," he sadly recorded. "The worst that we saw was that of a Negro woman who had been sick, being burned to death in a little cabin." Neighbors had heard her screams but were too frightened to venture into the streets.[42]

When the final count was in, forty-six blacks and two whites had been killed. Additionally, seventy-five were wounded, and over one hundred homes, schools, and churches were destroyed.[43]

Overcome by the death and destruction that lay before him, one writer expressed sorrowfully, "This is the bloom of civil rights—what the fruit will be, God alone can tell."[44]

Even before the riot had ended, people began laying blame.

Some citizens suspected that blacks had been planning an attack all along. Many in Memphis well remembered white agitators who had harangued Freedmen in the weeks and months preceding the riot: "You're what saved the country, and you ought to have just as much privileges as white men; if they do not give it to you, you ought to take them."[45] According to the *Memphis Daily Argus:*

> A negro woman made affidavit to the effect that the negroes have been plotting this defiance to the laws and its officers for the past four days; that the plan was to kill the police, sack and burn the city, and that was approved by the race for many miles around Memphis. It was not confined to this locality, but was wide spread and general. We do not know that the truth has been told by this woman but the stubbornness of the negroes engaged in the outbreak here gives a color of reasonableness to the conclusion.[46]

Reinforcing the editor's views were his own interviews with blacks during the riot. "They used expressions such as 'the d—d white trash,' and 'we would whip hell out of them,'" noted the outraged journalist.[47] Although this editor decried the burning of their homes and churches, he added that blacks had brought much of it on themselves by their behavior before and during the riots.[48]

The editor of the *Daily Memphis Avalanche* was inclined to be more circumspect, however, and placed the blame for the riots elsewhere:

> The Radicals have poisoned the mind of the negro—they have impressed him with the belief that he is equal, if not superior, to the white man, and the vengeance which has been threatened the Negro, if visited at all, should be upon the unprincipled men who have delivered him, and brought all these troubles upon his head. The negro is not to blame. He deserves our sympathy. During the late war, he was an arm of strength to the cause which has been lost. His kindness to the absent soldiers' family has won the affection of all, and in the name of humanity and justice we protest against any cruelty toward them.[49]

Almost as the above words were being written, two blacks near Memphis murdered their employer by bashing his head in with an ax. In an attempt to conceal the crime, the men ran the victim's wagon over a bridge, killing the oxen and smashing the wagon to bits. Although the two slyly reported the "accident" to authorities, the murderers could not explain the blood on the bridge. The incident threatened to reignite the fiery violence in Memphis.[50]

Although Memphis was perhaps the scene of the most sanguinary clash, similar confrontations between blacks and whites occurred all over the South—Richmond, Norfolk, Charleston, Chattanooga, Montgomery, Pensacola, Kinston, Savannah, Wilmington . . .

At New Orleans, where more than twenty men lay dead in the streets after the battle was over, witnesses were shocked upon viewing the aftermath. "The blood splashed walls, the masses of clotted gore . . . and other evidences of mob passions tell a fearful story which is sickening now to think of."[51] In the midst of the rioting, a black witness told the reporter, "there is not a Negro in New Orleans who is not organized and prepared."[52]

Yet in truth, no one, black or white, was totally prepared for the racial strife that followed the war. No one, that is, except those with an armchair seat from which they could relish the violence in safety. Sen. Benjamin Wade of Ohio, along with many of his peers, had longed for this ultimate race war, privately, if not publicly. "There is no doubt," wrote the fiery abolitionist, "that if by an insurrection they [the blacks] could contrive to slay one-half of their oppressors, the other half would hold them in the highest respect."[53]

It was just such chilling beliefs as these that Southern whites had suspected all along.

EPILOGUE

On the morning of August 14, 1866, four men walked onto the military post at Petersburg, Virginia, stacked their muskets in front of headquarters, then cautiously entered the commanding colonel's office. When the officer and his staff glanced up from their desks, none in the room were prepared for the sight that met their disbelieving gaze. Standing at attention before them were four individuals who seemed like ghosts from the past. Wrote a stunned local editor:

> A more ragged set of mortals had never appeared before the Colonel. . . . [One man] was a sort of walking . . . patchwork. His clothing had been tied and sewed and stuck together with string and thread and thorns until there did not appear to be a solitary square inch upon it which had not been tied up, sewed up, or stuck up in some way or other. His companions were not quite as badly off, one having a pair of blue Yankee pantaloons with only half a dozen rents in it; another hiding the raggedness of his grey pants with a flowing . . . Yankee overcoat, and the other . . . concealing the defects of his upper garments with an old oil cloth fly, awfully bedaubed with mud.[1]

When queried by the colonel on their condition, the spokesman for the group explained that following General Lee's evacuation of Petersburg the previous year, the four had been cut off from their units. Rather than surrender and die in prison, the men had made a vow with one another to never give up; as long as the Confederacy held out, so would they. Living in a cave along the Appomattox River, the four survived for the next seventeen months by hunting, fishing and raiding nearby cornfields. Upon learning from an old black that the South had indeed long ago lost the war, the reluctant Rebels at last sadly concluded that the end had come.

Upon gaining paroles from the astonished Yankee officer, the men quietly filed out of the office and wandered the streets of Petersburg for a short time. Not surprisingly, wherever the bedraggled quartet went, it was to the utter amazement of everyone who saw them. After receiving new suits of clothes from sympathetic civilians, and after being made "half drunk" in local saloons, the former Rebel soldiers at last boarded a train for their homes farther south.[2]

As incredible as the sight of these four wild men were to those in Petersburg, it was nothing compared with the sights the four would witness on the journey home.

During the spring of 1865, the Confederacy that the four men had last seen was a nation torn and ravaged by years of war. By the late summer of 1866, however, much of this destruction was only a grim memory. Many cities throughout the South had almost totally recovered. Charleston, Richmond, Atlanta, Baton Rouge, and other Southern towns were nearly unrecognizable a mere year after the war, so spectacular was their rerise. And smaller communities, like Okolona, Mississippi—towns that had been utterly wiped out by the war—not only had recovered lost ground, but were in fact surging ahead.

"No one believed that Okolona could be Okolona any more," wrote a surprised visitor. "It is now a well-built town of two or three thousand inhabitants, with a long street of brick stores, and many offshoots on the east, towards the railway depot."[3]

In one of the most devastated regions throughout the entire South, the Shenandoah Valley, little remained to remind residents of war but absent fences and a burnt barn or two. "No one would suppose an army *had* been in the Valley," wrote a shocked observer in the summer of 1866.[4]

Only a mere twelve months after the war, the wounds that had once scarred the land so savagely were quickly being erased. But while the physical transformation of the South would have seemed to the four men a nearly miraculous feat in such a short space of time, there was more than enough evidence at every hand to convince the soldiers that their nation had indeed lost the war and was now an occupied land.

Black soldiers in blue, erstwhile slaves, garrisoned the rebuilt cities and towns, and were now, in many instances, the unabashed enforcers of the new law in the land. Strange creatures with strange accents and carpetbags in their hands also strode the streets of the South carving new niches in politics and education and usurping old ones in business and commerce. In Louisiana alone, an estimated fifty thousand Northern "carpetbaggers" had arrived since war's end. Few cities in the South more typified this polyglot transformation than the birthplace of the Confederacy:

> Charleston was a city, first, of idle ragged negroes, who, with no visible means of support nevertheless sent an astonishing multi-

> tude of children to school; second, of small dealers, laborers, and German artisans, starving on the rebel custom; third, of widows and children of planters, keeping respectable boarding-houses, or pining in hopeless and unspeakable penury; fourth, of young men loafing in the saloons, and living on the profits of their mothers' boarding houses; fifth, of Jews and Massachusetts merchants, doing well on the semiloyal and negro custom; sixth, of utterly worthless and accursed political adventurers from the North, Bureau leeches, and promiscuous knaves, all fattening on the humiliation of the South and the credulity of the freedmen.[5]

And the noticeable absence of the South's old guard—its natural leaders—would have been nearly as startling to those returning Rebels as the enemy's occupation. With many former leaders dead, disenfranchised, or in exile, an increasing number of those filling the positions were aliens from the North or, worse, Southern Unionists—men who had been merely obnoxious and impotent curiosities in 1865, but now ensconced in places of power. Most painful of all, however, the symbol of the Lost Cause, the man on whom all hopes for independence had been pinned, remained imprisoned much as a common felon.

By the spring of 1866, after a year of agonizing separation, Varina Davis was finally allowed to visit her husband at Fort Monroe. After passing through three lines of sentries, each requiring a password, the anxious wife at last reached the cell of the man she loved. When the woman saw her husband's "shrunken form and glassy eyes," she nearly broke down.

"His cheekbones stood out like those of a skeleton," Varina recalled. "Merely crossing the room made his breath come in short gasps, and his voice was scarcely audible."[7]

Despite the fact that Jefferson Davis was more dead than alive, and even though the charges leveled at him for Lincoln's assassination and the Andersonville horrors had been dropped, many in the Federal government were determined to convict the ex-Confederate president on some charge. In wording reminiscent of the Spanish Inquisition, the crime of treason was finally directed at Davis by a Federal judge in Virginia:

> Jefferson Davis, yeoman, not having the fear of God before his eyes, nor weighing the duty of his said allegiance, but being moved and seduced by the institution of the devil, and wickedly

> devising against the peace and tranquility of the United States to subvert, and to stir, move, and incite insurrection, rebellion and war. . . .[8]

"I think his [the judge's] meanness and wickedness have affected his brain," said Mary Lee, wife of Gen. Robert E., after reading the incredible statement.[9]

Although this charge, like the others before it, was quietly dropped, and although Davis would be released the following year a free man, his personal humiliation and pain would continue. During the war, one of the Davis children, a little boy, had fallen from an upper window at the home and died. Now, in the summer of 1866, the couple learned to their great sorrow that the modest stone they had placed on the child's grave had been stolen; "probably," raged an Arkansas editor, "to be trafficked as a trophy in New England."[10]

"Every true heart at the South," wrote former Confederate general Wade Hampton to Davis in the summer of 1866, "feels that you are vicariously bearing the griefs of our people, & from every corner of our unhappy & desolate land constant prayers go up to Heaven for your deliverance."[11]

Of all the many changes that had taken place in the South since the end of the war, however, perhaps the most startling to the four men when they arrived home was the relationship between the races.

On the one side, blacks, formerly docile and respectful and under control, now displayed a surprisingly independent spirit and, in many cases, a barely concealed hatred not only for their former masters, but for all white Southerners in general. Newspapers were filled with accounts of murders, rapes, and crimes committed by the former slaves by day and chilling rumors spoke of mysterious black gatherings in the woods by night, as well as dark rumblings around bonfires of takeover and race war.

On the other side, whites, once in control, now resentful over the loss of power, plotted resistance and retaliation and a return to the days before defeat. With each new black crime and each new Yankee outrage, the ranks of white opposition grew until, wrote John Carroll of Tennessee, "there arose . . . a secret oath-bound organization among the Southern people. They wore masks and traveled in the night time. The insignia was a skull and cross-bones. Of this order I was a loyal member and woe unto the insolent negro or turbulent white man who incurred its displeasure!"[12]

It was, said another Southerner simply, "the creation of one feeling of terror as a counterpoise to another."[13]

Never entirely united before or even during the war, beset by enemies from without and enemies from within, white Southerners, high and low, were now, one year after the war, well down the road to becoming the "solid South."

Shortly after the surrender at Appomattox in 1865, Wade Hampton had urged his fellow Southerners to accept the inevitable and grant to literate or property-owning blacks the right to vote, thereby avoiding much anger, hostility, and perhaps future bloodshed.[14] Although his suggestion was not acted upon, and earned for the South Carolinian much enmity from Southern whites, few in retrospect could doubt that the general had the best interests of the South at heart. Nevertheless, moderate though he may have been on some issues, Hampton was outraged by the continual insults and injustices the defeated South was forced to endure following "peace." Finally, the angry general felt compelled to lay the case of his homeland at the feet of President Johnson:

> More than a year has elapsed since the South under the solemn promise of peace and amnesty, laid down [her] arms. . . . She had been assured in the most authoritative manner, that she had but to lower those arms, to be received again into full communion with the other States. . . . Four years of war—a war savage, bloody and cruel beyond nearly every other on record—left the South bleeding at every pore—her resources exhausted—her property stolen—her cities laid in ashes—her fields ravaged—her living sons ruined and many of her noblest sleeping under the soil they fought so bravely, though so fruitlessly to defend. . . . Such was the condition of the South when she laid down her arms and acknowledged the authority of the U.S. . . .
>
> Look back, Mr. President at the events which have marked this . . . most bitter and mournful year and say if the retrospect shows one effort made to conciliate her—one act of legislation that is not calculated to gall and irritate her—or one evidence that the dominant party at the North does not still cherish towards her, feelings of the bitterest and most vindictive hatred. The very first act of *peace,* consisted in pouring into our whole country a horde of barbarians—your brutal negro troops under

> their no less brutal and more degraded Yankee Officers. Every license was allowed to those wretches and the grossest outrages were committed by them with impunity. Their very presence amongst us at such a time, was felt as a direct and premeditated insult to the whole Southern people. Confederate soldiers returning home, weary and travel-stained, were seized by these negro soldiers, and the buttons of that grey jacket . . . were roughly and ignominiously torn off. . . .
>
> But there were not wanting other and darker features to fill up the gloomy canvass. Let me mention one case, not because it was an isolated one, for it was not, but because it shows with what perfect impunity the most horrible crimes could be, and were committed by the black devils who were charged with the preservation of peace and the maintainance [*sic*] of order in the South. A brave and gallant Confederate officer whilst walking in the streets of Columbus, Miss. was fired at by a Federal soldier. He promptly returned the fire, killing the man who had so wantonly assailed him. He was instantly surrounded by negro soldiers who beat him severely and wounded him. The Federal Officers ordered him taken to a Hospital, which was done, though he requested to be carried to his own home where he could receive the attention he needed. Whilst in the Hospital, a prisoner guarded by Federal Soldiers, *he was bayonetted to death. . . .*
>
> The whole South can tell of similar outrages.[15]

It is unclear whether Andrew Johnson replied to the letter or even read it. Five days before Hampton sent his comments, however, the president declared the entire issue null and void. "And I do further proclaim," he announced on August 20, 1866, "that the said insurrection is at an end, and that peace, order, tranquility, and civil authority now exist in and throughout the whole of the United States."[16]

Whether a much troubled and assailed Andrew Johnson actually believed his own words is open to debate, but if in his heart he did, he was perhaps the only man in America to do so. Had only Johnson's predecessor lived to serve out his second term, the words might well have been spoken a full year before . . . and spoken with truth. But Johnson's predecessor did not live to serve out his term and implement his policies, and as a consequence, the defeated South was plunged into decades of mistrust, hatred, and violence. Wrote Sara Rice Pryor:

> I question if, in any quarter of the country, the virtues of Abraham Lincoln—as exhibited in his spirit of forgiveness and forbearance—are more revered than in the very section which was the battle-ground of the fight for independence of his rule. It is certainly our conviction, that had he lived the South would never have suffered [such] shame and sorrow.[17]

Even Northerners, even if unsympathetic, had realized the impact upon Southerners of Lincoln's death. As the *Chicago Tribune* had asserted plainly, Lincoln was "the man who stood between them and retribution, who alone had the will and power to shield them. . . ."[18]

Without that shield, retribution, vengeance, reprisal, punishment—these had become the watchwords of the radicals and they had touched *all* in the South. The fruits of retribution had been laid at virtually every doorstep. But as Jefferson Davis had expressed, the conquerors had failed to realize the wisdom of the ancient proverb that he who builds a fire to consume his enemy is also destroyed. Thus, after months of "peace," no Southerner could have missed the symbolism of a small shipwreck in a winter storm near Cape Hatteras.

So many ships were lost through the years that this treacherous stretch of water off the North Carolina coast became known as the "graveyard of the Atlantic." One more wreck should not have been news. But in this case, it was. The schooner that ran aground had been a Confederate privateer during the war. Refitted by the victors, she began her new career as a merchant ship of the reunited nation. During her final disastrous voyage, the pilots were washed overboard and drowned in the icy waters. Without its eyes, the vessel soon ran aground. When rescuers arrived, they discovered to their horror the ship's crew hanging in the rigging, frozen to death.

Ironically, the vessel had been renamed *Retribution*.[19]

ENDNOTES

PROLOGUE: THE BETTER ANGEL

1. Raleigh *Daily Progress,* May 11, 1865.
2. *Chicago Tribune,* April 4, 1865.
3. Edward N. Hatcher, *The Last Four Weeks of the War* (Columbus, OH: 1891), 128; Washington, D.C., *Daily Constitutional Union,* April 4, 1865.
4. *Chicago Tribune,* April 4, 1865.
5. Ibid., May 13, 1865.
6. Springfield (Ohio) *Daily News and Republic,* April 11, 1865.
7. Allan Nevins, ed., *The Diary of George Templeton Strong* (New York: MacMillan, 1962), 574–75.
8. Washington, D.C., *Daily Constitutional Union,* April 3, 1865.
9. Springfield (Ohio) *Daily News and Republic,* April 7, 1865.
10. Wilmington *Delaware Republican,* May 4, 1865.
11. Ibid.
12. Margaret Leech, *Reveille in Washington, 1860–1865* (New York: Harper and Brothers, 1941), 379.
13. Letter dated April 10, 1865, Bell Collection, Delaware Public Archives, Hall of Records, Dover.
14. *New York Times,* April 10, 1865.
15. Emmy E. Werner, *Reluctant Witnesses: Children's Voices from the Civil War* (Boulder, CO: Westview Press, 1998), 136.
16. Richard Bak, *The Day Lincoln Was Shot: An Illustrated Chronicle* (Dallas: Taylor, 1998), 85.
17. Timothy S. Good, ed., *We Saw Lincoln Shot: One Hundred Eyewitness Accounts* (Jackson: University Press of Mississippi, 1995), 40.
18. Ibid., 55.
19. Bak, *The Day Lincoln Was Shot,* 85.
20. Leech, *Reveille in Washington,* 380.

21. Burke Davis, *The Long Surrender* (New York: Random House, 1985), 79.
22. John G. Nicolay and John Hay, *Abraham Lincoln: A History* (New York: Century, 1890), vol. 10, 283–84.
23. Michael Burlingame, ed., *Lincoln Observed: Civil War Dispatches of Noah Brooks* (Baltimore: Johns Hopkins University, 1998), 195.
24. Good, *We Saw Lincoln Shot,* 53.
25. Ibid.
26. Raleigh *Daily Progress,* May 11, 1865.
27. Bak, *The Day Lincoln Was Shot,* 89.
28. Springfield *Daily Illinois State Journal,* April 22, 1865.
29. George S. Bryan, *The Great American Myth* (1940; reprint, Chicago: Americana House, 1995), 182.
30. Bak, *The Day Lincoln Was Shot,* 92.
31. Springfield *Daily Illinois State Journal,* April 22, 1865.
32. Good, *We Saw Lincoln Shot,* 40.
33. Ibid. 53.

CHAPTER 1: THE BRIGHT DREAM

1. Mrs. Burton Harrison, *Recollections Grave and Gay* (New York: Charles Scribners Sons, 1916), 215.
2. Thomas C. DeLeon, *Four Years in Rebel Capitals* (1892; reprint, Spartanburg, SC: Reprint Company, 1975), 363.
3. Myrta Lockett Avary, *Dixie After the War* (New York: Doubleday, Page & Company, 1906), 107.
4. *New York Times,* April 30, 1865.
5. Katherine M. Jones. *Heroines of Dixie: Confederate Women Tell Their Story of the War* (Indianapolis: Bobbs-Merrill, 1955), 395.
6. Washington, D.C., *Evening Star,* April 12, 1865.
7. DeLeon, *Four Years in Rebel Capitals,* 367.
8. *Houston Chronicle,* June 19, 1947.
9. G. Clark letter, Appomattox Courthouse National Historic Site, Virginia.
10. William Miller Owen, *In Camp and Battle with the Washington Artillery of New Orleans* (Boston: Ticknor, 1885), 391.
11. Washington, D.C., *Daily Constitutional Union,* April 11, 1865.
12. Springfield (Ohio) *Daily News and Republic,* April 25, 1865.
13. *Chicago Tribune,* April 22, 1865.
14. Ibid.
15. Nicolay and Hay, *Abraham Lincoln,* 278.
16. *New York Times,* April 18, 1865.

17. Springfield *Daily Illinois State Journal,* April 29, 1865.
18. Nicolay and Hay, *Lincoln,* 279.
19. Gerald Schwartz, ed., *A Woman Doctor's Civil War* (Columbia: University of South Carolina, 1989), 129.
20. Springfield *Daily Illinois State Journal,* April 29, 1865; *New York Times,* April 18, 1865.
21. Springfield *Daily Illinois State Journal,* April 29, 1865.
22. Sidney Andrews, *The South since the War* (1866; reprint, Boston: Houghton Mifflin, 1971), 1.
23. Charles W. Mitchell, "Maryland and the Fort Sumter Crisis," *Maryland Historical Magazine* (Spring 2000): 91.
24. Schwartz, *A Woman Doctor's Civil War,* 132.
25. Noah Andre Trudeau, *Out of the Storm: The End of the Civil War, April-June 1865* (Baton Rouge: Louisiana State University, 1994), 222.

CHAPTER 2: OUTRAGE

1. *Chicago Tribune,* April 17, 1865.
2. Harold Bell Hancock, *Delaware during the Civil War: A Political History* (Wilmington: Historical Society of Delaware, n.d.), 160.
3. William Furry, ed., *The Civil War Journal of Reverend Francis Springer.* Excerpt published as pamphlet by Sangamon County (Illinois) Historical Society.
4. Raleigh *Daily Progress,* April 26, 1865.
5. Nevins, *The Diary of George Templeton Strong,* 583.
6. Good, *We Saw Lincoln Shot,* 36.
7. Ibid., 47.
8. Ibid., 54.
9. Springfield *Daily Illinois State Journal,* April 29, 1865; Indianapolis *Daily State Sentinel,* April 17, 1865.
10. *New York Times,* April 16, 1865.
11. *Indianapolis Daily Journal,* April 16, 1865.
12. Wilmington *Delaware Republican,* April 24, 1865.
13. *Indianapolis Daily Journal,* April 21, 1865; *New Orleans Picayune,* April 19, 1865.
14. Springfield *Illinois Daily State Journal,* April 17, 1865.
15. Ibid., April 21, 22, and 29, 1865; *Indianapolis Daily Journal,* April 16, 1865.
16. Springfield *Illinois Daily State Journal,* April 19, 1865; William Owner diary, June 7, 1865, Library of Congress; Washington, D.C., *Evening Star,* May 6, 1865; *Chicago Tribune,* April 17, 1865.
17. *Indianapolis Daily Journal,* April 21, 1865.

18. William Owner diary, loose clipping, 1865, Library of Congress.
19. Indianapolis *Daily State Sentinel,* April 24, 1865; *Fort Smith* (Arkansas) *New Era,* May 20, 1865.
20. *Montgomery Daily Mail,* May 15, 1865; Springfield *Daily News and Republic,* April 29, 1865; *New Orleans Picayune,* May 3, 1865.
21. Indianapolis *Daily State Sentinel,* April 17, 1865; *New Orleans Times,* May 2, 1865.
22. Washington, D.C., *Evening Star,* April 15 and 17, 1865.
23. Washington, D.C., *Daily Morning Chronicle,* April 20, 1865.
24. William Owner diary, loose clipping, 1865, Library of Congress.
25. Springfield (Ohio) *Daily News and Republic,* May 12, 1865.
26. *Chicago Tribune,* April 22, 1865.
27. Springfield *Illinois Daily State Journal,* April 27, 1865; Charles East, ed., *The Civil War Diary of Sarah Morgan* (Athens: University of Georgia, 1991), 608.
28. Ibid.
29. *Reminiscences of the Women of Missouri during the Sixties.* (n.d.; reprint, Dayton: Morningside House, 1988), 295–98.

CHAPTER 3: THE DAMNING SPOT

1. Abraham Lincoln pamphlets, vol. 1, A-L, Kansas State Historical Society, Topeka.
2. Furry, *The Civil War Journal of Reverend Francis Springer.*
3. *Chicago Tribune,* April 17, 1865.
4. Ibid.
5. Springfield (Ohio) *Daily News and Republic,* May 1, 1865.
6. Hudson Strode, *Jefferson Davis—Tragic Hero: 1864–1889, The Last Twenty-five Years* (New York: Harcourt, Brace & World, 1964), 199.
7. Avary, *Dixie after the War,* 90.
8. Good, *We Saw Lincoln Shot,* 69.
9. Springfield (Ohio) *Daily News and Republic,* April 27, 1865.
10. Townsend Downes diary, April 15, 1865, Delaware Public Archives, Hall of Records, Dover.
11. *Chicago Tribune,* April 21, 1865; Springfield *Illinois Daily State Journal,* April 29, 1865; Wilmington *Delaware Republican,* May 1, 1965.
12. *Chicago Tribune,* April 23, 1865; Leavenworth *Daily Conservative,* April 23, 1865.
13. Springfield (Ohio) *Daily News and Republic,* April 26, 1865.
14. Trudeau, *Out of the Storm,* 230.

15. Indianapolis *Daily Journal,* April 16, 1865; Thomas Reed Turner, *Beware the People Weeping: Public Opinion and the Assassination of Abraham Lincoln* (Baton Rouge: Louisiana State University, 1982), 27.
16. Ibid.; *New Orleans Daily Picayune,* May 6, 1865.
17. Asia Booth, *The Unlocked Book: A Memoir of John Wilkes Booth By His Sister Asia Booth Clarke* (New York: Benjamin Blom, 1971), 202.
18. *New Orleans Times,* May 2, 1865.
19. Leech, *Reveille in Washington,* 406.
20. J. R. Perkins, *Trails, Rails and War: The Life of General G. M. Dodge* (Indianapolis: Bobbs-Merrill, 1929), 169; *Chicago Tribune,* April 22, 1865.
21. Ibid.; Indianapolis *Daily State Journal,* April 18, 1865.
22. Davis, *Long Surrender,* 79.
23. Avary, *Dixie after the War,* 90.
24. *Chicago Tribune,* May 10, 1865.
25. Davis, *Long Surrender,* 105.
26. *Chicago Tribune,* April 17, 1865.
27. Trudeau, *Out of the Storm,* 234.

CHAPTER 4: THE FUGITIVE

1. Davis, *Long Surrender,* 54.
2. Ibid., 60.
3. Ibid., 68.
4. Ibid., 71.
5. Ibid., 72.
6. *Houston Tri-Weekly Telegraph,* May 8, 1865.
7. Mary Sanders, ed., *Diary in Gray: The Civil War Letters and Diary of Jared Young Sanders* (Baton Rouge: Louisiana Genealogical and Historical Society, 1994), 94.
8. John Newman Edwards, *Shelby and His Men; or, The War in the West* (Waverly, MO: General Joseph Shelby Memorial Fund, 1993), 517.
9. Davis, *Long Surrender,* 84.
10. Jefferson Davis, *The Rise and Fall of the Confederate Government* (1881; reprint, New York: Yoseloff, 1958), 683.
11. Ibid., 86.
12. Ibid., 93.
13. Trudeau, *Out of the Storm,* 238.
14. Ibid., 239.
15. Carolyn L. Harrell, *When the Bells Tolled for Lincoln: Southern Reaction to the Assassination* (Macon, GA: Mercer University, 1997), 43–44.

16. John F. Marszalek, *Sherman: A Soldier's Passion for Order* (New York: The Free Press, 1993), 343–44.
17. Springfield (Ohio) *Daily News and Republic,* May 19, 1865.
18. Ulysses S. Grant, *Ulysses S. Grant: Memoirs and Selected Letters, Personal Memoirs of U. S. Grant, Selected Letters 1839–1865* (New York: Library of America, 1990), 1089.

CHAPTER 5: GRAPEVINE BATTERIES

1. G. Glenn Clift, ed., *The Private War of Lizzie Hardin: A Kentucky Confederate Girl's Diary of the Civil War in Kentucky, Virginia, Tennessee, Alabama, and Georgia* (Frankfort: Kentucky Historical Society, 1963), 224.
2. Charles M. McGee, Jr., and Ernest M. Lander, Jr., eds., *A Rebel Came Home* (Columbia: University of South Carolina, 1961), 83.
3. William Kauffman Scarborough, ed., *The Diary of Edmund Ruffin* (Baton Rouge: Louisiana State University, 1989), vol. 3, 861.
4. Joseph T. Durkin, ed., *John Dooley: Confederate Soldier, His War Journal* (South Bend, IN: University of Notre Dame, 1963), 176–77.
5. Clift, *Private War of Lizzie Hardin,* 235.
6. Ibid., 223.
7. Emma LeConte, *When the World Ended: The Diary of Emma LeConte* (New York: Oxford University, 1957), 97.
8. Durkin, *John Dooley,* 200.
9. George Cary Eggleston, *A Rebel's Recollections* (Bloomington: Indiana University, 1959), 182–83.
10. Clift, *Lizzie Hardin,* 231.
11. Ibid., 233.
12. Robert Manson Myers, ed., *The Children of Pride: A True Story of Georgia and the Civil War* (New Haven, CT: Yale University, 1972), 1268.
13. Rev. Cornelius Walker diary, April 18, 1865, Museum of the Confederacy, Richmond, Virginia.
14. John Q. Anderson, ed., *Brokenburn: The Journal of Kate Stone, 1861–1868* (Baton Rouge: Louisiana State University, 1955), 331.
15. Clift, *Private War of Lizzie Hardin,* 231.
16. *Montgomery Daily Mail,* April 24 and 29, 1865.
17. Mrs. A. T. Smythe, Miss M. B. Poppenheim, and Mrs. Thomas Taylor, *South Carolina Women in the Confederacy* (Columbia, SC: State, 1903), 286.
18. Durkin, *John Dooley,* 177.
19. Ibid.

20. *Sad Earth, Sweet Heaven: The Diary of Lucy Rebecca Buck* (Buckingham, AL: Buck, 1992).
21. Clift, *Private War of Lizzie Hardin,* 232.
22. Spencer Bidwell King, Jr., ed., *The War-Time Journal of a Georgia Girl, 1864–1865* (Macon, GA: Ardivan, 1960), 155.
23. *Greensboro* (Alabama) *Beacon,* April 21, 1865.
24. Bell Irvin Wiley, ed., *Fourteen Hundred and 91 Days in the Confederate Army: A Journal Kept by W. W. Heartsill* (Wilmington, NC: Broadfoot, 1987), 242–43.
25. Avary, *Dixie after the War,* 83.
26. Anderson, *Brokenburn: The Journal of Kate Stone,* 333.
27. LeConte, *When the World Ended,* 141.
28. King, ed., *The War-Time Journal of a Georgia Girl,* 173–74.
29. Frances Hewitt Fearn, *Diary of a Refugee* (New York: Moffatt, Yard, 1910), electronic edition, 114–15.
30. King, *War-Time Journal,* 173–74.
31. Virginia Ingrahm Burr, ed., *The Secret Eye: The Journal of Ella Gertrude Clanton Thomas, 1848–1889* (Chapel Hill: University of North Carolina, 1990), 277.
32. Durkin, *John Dooley,* 197.
33. McGee, and Lander, eds., *A Rebel Came Home,* 83.
34. James P. Shelton, ed., *The Reconstruction: A Documentary History of the South after the War, 1865–1877* (New York: G. P. Putnam's Sons, 1963), 14.
35. Myers, *Children of Pride,* 1268.
36. Avary, *Dixie after the War,* 83.
37. Turner, *Beware the People Weeping,* 95.
38. Raleigh *Daily Progress,* May 17, 1865.
39. *Frankfort* (Kentucky) *Commonwealth,* June 13, 1865.
40. Anderson, *Journal of Kate Stone,* 333.

CHAPTER 6: EVERY MAN'S HAND

1. *Chicago Tribune,* April 17, 1865.
2. Indianapolis *Daily State Journal,* April 19, 1865; *Memphis Daily Avalanche,* April 4, 1866.
3. *Chicago Tribune,* April 17, 1865.
4. *New Orleans Daily Picayune,* April 30, 1865.
5. Ibid., April 25, 1865.
6. Priscilla Bond diary, Special Collections, Louisiana State University, May 17, 1865; Washington, D.C., *Evening Star,* April 28, 1865.

7. *Council Bluffs* (Iowa) *Bugle,* May 11, 1865.
8. Springfield *Daily Illinois State Journal,* April 29, 1865.
9. Ibid.
10. Ibid.
11. Trudeau, *Out of the Storm,* 232.
12. Springfield *Daily Illinois State Journal,* April 29, 1865.
13. Springfield (Ohio) *Daily News and Republic,* May 3, 1865.
14. *New Orleans Times,* May 3, 1865; Springfield (Ohio) *Daily News and Republic,* June 5, 1865; Washington, D.C., *Evening Star,* April 21, 1865.
15. Baton Rouge *Weekly Advocate,* May 19, 1865; *New York Times,* June 1, 1865.
16. *Chicago Tribune,* April 29, 1865.
17. *Chicago Tribune,* May 4, 1865; *Montgomery* (Alabama) *Daily Mail,* June 16, 1865.
18. Dorothy Meserve Kunhardt and Phillip B. Kunhardt, Jr., *Twenty Days* (New York: Harper and Row, 1965), 182.
19. *Chicago Tribune,* May 4, 1865.
20. Ibid., April 28, 1865.
21. *New Orleans Daily Picayune,* May 6, 1876; Turner, *Beware the People Weeping,* 121.
22. Washington, D.C., *Evening Star,* May 1, 1865.
23. *Chicago Tribune,* April 24, 1865.
24. *New York Times,* April 25, 1865.
25. *Chicago Tribune,* May 2, 1865.
26. Nicolay and Hay, *Abraham Lincoln,* 321.
27. Washington, D.C., *Evening Star,* April 25, 1865; Nicolay and Hay, *Abraham Lincoln,* 321; Kunhardt and Kunhardt, *Twenty Days,* 221.
28. *New York Times,* April 29, 1865.
29. Wilmington *Delaware Republican,* May 11, 1865.

CHAPTER 7: GOD'S CURSE

1. Katherine M. Jones, *Ladies of Richmond: Confederate Capital* (New York: Bobbs-Merrill, 1962), 298.
2. Ibid.
3. *New York Times,* May 7, 1865.
4. King, *War-Time Journal of a Georgia Girl,* 204–205.
5. Clift, *Private War of Lizzie Hardin,* 242, 245.
6. Mary D. Robertson, ed., *A Confederate Lady Comes of Age: The Journal of Pauline DeCaradeuc Heyward, 1863–1888* (Columbia: University of South Carolina, 1992), 75.
7. Davis, *Long Surrender,* 135.

8. Joseph Howard Parks, *General Edmund Kirby Smith, C.S.A.* (Baton Rouge: Louisiana State University, 1954), 460.
9. Sanders, *The Civil War Letters and Diary of Jared Young Sanders,* 93.
10. Edwards, *Shelby and His Men,* 523.
11. Ina Woestemeyer Van Noppen, *Stoneman's Last Raid* (Boone, NC: n.p., 1961), 99.
12. Ibid., 100; *New York Times,* May 11, 1865.
13. *New York Times,* May 4, 1865.
14. Van Noppen, *Stoneman's Last Raid,* 100.
15. Ibid., 101.
16. Trudeau, *Out of the Storm,* 294.
17. Davis, *Rise and Fall,* 701.
18. Trudeau, *Out of the Storm,* 294.
19. C. W. Raines, ed., *Six Decades in Texas; or, Memoirs of Francis Richard Lubbock, Governor of Texas in War Time, 1861–63* (Austin, TX: B. C. Jones, 1900), 572.
20. Ibid., 573.
21. Trudeau, *Out of the Storm,* 295.
22. Davis, *Long Surrender,* 150–51.
23. Raines, *Six Decades in Texas,* 573.
24. William C. Davis, *Jefferson Davis: The Man and His Hour* (New York: Harper Collins, 1991), 640.
25. Trudeau, *Out of the Storm,* 296.
26. Ibid., 295.
27. Davis, *Long Surrender,* 149.
28. Trudeau, *Out of the Storm,* 296.
29. Davis, *Long Surrender,* 155.
30. LeConte, *When the World Ended,* 103.
31. James C. Bonner, ed., *The Journal of a Milledgeville Girl, 1861–1867* (Athens: University of Georgia, 1964), 74–75.
32. East, *Civil War Diary of Sarah Morgan,* 611.
33. Kunhardt, *Twenty Days,* 301.
34. *Chicago Tribune,* May 6, 1865.
35. *Pekin* (Illinois) *Register,* May 10, 1865.

CHAPTER 8: IN DURANCE VILE

1. *The War of the Rebellion: A Compilation of the Official Records of the Union and Confederate Armies* (Washington, D.C.: Government Printing Office, 1880–1901), ser. 2, vol. 8, "Prisoners of War, etc.," 563–564.
2. Washington, D.C., *Evening Star,* May 24, 1865.
3. Alexandria *Louisiana Democrat,* July 11, 1866.

4. Ibid.
5. *Official Records,* ser. 2, vol. 8, "Prisoners," 564.
6. Alexandria *Louisiana Democrat,* July 11, 1866.
7. *Official Records,* ser. 2, vol. 8, "Prisoners," 564–65; *Greensboro* (North Carolina) *Patriot,* March 16, 1866; *New York Times,* June 8, 1865.
8. *Montgomery* (Alabama) *Daily Mail,* June 8, 1865.
9. Alexandria *Louisiana Democrat,* July 11, 1866.
10. Springfield (Ohio) *Daily News and Republic,* June 9, 1865.
11. Strode, *Jefferson Davis,* 232.
12. Charles Adams, "The Trial of the Century That Never Was," *Southern Partisan* (first quarter 1998): 18.
13. Jackson *Daily Mississippian,* September 14, 1865.
14. *Fort Smith* (Arkansas) *New Era,* May 27, 1865.
15. William C. Davis, *Jefferson Davis,* 646.
16. Davis, *Long Surrender,* 145; *Raleigh Daily Progress,* May 19, 1865.
17. *Fort Smith* (Arkansas) *New Era,* June 17, 1865.
18. J. William Jones, *The Davis Memorial Volume; or, Our Dead President, Jefferson Davis, and the World's Tribute to His Memory* (Waco, TX: Yeager, 1890), 401–2.
19. Michael Golay, *A Ruined Land* (New York: John Wiley, 1999), 230.
20. *Chicago Tribune,* May 16, 1865.
21. Washington, D.C., *Evening Star,* May 23, 1865.
22. *Fort Smith* (Arkansas) *New Era,* May 27, 1865; Adams, "The Trial of the Century," 18; Springfield (Ohio) *Daily News and Republic,* May 20, 1865; *New York Times,* July 16, 1865.
23. *Owensboro* (Kentucky) *Monitor,* August 2, 1865.
24. Alexandria *Louisiana Democrat,* July 11, 1866.
25. Springfield (Ohio) *Daily News and Republic,* May 31, 1865.
26. *Recollections and Reminiscences, 1861–1865* (South Carolina Division, United Daughters of the Confederacy, 1990), 30.
27. Alexandria *Louisiana Democrat,* July 11, 1866.
28. "How Jefferson Davis Was Shackled," *Confederate Veteran* (1909): 558.
29. Scarborough, *Diary of Edmund Ruffin,* 922.
30. Robertson, *Confederate Lady Comes of Age,* 76.

CHAPTER 9: INFAMOUS

1. Hodding Carter, *The Angry Scar: The Story of Reconstruction* (Garden City, NY: Doubleday, 1959), 82.
2. Donald Lankiewicz, "Journey to Asylum: A Secretary of State Runs for His Life," *Civil War Times Illustrated* (December 1987): 18.
3. Trudeau, *Out of the Storm,* 384; Davis, *Long Surrender,* 43.

4. Jones, *Heroines of Dixie,* 405.
5. LeConte, *When the World Ended,* 108.
6. Benjamin H. Hill, Jr., *Senator Benjamin H. Hill of Georgia: His Life, Speeches and Writings* (Atlanta: H. C. Hudgins, 1891), 46.
7. Raines, *Six Decades in Texas,* 580.
8. *Chicago Tribune,* April 17, July 3, 1865; *St. Louis Dispatch,* April 18, 1865.
9. *Official Records,* ser. 2, vol. 8, "Prisoners," 726.
10. Carter, *Angry Scar,* 25.
11. *Fort Smith* (Arkansas) *New Era,* June 10, 1865.
12. Carter, *Angry Scar,* 44.
13. Robert Selph Henry, ed., *As They Saw Forrest: Some Recollections and Comments of Contemporaries* (Jackson, TN: McCowat-Mercer, 1956), 222.
14. Alexandria *Louisiana Democrat,* August 9, 1865.
15. Marszalek, *Sherman,* 355.
16. Mount Sterling (Kentucky) *Sentinel,* July 28, 1865.
17. Trudeau, *Out of the Storm,* 362.
18. Ibid., 361–62; Turner, *Beware the People Weeping,* 68.
19. *Livingston* (Alabama) *Journal,* July 15, 1865; William Hanchett, *The Lincoln Murder Conspiracies* (Urbana: University of Illinois, 1986), 29.
20. Springfield (Ohio) *Daily News and Republic,* April 27, and May 1, 1865.
21. *Anderson* (South Carolina) *Intelligencer,* November 2, 1865.
22. Springfield (Ohio) *Daily News and Republic,* April 25, 1865.
23. *Official Records,* ser. 2, vol. 8, "Prisoners," 773–74.
24. Baton Rouge *Tri-Weekly Advocate,* September 11, 1865.
25. *Recollections and Reminiscences,* 161.
26. Ibid., 11.
27. Joan Tracy Armstrong, *History of Smyth County, Virginia: Ante-Bellum Years Through the Civil War* (Marion, VA: Smyth County Historical and Museum Society, 1986), vol. 2, 145.
28. Edwin W. Beitzell, *Point Lookout Prison Camp for Confederates* (Abell, MD: 1972), 91.
29. *Recollections and Reminiscences,* 291.
30. Louis Leon, *Diary of a Tarheel Confederate Soldier* (Charlotte, NC: Stone, 1913) electronic edition, 68.
31. Milton Asbury Ryan, *Experience of a Confederate Soldier in Camp and Prison in the Civil War, 1861–1865.* Electronic edition. Copy in possession of Carter House, Franklin, Tennessee.
32. Ibid.
33. *Recollections and Reminiscences,* 302.

34. Armstrong, *History of Smyth County,* 145.
35. Gustavus W. Dyer and John Trotwood Moore, eds., "William Henry Blackburn," *The Tennessee Civil War Veterans Questionnaires* (Greenville, SC: Southern Historical Press, 1985).
36. Baton Rouge *Tri-Weekly Advocate,* September 11, 1865.

CHAPTER 10: DEATH OF THE DREAM

1. Parks, *General E. Kirby Smith,* 456–57.
2. Ibid.
3. Thomas W. Cutrer and T. Michael Parrish, eds., *Brothers in Gray: The Civil War Letters of the Pierson Family* (Baton Rouge: Louisiana State University, 1997), 259.
4. Robert S. Weddle, *Plow-Horse Cavalry: The Caney Creek Boys of the Thirty-Fourth Texas* (Austin, TX: Madrona, 1974), 158.
5. Ibid., 160–61.
6. Parks, *General E. Kirby Smith,* 478n; Edwards, *Shelby and His Men,* 540.
7. Trudeau, *Out of the Storm,* 353.
8. Edwards, *Shelby,* 534–35.
9. Anderson, *Journal of Kate Stone,* 345–46.
10. Alexandria *Louisiana Democrat,* June 14, 1865.
11. Parks, *Smith,* 475; Trudeau, *Storm,* 340.
12. Ibid., 357; Edwards, *Shelby,* 545.
13. Scarborough, *Ruffin Diary,* 884.
14. Ibid., 854–55.
15. Ibid., 850–51.
16. Ibid., 946, 947.
17. Ibid., 950.
18. *New York Times,* July 8, 1865.
19. Alexandria *Louisiana Democrat,* July 26, 1865; Elizabeth Steger Trindal, *Mary Surratt: An American Tragedy* (Gretna, LA: Pelican, 1996), 218.
20. Alexandria *Louisiana Democrat,* July 26, 1865.
21. Trudeau, *Out of the Storm,* 375.
22. Ibid., 374.
23. Alexandria *Louisiana Democrat,* July 26, 1865.
24. Ibid.
25. Owner diary, July 12, 1865.
26. Edwards, *Shelby,* 547.

CHAPTER 11: SILENCE OF THE GRAVEYARD

1. C. Vann Woodward, ed., *Mary Chesnut's Civil War* (New Haven, CT: Yale University, 1981), 790.
2. Jones, *Heroines of Dixie,* 405.

3. McGee and Lander, *A Rebel Came Home,* 85.
4. Belinda Hurmence, *Before Freedom: 48 Oral Histories of Former North and South Carolina Slaves* (New York: Mentor, 1990), 40.
5. King, *War-Time Journal of a Georgia Girl,* 212.
6. *Nashville* (Tennessee) *Daily Press,* May 27, 1865.
7. Thomas Goodrich, *Black Flag: Guerrilla Warfare on the Western Border, 1861–1865* (Bloomington: Indiana University, 1995), 55.
8. Ronnie C. Tyler and Lawrence R. Murphy, eds., *The Slave Narratives of Texas* (Austin, Texas: Encino, 1974), 100.
9. *Houston* (Texas) *Tri-Weekly Telegraph,* April 28, 1865.
10. Katherine M. Jones, *When Sherman Came: Southern Women and the "Great March"* (Indianapolis: Bobbs-Merrill, 1964), 303.
11. *Houston* (Texas) *Tri-Weekly Telegraph,* April 28, 1865.
12. Janie Smith letter, April 12, 1865, Eisenschiml Collection, Box 9, Illinois State Historical Library, Springfield.
13. *Houston* (Texas) *Tri-Weekly Telegraph,* April 21, 1865.
14. Ibid.
15. Janie Smith letter.
16. *Houston* (Texas) *Tri-Weekly Telegraph,* April 28, 1865.
17. Mary Stevenson, ed., *The Diary of Clarissa Adger Bowen, Ashtabula Plantation, 1865 and the Pendleton-Clemson Area, South Carolina, 1776–1889* (Pendleton, SC: Foundation for Historic Restoration, n.d.), 55.
18. Tyler and Murphy, *Slave Narratives,* 115.
19. Hurmence, *Before Freedom,* 41.
20. Woodward, *Mary Chesnut,* 823–24.
21. Hurmence, *Freedom,* 48–49.
22. Malcolm C. McMillan, *The Alabama Confederate Reader* (Tuscaloosa: University of Alabama, 1963), 421.
23. Janie Smith letter.
24. Myers, *Children of Pride,* 1274.
25. Woodward, *Mary Chesnut,* 866.
26. *Recollections and Reminiscences,* 138.
27. Woodward, *Mary Chesnut,* 801.
28. Clift, *Private War of Lizzie Hardin,* 238.
29. Woodward, *Mary Chesnut,* 807.
30. Ibid., 802.
31. Ibid.
32. Ibid., 804.
33. Stevenson, ed., *Diary of Clarissa Adger Bowen,* 74.
34. King, *War-Time Journal,* 283.
35. *Houston* (Texas) *Tri-Weekly Telegraph,* April 28, 1865.
36. *Chattanooga Daily Rebel,* April 25, 1865.

37. *Houston* (Texas) *Tri-Weekly Telegraph,* April 28, 1865.
38. Hurmence, *Before Freedom,* 41.

CHAPTER 12: THE ROAD BACK

1. LeConte, *When the World Ended,* 98.
2. Tyler and Murphy, *Slave Narratives,* 105.
3. McMillan, *Alabama Confederate Reader,* 430.
4. *Anderson* (South Carolina) *Intelligencer,* August 3, 1865; Dyer and Moore, "E.M. Lively," *Tennessee Veterans.*
5. *Anderson* (South Carolina) *Intelligencer,* August 3, 1865.
6. Matthew Jack Davis manuscript, "War Sketches as Seen and Remembered by the Writer, Matthew Jack Davis of Co. K 19 Mississippi Infantry," Lucas Collection, Sherman, Texas, Public Library, 36–39.
7. J. T. Bowden, "How a Confederate Got Home in 1865," *Confederate Veteran* (1909): 59.
8. Dyer and Moore, "William Baldridge," *Tennessee Veterans.*
9. John Jones poem, copy in possession of Ronald Leonard, Cana, Virginia.
10. Jesse Edwards letter, June 20, 1865, Chaplain A. S. Billingsley letter, June 23, 1865, copies in possession of Ronald Leonard, Cana, Virginia.
11. "War Was the Place: A Centennial Collection of the Confederate Soldiers Letters," *Chattahoochee Valley Historical Society Bulletin* (November 1961): 113.
12. Ibid.
13. Ibid., 113–17.
14. Marcus Morton Rhoades diary, June 17, 1865, Western Historical Manuscript Collection, Columbia, Missouri; Davis, "War Sketches," 34.
15. Meridian (Mississippi) *Daily Clarion,* June 21, 1865; *Memphis Daily Argus,* June 20, 1865; Alexandria *Louisiana Democrat,* June 14, 1865.
16. *Memphis Daily Argus,* June 20, 1865.
17. Ibid.
18. *Memphis Daily Argus,* June 16, June 20, 1865.
19. Washington, D.C., *Evening Star,* June 30, 1865.
20. Dyer and Moore, "Samuel Adkisson" and "D.P. Hickman," *Tennessee Veterans.*
21. Gary W. Gallagher, *The Confederate War* (Cambridge, MA: Harvard University, 1997), 167.
22. I. G. Bradwell, "Making Our Way Home from Appomattox," *Confederate Veteran* (1921): 102.
23. Ibid.
24. John Richard Dennett, *The South as It Is: 1865–1866* (New York: Viking, 1965), 225.

25. William C. Davis, ed., *Diary of a Confederate Soldier: John S. Jackman of the Orphan Brigade* (Columbia: University of South Carolina, 1990), 168.
26. Davis, "War Sketches," 41.

CHAPTER 13: GLORIOUS IN THE DUST

1. Joseph McClure, "Wounded Texan's Trip Home on Crutches," *Confederate Veteran* (1909): 163.
2. Dyer and Moore, "Robert Preston Adair," *Tennessee Veterans.*
3. Sanders, *Diary in Gray,* 95.
4. William D. Cater, ed., *As It Was* (San Antonio, TX: n.p., 1981), 228.
5. Dyer and Moore, "John H. Frierson," *Tennessee Veterans.*
6. Ibid., "Zachary Taylor Dyer" and "Thomas Perkins."
7. *Recollections and Reminiscences,* 472; William Walsh manuscript, Lucas Collection, file #140, Sherman, Texas, Public Library.
8. Parthenia Antoinette Hague, *A Blockaded Family: Life in Southern Alabama During the Civil War* (1888; reprint, Boston: Houghton Mifflin, 1971), 168.
9. Ibid., 167.
10. Wiley, ed., *Fourteen Hundred and 91 Days in the Confederate Army,* 239.
11. Jackson *Daily Mississippian,* July 27, 1865.
12. William A. Fletcher, *Rebel Private, Front and Rear: Memoirs of a Confederate Soldier* (New York: Dutton, 1995), 201–5.
13. Ibid., 208–9.
14. Anderson (South Carolina) *Intelligencer,* July 27, 1865.
15. King, *War-Time Journal of a Georgia Girl,* 184.
16. Bradwell, "Appomattox," 103.
17. Edward Crenshaw diary, Alabama Department of Archives and History, Montgomery, May 22, 1865.
18. William Pitt Chambers journal, Mississippi Department of Archives and History, Jackson, April 26, 1865.
19. Dyer and Moore, *Tennessee Veterans.*
20. Lucille Griffith, *Alabama: A Documentary History to 1900* (Tuscaloosa: University of Alabama, 1968), 435.
21. Frank M. Mixson, *Reminiscences of a Private* (n.d.; reprint, Camden, SC: J. J. Fox, 1990), 129.
22. Laura Virginia Hale, *Four Valiant Years in the Lower Shenandoah Valley, 1861–1865* (Front Royal, VA: Hathaway, 1986), 514.
23. Mary Iona Chadick diary, 1862–1865, folder 2, Alabama Department of Archives and History, Montgomery, May 4, 1865.
24. King, *War-Time Journal of a Georgia Girl,* 184.
25. Ibid., 182.

26. Sara Agnes Rice Pryor, *Reminiscences of Peace and War* (New York: Macmillan, 1906), 382–83.
27. Andrew Buni, ed., "Reconstruction in Orange County, Virginia: A Letter from Hannah Garlick Rawlings to Her Sister, Clarissa Lawrence Rawlings, August 9, 1865," *The Virginia Magazine of History and Biography* (1967): 463.
28. *Recollections and Reminiscences,* 321.
29. King, *War-Time Journal,* 182, 232.
30. Bell Irvin Wiley, ed., *"This Infernal War": The Confederate Letters of Sgt. Edwin H. Fay* (Austin: University of Texas, 1958), 448.
31. Priscilla Bond diary, June 16 and June 26, 1865.
32. Ibid., July 6 or 7, 1865.
33. Myrta Lockett Avary, *A Virginia Girl during the War* (New York: Appleton, 1903), 381.
34. *Recollections and Reminiscences,* 351.
35. Jesse Loving manuscript, Lucas Collection, Sherman, Texas, Public Library, 10–12.
36. Gary Gallagher, ed., *Fighting for the Confederacy: The Personal Recollections of General Edward Porter Alexander* (Chapel Hill: University of North Carolina, 1989), 552.
37. Milton Asbury Ryan, *Experience of a Confederate Soldier in Camp and Prison in the Civil War 1861–1865,* electronic edition; Mark K. Christ, *Rugged and Sublime: The Civil War in Arkansas* (Fayetteville: University of Arkansas, 1994), 160.
38. Cornelius H. Carlton diary, Virginia State Library, Archives Division, Richmond, April 14, 1865.
39. Mixson, *Reminiscences,* 129.
40. Fletcher, *Rebel Private,* 211.
41. Bowden, "How a Confederate Got Home," 59.
42. W. A. Callaway, "Reminiscences of War at the Close," *Confederate Veteran* (1909): 505.
43. Cater, 233.
44. Christ, *Rugged and Sublime,* 160; *Macon* (Mississippi) *Beacon,* June 30, 1866.
45. *Selma* (Alabama) *Morning Times,* December 11, 1865.
46. Mary D. Moody letter, May 4, 1865, Moody Family Letters, Museum of the Confederacy, Richmond, Virginia.
47. *Selma* (Alabama) *Morning Times,* December 11, 1865.
48. John R. Hildebrand, ed., *A Mennonite Journal, 1862–1865* (Shippensburg, PA: Burd Street Press, 1996), April 17 and May 1, 1865.
49. DeLeon, *Four Years in Rebel Capitals,* 366–67.

CHAPTER 14: THE YEAR OF JUBILO

1. Tyler and Murphy, *Slave Narratives,* 115.
2. Ibid., 121.
3. Ibid., 120.
4. Eggleston, *A Rebel's Recollections,* 185.
5. Tyler and Murphy, *Slave Narratives.* 105.
6. Hurmence, *Before Freedom,* 83.
7. *Council Bluffs* (Iowa) *Bugle,* July 13, 1865.
8. *New York Times,* June 4, 1865.
9. King, *War-Time Journal,* 293.
10. Tyler and Murphy, *Slave Narratives,* 124.
11. Ibid., 127.
12. Virginia Clare, *Thunder and Stars: The Life of Mildred Rutherford* (Oglethorpe, Georgia: Oglethorpe University, 1941), 106–07.
13. *Recollections and Reminiscences,* 388.
14. Tyler and Murphy, *Slave Narratives.* 120.
15. Carter, *Angry Scar,* 35.
16. Arney Robinson Childs, ed., *The Private Journal of Henry William Ravenel, 1859–1887* (Columbia: University of South Carolina, 1947), 244.
17. Dennett, *South,* 14.
18. Carter, *Angry Scar,* 55.
19. Tyler and Murphy, 113.
20. Jo Ella Powell Exley, ed., *Texas Tears and Texas Sunshine: Voices of Frontier Women* (College Station: Texas A & M University, 1985), 155–56.
21. Jackson *Daily Mississippian,* September 14, 1865.
22. Carter, *Angry Scar,* 49.
23. Mary Elizabeth Massey, *Dixie: Women in the Civil War* (Lincoln: University of Nebraska, 1966), 286.
24. Tyler and Murphy, *Slave Narratives,* 113–14.
25. Childs, *Private Journal,* 244.
26. Tyler and Murphy, *Slave Narratives,* 113.
27. Gordon Carroll, ed., *The Desolate South, 1865–1866: A Picture of the Battlefields and of the Devastated Confederacy* (Boston: Little, Brown, 1956), 205.
28. Alexandria *Louisiana Democrat,* June 28 and August 30, 1865.
29. George Rawick, ed., "Walter Calloway," *The American Slave: A Composite Autobiography* (Westport, CT: Greenwood, 1972–79), electronic edition: *American Slave Narratives: An Online Anthology.*
30. Hurmence, *Before Freedom,* 50.
31. Mount Sterling (Kentucky) *Sentinel,* September 29, 1865.

32. Jackson *Daily Mississippian,* September 13, 1865.
33. Ibid.
34. Jackson *Daily Mississippian,* August 22, 1865.
35. *Montgomery* (Alabama) *Daily Mail,* April 1, 1866.
36. King, *War-Time Journal of a Georgia Girl,* 331.
37. Alexandria, *Louisiana Democrat,* November 22, 1865.
38. Jennie Vass memoir, Museum of the Confederacy, Richmond, Virginia.
39. Jackson *Daily Mississippian,* July 27, 1865.
40. Rawick, "Fountain Hughes," *American Slave.*
41. Fearn, *Diary of a Refugee,* 135.
42. *Montgomery* (Alabama) *Daily Mail,* February 22, 1866.
43. Thaddeus Stevens speech transcript, December 18, 1865, Library of Congress.
44. Thomas Affleck papers, "America," Special Collections, Louisiana State University, Baton Rouge, scrapbook, box 51, folder #7.
45. Mount Sterling (Kentucky) *Sentinel,* September 8, 1865.
46. Orville Vernon Burton, *In My Father's House Are Many Mansions: Family and Community in Edgefield, South Carolina* (Chapel Hill: University of North Carolina, 1985), 229–30.
47. *Fort Smith* (Arkansas) *Herald,* August 4, 1866.
48. Lucille Griffith, *Alabama: A Documentary History to 1900* (Tuscaloosa: University of Alabama, 1968), 440.
49. Jones, *Ladies of Richmond,* 322.
50. Carroll, *Desolate South,* 113.
51. Fearn, *Diary of a Refugee,* 141.
52. Rawick, "John Quincy Adams," *American Slave.*
53. Andrews, *The South since the War,* 23.
54. Richard L. Troutman, ed., *The Heavens Are Weeping: The Diaries of George Richard Browder, 1852–1886* (Grand Rapids, MI: Zondervan, 1987), 205.
55. O. F. Weisiger letter, May 29, 1865, Virginia Military Institute Archives, Lexington, MS # 285.
56. Hurmence, *Before Freedom,* 68–69.

CHAPTER 15: SWALLOWING THE DOG

1. Stephen V. Ash. "White Virginians under Federal Occupation," *The Virginia Magazine of History and Biography* (April 1990): 190.
2. Charlotte (North Carolina) *Western Democrat,* June 6, 1865.
3. Childs, *Ravenel Journal,* 302.
4. Charlotte (North Carolina) *Western Democrat,* June 6, 1865.

5. Dyer and Moore, "William Carroll Boze," *Tennessee Veterans;* Davis, *Diary of a Confederate Soldier*, 169.
6. LeConte, *When the World Ended,* 107.
7. "After Appomattox," *Confederate Veteran* (1923): 196–98.
8. Clipping dated June 28, 1912, in Civil War Memories of Robert C. Carden Company B, 16th Tennessee Infantry (published as a series by Boone, Iowa, *Independent,* 1912). Clippings in possession of descendant, Robert C. Carden, and published online.
9. *Reminiscences of the Women of Missouri,* 195.
10. July 12, 1912, in *Civil War Memories of Robert C. Carden.*
11. LeConte, *When the World Ended,* 107–8.
12. Goodrich, *Black Flag,* 44.
13. Avary, *Dixie after the War,* 70–71.
14. Andrews, *South since the War,* 290.
15. Jackson *Daily Mississippian,* September 24, 1865.
16. Myers, *Children of Pride,* 1290.
17. Moses F. T. Evans letter, dated June 14, 1865, to "My dear Sister Mary," Virginia State Library, Archives Division, Richmond.
18. Francis Butler Simkins and James Welch Patton, *The Women of the Confederacy* (1936; reprint, St. Clair Shores, MI: Scholarly, 1976), 245.
19. Jackson *Tri-Weekly Mississippian,* July 20, 1865.
20. Ibid.
21. Ibid., November 19, 1865.
22. Pryor, *Reminiscences of Peace and War,* 377.
23. LeConte, *When the World Ended,* 107–08.
24. Washington, D.C., *Evening Star,* May 1, 1865.
25. Owner diary, September 29, 1865.
26. *Houston* (Texas) *Tri-Weekly Telegraph,* May 15, 1865.
27. LeConte, *When the World Ended,* 111.
28. *Official Records,* ser. 1, vol. 48, part 2, 250.
29. Robert A. Austin manuscript, copy in possession of Hubert Dye, Jr., Olathe, Kansas, 13–14.
30. Clipping dated June 18, 1912, in Civil War Memories of Robert C. Carden.
31. Mount Sterling (Kentucky) *Sentinel,* September 8, 1865.
32. Avary, *Virginia Girl,* 363.
33. Cornelia Phillips Spencer, *The Last Ninety Days of the War* (1866; reprint, Wilmington, NC: Broadfoot, 1993) 171.
34. King, *War-Time Journal,* 239.
35. Salem (North Carolina) *Peoples Press,* May 27 and August 19, 1865.
36. King, *War-Time Journal,* 239.

37. James H. McNeilly, "Surrender and Homeward Bound," *Confederate Veteran* (1923): 515.
38. John H. Worsham, *One of Jackson's Foot Cavalry: His Experience and What He Saw during the War, 1861–1865* (New York: Neale, 1912), 293–94.
39. Carter, *Angry Scar,* 44–45.
40. A. E. Lloyd manuscript, Museum of the Confederacy, Richmond, Virginia, 12.
41. *Recollections and Reminiscences,* 291.
42. King, *War-Time Journal,* 276.
43. James Whitman, "Incidents of Reconstruction," *Confederate Veteran* (1923): 221.
44. Clift, *Private War of Lizzie Hardin,* 274; Ann L. B. Brown, "Fort Delaware: The Most Dreaded Northern Prison," *Civil War Quarterly* 10 (September 1987): 40; Washington, D.C., *Evening Star,* April 26, 1865; *Official Records,* ser. 2, vol. 8, 515; *Alton* (Illinois) *Telegraph,* May 12, 1865.
45. *Memphis* (Tennessee) *Daily Avalanche,* March 24, 1866.
46. Alexandria *Louisiana Democrat,* July 11, 1866.
47. Ibid.
48. *Official Records,* ser. 2, vol. 8, 740.
49. Alexandria *Louisiana Democrat,* July 11, 1866.
50. Carroll, *The Desolate South,* 119–20.

CHAPTER 16: SUCH DAMNED REBELS

1. Alexandria *Louisiana Democrat,* January 3, 1866.
2. Kate D. Foster diary, Mississippi Department of Archives and History, Jackson.
3. Robertson, ed., *A Confederate Lady Comes of Age,* 74.
4. Shelton, ed., *Reconstruction,* 15.
5. Monroe F. Cockrell, ed., *Gunner with Stonewall: Reminiscences of William Thomas Poague* (Jackson, TN: McCowat-Mercer, 1957), 160–61.
6. King, *War-Time Journal,* 251.
7. Durkin, *John Dooley,* 183.
8. LeConte, *When the World Ended,* 106.
9. King, *War-Time Journal,* 259.
10. Ibid., 338.
11. Stevenson, *Diary of Clarissa Adger Bowen,* 76.
12. LeConte, *When the World Ended,* 113.
13. Bradwell, "Making Our Way Home," 103.
14. DeLeon, *Four Years in Rebel Capitals,* 369.

15. Shelton, ed., *Reconstruction,* 16.
16. LeConte, *When the World Ended,* 108–09.
17. Anderson, ed., *Brokenburn,* 351.
18. King, *War-Time Journal,* 379.
19. James I. Robertson, Jr., "Danville under Military Occupation, 1865," *The Virginia Magazine of History and Biography,* (1967): 347.
20. Exley, *Texas Tears,* 157.
21. Francis Butler Simkins and Robert Hilliard Woody, *South Carolina during Reconstruction* (1932; reprint, Gloucester, MA: Peter Smith, 1966), 20.
22. *New Orleans Daily Picayune,* April 23, 1865.
23. Mount Sterling (Kentucky) *Sentinel,* September 8, 1865.
24. Robertston, "Danville," 343.
25. McNeilly, "Surrender," 514.
26. Jackson *Daily Mississippian,* September 24, 1865.
27. Exley, *Texas Tears,* 149.
28. Baton Rouge (Louisiana) *Tri-Weekly Advocate,* August 9, 1865.
29. Robertson, ed., *Confederate Lady,* 80.
30. *Montgomery* (Alabama) *Daily Mail,* June 16, 1865.
31. Ibid., December 12, 1865.
32. Ibid., March 23, 1866.
33. Exley, *Texas Tears,* 149.
34. Alexandria *Louisiana Democrat,* August 9, 1865.
35. Robertson, ed., *Confederate Lady,* 79; Avary, *Dixie After the War,* 114; *Montgomery* (Alabama) *Daily Mail,* February 16, 1866.
36. Owner diary, October 17, 1865.
37. Exley, *Texas Tears,* 148; Springfield (Ohio) *Daily News and Republic,* May 25, 1865.
38. Bettie Pearl Fisher Hill manuscript, "Biography of Elizabeth Caroline Tinsley Fisher," Carrollton, Georgia, Public Library.
39. *Memphis* (Tennessee) *Daily Avalanche,* May 1, 1866.
40. *New Orleans Daily Picayune,* April 14, 1865; Gordon A. Cotton, *The Murder of Minerva Cook* (Vicksburg, MS: the author, 1993), 20–21.
41. William Best Hesseltine, *Civil War Prisons: A Study in Civil War Psychology* (New York: Frederick Ungar, 1930), 239.
42. Trudeau, *Out of the Storm,* 375–76.
43. Owner diary, September 23, 1865.
44. *Official Records,* ser. 2, vol. 8, 773–74.
45. Strode, *Jefferson Davis,* 267.
46. *New York Times,* November 11, 1865.
47. Pekin (Illinois) *Tazewell Register,* November 15, 1865.

48. *New York Times,* November 11, 1865.
49. Trudeau, *Out of the Storm,* 377.
50. *New York Times,* November 11, 1865.
51. *Natchez* (Mississippi) *Daily Courier,* November 29, 1865.
52. Statesville (North Carolina) *American,* November 14, 1865.
53. *Natchez* (Mississippi) *Daily Courier,* November 29, 1865.
54. *Selma* (Alabama) *Morning Times,* December 11, 1865.
55. King, *War-Time Journal,* 314.
56. Clift, *Private War of Lizzie Hardin,* 239.
57. Daniel E. Sutherland, ed., *A Very Violent Rebel: The Civil War Diary of Ellen Renshaw House* (Knoxville: University of Tennessee, 1996), 184.

CHAPTER 17: DEATH BY PEACE

1. Barbara Babcock Millhouse, ed., *Recollections of Major A. D. Reynolds, 1847–1925* (Winston-Salem, NC: Reynolds House, 1978), 18–21.
2. Ibid.; Salem (North Carolina) *People's Press,* June 24, 1865.
3. Eggleston, *Rebel's Recollections,* 182.
4. Ibid., 181.
5. David Paul Smith, *Frontier Defense in the Civil War: Texas' Rangers and Rebels* (College Station: Texas A & M University, 1992), 173–74.
6. J. W. Wilbarger, *Indian Depredations in Texas* (1888; reprint, Austin, TX: Eakin, 1985), 646–48.
7. Ibid., 647–48.
8. Andrews, *South,* 355–56.
9. Affleck papers, "Dallas Herald, June 30, 1866."
10. Jackson *Daily Mississippian,* August 2, 1865.
11. Ibid., semi-weekly edition, August 25, 1865.
12. *Montgomery* (Alabama) *Daily Mail,* January 14, 1865.
13. John N. Edwards, *Noted Guerrillas; or, the Warfare on the Border* (St. Louis: Bryan, Brand, 1877) 333–34.
14. Goodrich, *Black Flag,* 164.
15. Owner diary, April 18, 1865.
16. John W. Carroll, *Autobiography and Reminiscences,* Manuscript, Tennessee State Library and Archives, Nashville, 45.
17. Thomas B. Alexander, *Political Reconstruction in Tennessee* (Nashville: Vanderbilt University, 1950), 62.
18. Carroll, *Desolated South,* 126.
19. *Natchez* (Mississippi) *Daily Courier,* December 20, 1865.
20. Alexander, *Political Reconstruction,* 63–64.
21. Ibid., 62.

22. John W. Carroll, *Autobiography,* 42.
23. Sutherland, *House Diary,* 181, 186.
24. Ibid., 184–85.
25. Alexander, *Political Reconstruction,* 66.
26. *Council Bluffs* (Iowa) *Bugle,* June 22, 1865.
27. Alexander, *Political Reconstruction,* 64.
28. Ibid., 67.
29. *Memphis Daily Avalanche,* May 1, 1866.
30. Owner diary, October 2, 1865.
31. *Council Bluffs* (Iowa) *Bugle,* June 22, 1865.
32. Ibid.
33. Alexander, *Political Reconstruction,* 66.
34. Owner diary, October 2, 1865.
35. Sutherland, ed., *House Diary,* 181.
36. Andrews, *South,* 112.
37. Ibid., 113.
38. Ibid., 114.
39. *New Orleans Daily Picayune,* May 7, 1865.
40. Washington, D.C., *Evening Star,* May 10, 1865.
41. *New Orleans Daily Picayune,* May 7, 1865.
42. George Wilson Booth, *Personal Reminiscences of a Maryland Soldier in the War Between the States, 1865–1865,* (1898; reprint, Gaithersburg MD: Butternut Press, 1986), 176; *New York Times,* May 6, 1865; *Official Records,* ser. 2, vol. 8, 515; *Macon* (Mississippi) *Beacon,* June 30, 1866.
43. Mount Sterling (Kentucky) *Sentinel,* September 15, 1865.
44. *Montgomery* (Alabama) *Daily Mail,* June 14, 1865.
45. *Lexington* (Kentucky) *Observer and Reporter,* April 23, 1865.
46. John W. Tuttle diary, May 31, 1865, Special Collections, Kentucky Historical Society, Frankfort.
47. Lucas Collection, loose clippings, folder #103, Sherman, Texas, Public Library.
48. *Livingston* (Alabama) *Journal,* September 2, 1865.
49. Ibid.
50. Jackson *Daily Mississippian,* September 15, 1865.
51. Clipping dated July 19, 1912, Civil War Memories of Robert C. Carden.
52. Albert Castel, *William Clarke Quantrill: His Life and Times* (Norman: University of Oklahoma, 1999), 221.
53. Goodrich, *Black Flag,* 164.

CHAPTER 18: THROUGH A GLASS DARKLY

1. Mary Elizabeth Carter Rives diary, May 12, 1965, Special Collections, Louisiana State Univeristy, Baton Rouge.
2. Woodward, *Mary Chesnut,* 800.
3. Clift, *Private War of Lizzie Hardin,* 258.
4. *Montgomery Daily Mail,* June 14, 1865.
5. Washington, D.C., *Evening Star,* June 30, 1865.
6. Ibid., June 1, 1865.
7. *New York Times,* August 5, 1865.
8. Violet Hall, "Reconstruction: 1866," WPA Papers from the Louisiana Writers' Project, Louisiana Collection, Louisiana State Library, Baton Rouge, 17.
9. Christ, *Rugged and Sublime,* 160; Griffith, *History of Alabama,* 445.
10. Goodrich, *Black Flag,* 160.
11. Pryor, *Reminiscences of Peace and War,* 383 and 394.
12. Stephen V. Ash, *When the Yankees Came: Conflict and Chaos in the Occupied South, 1861–1865* (Chapel Hill: University of North Carolina, 1995), 209.
13. Jones, *Ladies of Richmond,* 310–11.
14. Anderson, *Journal of Kate Stone,* 364–65.
15. Sanders, *Diary in Gray,* 96.
16. Louisville (Kentucky) *True Presbyterian,* June 15, 1864.
17. Clift, *Private War of Lizzie Hardin,* 233.
18. William E. Watt diary, April 9 and 22, 1865, Museum of the Confederacy, Richmond.
19. Wiley, *This Infernal War,* 443.
20. Henry Grider letter, September 12 or 13, 1865, Milliken Collection, Kentucky Museum, Bowling Green.
21. Massey, *Dixie,* 323.
22. Simkins and Woody, *South Carolina,* 26.
23. Pryor, *Reminiscences,* 393.
24. Dennett, *South,* 12.
25. Baton Rouge (Louisiana) *Weekly Advocate,* June 16, 1866.
26. Carroll, *Desolated South,* 304.
27. Washington, D.C., *Evening Star,* July 7, 1865.
28. *Owensboro* (Kentucky) *Monitor,* July 12, 1865.
29. *Montgomery* (Alabama) *Daily Mail,* January, 16, 1866.
30. Laura Elizabeth Lee Battle, *Forget-Me-Nots of the Civil War: A Romance, Containing Reminiscences and Original Letters of Two Confederate Soldiers* (St. Louis: A. R. Fleming, 1909), Electronic edition, 177.
31. Simkins and Patton, *The Women of the Confederacy,* 256.

32. Simkins and Woody, *South Carolina,* 22.
33. Simkins and Patton, *Women of the Confederacy,* 256.
34. Alexandria *Louisiana Democrat,* October 25, 1865.
35. Jesse Johnson Finley, letter to parents, February 28, 1866, Jesse Johnson Finley Family Collection, Museum of the Confederacy, Richmond, Virginia.
36. King, *War-Time Journal,* 317.
37. *Council Bluffs* (Iowa) *Bugle,* July 13, 1865.
38. *Recollections and Reminiscences,* 32.
39. Clipping dated June 14, 1912, Civil War Memories of Robert Carden.
40. Dyer and Moore, "John Bishop," *Tennessee Veterans.*
43. Ibid., "William David Beard."
42. Ibid., "Henry Barksdale."
43. DeLeon, *Four Years in Rebel Capitals,* 371.
44. King, *War-Time Journal,* 332.
45. Simkins and Woody, *South Carolina,* 18.
46. Meridian (Mississippi) *Daily Clarion,* August 11, 1865.
47. *Montgomery* (Alabama) *Daily Mail,* April 8, 1866.
48. Washington, D.C., *Evening Star,* June 21, 1865.
49. *Confederate Reminiscences and Letters, 1861–1865* (Atlanta: Georgia Division United Daughters of the Confederacy, 1996), vol. 2, 88.
50. Callaway, "Reminiscences," 505.
51. Simkins and Patton, *Women of the Confederacy,* 245.
52. Gallagher, *Confederate War,* 162.
53. *New York Times,* July 9, 1865.
54. Washington, D.C., *Evening Star,* July 3, 1865.
55. Simkins and Woody, *South Carolina,* 19.
56. Myers, *Children of Pride,* 1303.
57. Simkins and Woody, *South Carolina,* 18.
58. Myers, *Children of Pride,* 1281.
59. Simkins and Woody, *South Carolina,* 18.
60. Worsham, *Jackson's Foot Cavalry,* 293.
61. John B. Gordon, *Reminiscences of the Civil War* (New York: Charles Scribner's Sons, 1904), 453.
62. Traylor Russell, *History of Titus County, Texas* (Waco, TX: W. M. Morrison, 1965), 95–96.
63. Jones, *Ladies of Richmond,* 311–12.
64. Ibid.
65. *Montgomery* (Alabama) *Daily Mail,* February 22, 1866.
66. Ibid., May 25, 1865.

67. Daniel E. Sutherland, "Virginia's Expatriate Artists: A Post-Civil War Odyssey," *The Virginia Magazine of History and Biography* (April 1983): 134.
68. Alexandria *Louisiana Democrat,* June 14, 1865.
69. Robertson, *Confederate Lady Comes of Age,* 76.
70. *Montgomery* (Alabama) *Daily Mail,* December 12, 1865.
71. Ibid., February 28, 1866.

CHAPTER 19: THE BEST BLOOD

1. Pryor, *Reminiscences of Peace and War,* 385.
2. *Memphis Daily Avalanche,* March 31, 1866.
3. Carroll, *Desolated South,* 136–37.
4. Andrews, *South,* 10–11.
5. Samuel Carter III, *The Last Cavaliers: Confederate and Union Cavalry in the Civil War* (New York: St. Martin's, 1979), 320.
6. *Fayetteville* (North Carolina) *News,* June 5, 1866.
7. *Reminiscences of the Women of Missouri,* 15–16.
8. *Lexington* (Kentucky) *Observer and Reporter,* October 4, 1865.
9. Andrews, *South,* 340.
10. Shelton, ed., *The Reconstruction,* 112–13.
11. *Montgomery* (Alabama) *Daily Mail,* January 28, 1866.
12. Wiley Sword, *Southern Invincibility: A History of the Confederate Heart* (New York: St. Martin's, 1999), 337.
13. Durkin, *John Dooley,* 10.
14. *Lexington* (Kentucky) *Observer and Reporter,* September 13, 1865.
15. Stevenson, *Diary of Clarissa Adger Bowen,* 74.
16. *Montgomery* (Alabama) *Daily Mail,* May 31, 1865.
17. Baton Rouge (Louisiana) *Tri-Weekly Advocate,* August 11, 1865.
18. Alexandria *Louisiana Democrat,* August 9, 1865; *Alton* (Illinois) *Telegraph,* June 9, 1865.
19. Mount Sterling (Kentucky) *Sentinel,* September 1, 1865.
20. *Fort Smith* (Arkansas) *New Era,* July 15, 1865.
21. *House Report 101,* 30th Congress, 1st Session, "Memphis Riots and Massacres," 82.
22. Alexandria *Louisiana Democrat,* August 9, 1865.
23. Mount Sterling (Kentucky) *Sentinel,* September 29, 1865.
24. Kate Cumming diary, September 11, 1865, Alabama Department of Archives and History, Montgomery.
25. *Montgomery* (Alabama) *Daily Mail,* January 14, 1866; *New York Times,* June 8, 1865.
26. Strode, *Jefferson Davis,* 274.

27. *Official Records,* ser. 2, vol. 8, 841.
28. Ibid., 962.
29. *Greensboro* (North Carolina) *Patriot,* September 9, 1865.
30. *New Orleans Daily Picayune,* May 12, 1865.
31. *New York Times,* July 15, 1865; Jackson *Daily Mississippian,* July 26, 1865.
32. *Owensboro* (Kentucky) *Monitor,* May 31, 1865.
33. Hancock, *Delaware during the Civil War,* 168.
34. *Montgomery* (Alabama) *Daily Mail,* January 13, 1866.
35. Washington, D.C., *Evening Star,* June 30, 1865.
36. Strode, *Jefferson Davis,* 292.
37. *Montgomery* (Alabama) *Daily Mail,* March 4, 1866.
38. Albert Castel, *The Presidency of Andrew Johnson* (Lawrence: The Regents Press of Kansas, 1979), 22, 27–30; Charlotte (North Carolina) *Western Democrat,* February 13, 1866; Alexandria *Louisiana Democrat,* July 26, 1865.
39. Castel, *Johnson,* 51.
40. Ibid., 22.
41. Charlotte (North Carolina) *Western Democrat,* July 18, 1865.
42. "How Jefferson Davis Was Shackled," *Confederate Veteran* (1909): 558.

CHAPTER 20: ON BLOODLESS BATTLEFIELDS

1. King, *War-Time Journal of a Georgia Girl,* 231.
2. Earl Schenck Miers, ed., *A Rebel War Clerk's Diary* (New York: Sagamore, 1958), 537.
3. Avary, *Virginia Girl,* 354.
4. Battle, *Forget-Me-Nots,* 187.
5. Shelton, *The Reconstruction,* 16.
6. *Confederate Reminiscences,* 88.
7. Pryor, *Reminiscences of Peace and War,* 391.
8. Ibid.
9. *Montgomery* (Alabama) *Daily Mail,* January 28, 1866.
10. *Memphis Daily Avalanche*, April 1 or 3, 1866.
11. Ibid.
12. Ibid., April 17, 1866.
13. Childs, *Private Journal,* 231.
14. *Greensboro* (North Carolina) *Patriot,* July 22, 1865; J. G. de Roulhac Hamilton, *Reconstruction in North Carolina* (Gloucester, MA: Peter Smith, 1964), 167; Salem (North Carolina) *Peoples Press,* August 5, 1865; Fort Smith (Arkansas) *Herald,* July 24, 1866.
15. Hamilton, *Reconstruction in North Carolina,* 168.

16. *Montgomery* (Alabama) *Daily Mail,* January 10, 1866.
17. Baton Rouge (Louisiana) *Tri-Weekly Advocate,* August 23, 1865.
18. *Montgomery* (Alabama) *Daily Mail,* January 18, 1866.
19. King, *War-Time Journal,* 371.
20. Charleston *South Carolina Leader,* November 25, 1865.
21. Carter, *Angry Scar,* 25.
22. Springfield (Ohio) *Daily News and Republic,* May 3, 1865.
23. Affleck Papers, "America," Special Collections, Louisiana State University.
24. Fearn, *Diary of a Refugee,* 114.
25. Statesville (North Carolina) *American,* November 14, 1865.
26. Alexandria *Louisiana Democrat,* December 20, 1865.
27. Gallagher, *Confederate War,* 169.
28. Buni, "Reconstruction in Orange County," 463.
29. *Weekly Panola* (Mississippi) *Star,* July 22, 1865.
30. Baton Rouge (Louisiana) *Tri-Weekly Advocate,* September 1, 1865.
31. Ibid.
32. *Council Bluffs* (Iowa) *Bugle,* July 13, 1865.
33. *The Columbia Book of Civil War Poetry* (New York: Columbia University, 1994), 419–22.
34. Burr, *Secret Eye,* 266.
35. Harrison, *Recollections Grave and Gay,* 218.
36. DeLeon, *Four Years in Rebel Capitals,* 369.
37. Ibid.
38. Pryor, *Reminiscences of Peace and War,* 310.
38. Shelton, *Reconstruction,* 136.
40. Washington, D.C., *Evening Star,* July 5, 1865.
41. Ibid.
42. *Mobile* (Alabama) *Nationalist,* January 11, 1866.
43. Anderson (South Carolina) *Intelligencer,* July 20, 1865.
44. DeLeon, *Four Years,* 365.
45. Richard Taylor, *Destruction and Reconstruction: Personal Experiences of the Late War* (New York: D. Appleton, 1879), 236.
46. Affleck Papers, "America," Special Collections, Louisiana State University.
47. King, *War-Time Journal,* 317.
48. Andrews, *South,* 4.
49. Ibid., 5.
50. Mount Sterling (Kentucky) *Sentinel,* August 4, 1865.
51. Owner diary, December 12, 1865.
52. Childs, *Private Journal,* 251.

53. *Montgomery* (Alabama) *Daily Mail,* January 18, 1866.
54. Ibid., January 10, 1866.
55. Roberta Sue Alexander, "Hostility and Hope: Black Education in North Carolina during Presidential Reconstruction, 1865–1867," *North Carolina Historical Review* (April 1976), 118; Griffith, *History of Alabama,* 443.
56. Jackson *Daily Mississippian,* August 8, 1865.
57. Meridian (Mississippi) *Daily Clarion,* June 22, 1865.
58. King, *War-Time Journal,* 317, 345.
59. Jackson *Daily Mississippian,* September 15, 1865; Alexandria *Louisiana Democrat,* February 14, 1866.
60. Childs, *Private Journal,* 270.
61. Dorothy Sterling, ed., *The Trouble They Seen: Black People Tell the Story of Reconstruction* (Garden City, NY: Doubleday, 1976), 28.
62. Alexander, "Hostility and Hope," 118.
63. Jones, *Ladies of Richmond,* 309.
64. Baton Rouge (Louisiana) *Weekly Advocate,* May 12, 1866.
65. King, *War-Time Journal,* 344.
66. Childs, *Private Journal,* 240.
67. Alexandria *Louisiana Democrat,* September 20, 1865.

CHAPTER 21: THE SECOND SNAKEBITE

1. William Gillespie McBride, "Blacks and the Race Issue in Tennessee Politics, 1865–1876," manuscript, Tennessee State Library and Archives, Nashville, 37–38.
2. William L. Richter, *The Army in Texas during Reconstruction, 1865–1870* (College Station: Texas A & M University, 1987), 33.
3. Andrews, *South,* 218.
4. Anderson (South Carolina) *Intelligencer,* November 30, 1865.
5. Tyler and Murphy, *Slave Narratives of Texas,* 125.
6. Clift, *Private War of Lizzie Hardin,* 280.
7. *Augusta* (Georgia) *Daily Chronicle,* September 18 and 19, 1865.
8. *Louisville* (Kentucky) *Democrat,* September 15, 1865.
9. Mount Sterling (Kentucky) *Sentinel,* September 8, 1865.
10. Hancock, *Delaware during the Civil War,* 166.
11. Nathaniel Cameron Papers, contract, Alabama State Library and Archives, Montgomery.
12. Anderson (South Carolina) *Intelligencer,* July 27, 1865.
13. Augusta *Loyal Georgian,* March 3, 1866.
14. Ibid.
15. Andrews, *South,* 220.

16. Sterling, ed. *The Trouble They Seen,* 7.
17. *Mobile* (Alabama) *Nationalist,* March 22, 1866.
18. Sterling, *The Trouble They Seen,* 8.
19. Tyler and Murphy, *Slave Narratives,* 123.
20. Rawick, *The American Slave,* "Fountain Hughes."
21. Tyler and Murphy, *Slave Narratives,* 123.
22. Ibid., 114.
23. Ibid., 114–15.
24. *Montgomery* (Alabama) *Daily Mail,* May 15, 1865.
25. Tyler and Murphy, *Slave Narratives,* 121.
26. Annie Heloise Abel, *The American Indian Under Reconstruction* (Cleveland: Arthur H. Clark, 1925), 273.
27. Golay, *A Ruined Land,* 220.
25. *Lexington* (Kentucky) *Observer and Reporter,* June 28, 1865.
29. Callaway, "Reminiscences of War," 505.
30. Daniel E. Huger Smith, Alice R. Huger Smith and Arney R. Childs, eds., *Mason Smith Family Letters, 1860–1868* (Columbia: University of South Carolina, 1950), 232–33.
31. Ash, "White Virginians under Federal Occupation," 191.
32. Sanders, *Diary in Gray,* 97.
33. Woodward, *Mary Chesnut,* 803.
34. Civil War Correspondence: Middle Tennessee, vol. 3, Tennessee State Library and Archives, Nashville, 304.
35. J. B. Killebrew manuscript, vol. 1, Tennessee State Library and Archives, Nashville, 107.
36. Grider letter, September 12 or 13, 1866, Milliken Collection, Kentucky Museum, Bowling Green.
37. Mary Elizabeth Carter Rives diary, October 9 and November 1, 1865, Special Collections, Louisiana State University.
38. Edward Younger, ed., *Inside the Confederate Government: A Diary of Robert Garlick Hill Kean* (New York: Oxford University, 1957), 210.
39. Myers, *Children of Pride,* 1282–83.
40. Charlotte (North Carolina) *Western Democrat,* January 16, 1866.
41. *Mobile* (Alabama) *Nationalist,* March 22, 1866.
42. Ibid., August 2, 1866.
43. King, *War-Time Journal of a Georgia Girl,* 278; Marget Mackay Jones, ed., *The Journey of Catherine Devereaux Edmonston, 1860–1866,* Manuscript, Kentucky Historical Society, Frankfort, 105.
44. Peter R. Henriques, ed., "The Civil War Diary of Anne Frobel, Part II," *Northern Virginia Heritage: A Journal of Local History* (June 1987): 16.

45. C. Vann Woodward and Elisabeth S. Muhlenfeld, eds., *The Private Mary Chesnut: The Unpublished Civil War Diaries* (New York: Oxford University, 1984), 242.

CHAPTER 22: STANDING ON A VOLCANO

1. "Biography of Dr. Fuller," draft, Jabez Lamar Monroe Curry Papers, Alabama Department of Archives and History, Montgomery, 39.
2. Jackson *Daily Mississippian,* September 9, 1865.
3. *Natchez* (Mississippi) *Daily Courier,* December 19, 1865.
4. Childs, *Private Journal,* 252.
5. *Greensboro* (North Carolina) *Patriot,* September 30, 1865.
6. Troutman, *Heavens Are Weeping,* 204–5.
7. Lexington (Kentucky) *Observer and Reporter,* September 9, 1865.
8. Jackson *Daily Mississippian,* November 4, 1865.
9. Anderson (South Carolina) *Intelligencer,* March 8, 1866.
10. *Montgomery* (Alabama) *Daily Mail,* January 9, 1866.
11. Jackson *Daily Mississippian,* July 29, 1865.
12. Ibid.
13. Ibid., July 30, 1865.
14. *Macon* (Mississippi) *Beacon,* August 18, 1865; *Natchez* (Mississippi) *Daily Courier,* November 28, 1865.
15. Raleigh (North Carolina) *Daily Progress,* August 3, 1865.
16. Avary, *Dixie After the War,* 384.
17. Alexandria *Louisiana Democrat,* January 17, 1866.
18. Charlotte (North Carolina) *Western Democrat,* January 16, 1866.
19. Ramsdell, *Reconstruction in Texas,* 82.
20. *Greensboro* (North Carolina) *Patriot,* September 30, 1865.
21. Ibid., September 9, 1865.
22. Nashville *Colored Tennessean,* March 24, 1866.
23. Massey, *Dixie,* 287.
24. Avary, *Dixie After the War,* 384.
25. King, *War-Time Journal of a Georgia Girl,* 351, 348.
26. Dennett, *South,* 5.
27. Elizabeth W. Allston Pringle, *Chronicles of Chicora Wood* (Boston: Christopher, 1940), 260–65
28. Ibid., 269–75.
29. *Macon* (Mississippi) *Beacon,* August 25, 1865.
30. William L. Richter, *Overreached on All Sides: The Freedmen's Bureau Administrators in Texas, 1865–1868* (College Station: Texas A & M University, 1991), 26.

31. Salem (North Carolina) *People's Press,* May 27, 1865.
32. Woodward and Muhlenfeld, *Private Mary Chesnut,* 243.
33. Dennett, *South,* 240–1.
34. Wadesborough *North Carolina Argus,* October 21, 1865.
35. Salem (North Carolina) *People's Press,* August 5, 1865.
36. Charleston *South Carolina Leader,* December 9, 1865.
37. *Mobile* (Alabama) *Nationalist,* January 11, 1866.
38. Ira Berlin, Barbara J. Fields, Steven F. Miller, Joseph P. Reidy, and Leslie S. Rowland, *Free at Last: A Documentary History of Slavery, Freedom and the Civil War* (New York: New Press, 1993), 537.
39. Ibid.
40. *Mobile* (Alabama) *Nationalist,* January 11, 1866.
41. Ibid., January 18, 1866.
42. *New Orleans Tribune,* December 14, 1865.
43. *Memphis Daily Avalanche,* April 5, 1866.
44. Ibid.
45. *Montgomery* (Alabama) *Daily Mail,* March 4, 1866.
46. Owner diary, June 13, 1865.
47. Jackson *Tri-Weekly Mississippian,* July 20, 1865.
48. King, *War-Time Journal of a Georgia Girl,* 314.

CHAPTER 23: SOME FINE MORNING

1. Owner diary, June 19, 1865.
2. Younger, *Inside the Confederate Government,* 209–10.
3. Wadesborough *North Carolina Argus,* October 21, 1865.
4. Childs, *Private Journal of Henry William Ravenel,* 258.
5. *Greensboro* (North Carolina) *Patriot,* February 2, 1866.
6. Henriques, "Diary of Anne Frobel," 16.
7. King, *War-Time Journal,* 367; *Selma* (Alabama) *Morning Times,* December 11, 1865.
8. Smith, et al., *Mason Smith Family Letters,* 232.
9. Berlin et al., *Free at Last,* 520.
10. Charleston *South Carolina Leader,* October 21, 1865.
11. *Mobile* (Alabama) *Nationalist,* February 22, 1866.
12. Ibid.
13. *Montgomery* (Alabama) *Daily Mail,* March 23, 1866.
14. Salem (North Carolina) *People's Press,* September 23, 1865.
15. Baton Rouge (Louisiana) *Tri-Weekly Advocate,* August 11, 1865.
16. *Lexington* (Kentucky) *Observer and Reporter,* April 26, 1865; *New York Times,* July 16, 24, 1865.
17. Salem (North Carolina) *People's Press,* September 30, 1865.

18. *Montgomery* (Alabama) *Daily Mail,* December 12, 1865.
19. *Fort Smith* (Arkansas) *New Era,* July 8, 1865.
20. Lexington (Kentucky) *Observer and Reporter,* August 5, 1865.
21. Ibid., September 23, 1865.
22. Bobby L. Lovett, "Memphis Riots: White Reaction to Blacks in Memphis, May 1865–July 1866," *Tennessee Historical Quarterly* (spring 1979): 10–11.
23. Ibid.
24. *House Report 122,* 39th Congress, 1st Session, "Riot at Memphis," 2; *Fayetteville* (North Carolina) *News,* June 5, 1866.
25. George C. Rable, *But There Was No Peace: The Role of Violence in the Politics of Reconstruction* (Athens: University of Georgia, 1984), 37.
26. Berlin et al., *Free at Last,* 515.
27. Lexington (Kentucky) *Observer and Reporter,* October 14, 1865.
28. *House Report 101,* 67.
29. Ibid., 64.
30. Ibid., 104.
31. Ibid., 90.
32. Ibid., 80.
33. Joe M. Richardson, ed., "The Memphis Race Riot and Its Aftermath: Report by a Northern Missionary," *Tennessee Historical Quarterly* (1965): 66.
34. *Memphis Daily Argus,* May 3, 1866.
35. Ibid.
36. Ibid.
37. Ibid.
38. *Fayetteville* (North Carolina) *News,* June 5, 1866.
38. *Memphis Daily Argus,* May 3, 1866.
40. Ibid.
41. Ibid., May 4, 1866.
42. Ibid.
43. *House Report 101,* 36.
44. *Memphis Daily Argus,* May 3, 1866.
45. *House Report 101,* 87.
46. *Memphis Daily Argus,* May 3, 1866.
47. Ibid.
48. Ibid., May 4, 1866.
49. *The Daily Memphis Avalanche,* May 3, 1866.
50. Ibid., April 17, 1866.
51. Alexandria *Louisiana Democrat,* August 8, 1866.
52. Ibid.
53. Carter, *Angry Scar,* 25.

EPILOGUE

1. *Petersburg* (Virginia) *Index,* August 15, 1866.
2. Ibid.
3. Shelton, *Reconstruction,* 60.
4. Wadesborough *North Carolina Argus,* July 5, 1866.
5. Gordon Carroll, ed., *The Desolate South,* 212.
6. Shelton, ed., *Reconstruction,* 145.
7. Strode, *Jefferson Davis,* 280.
8. Ibid., 279.
9. Ibid.
10. *Fort Smith* (Arkansas) *Herald*, August 2, 1866.
11. Strode, 290.
12. Carroll, *Autobiography,* 43–44.
13. Shelton, ed., *Reconstruction,* 62.
14. Carter, *Angry Scar,* 45.
15. Charles E. Cauthen, ed., *Family Letters of the Three Wade Hamptons, 1782–1901* (Columbia: University of South Carolina, 1953), 126–30.
16. Robert B. Murray, "The End of the Rebellion," *North Carolina Historical Review* (October 1967): 336.
17. Pryor, *Reminiscences of Peace and War,* 360.
18. *Chicago Tribune*, April 17, 1865.
19. Charlotte (North Carolina) *Western Democrat*, January 23, 1866.

MANUSCRIPTS, DIARIES, AND LETTERS, ETC.

Affleck, Thomas. Papers. Special Collections, Louisiana State University, Baton Rouge.

Austin, Robert A. Manuscript. Hubert Dye, Jr., Collection, Olathe, Kansas.

Bell Letter. Bell Collection, 1865, Delaware Public Archives, Hall of Records, Dover.

Billingsley, Chaplain A. S. Letter. Ronald Leonard Collection, Cana, Virginia.

Bond, Priscilla. Diary. Special Collections. Louisiana State University, Baton Rouge.

Cameron, Nathaniel. Papers. Alabama Department of Archives and History, Montgomery.

Carlton, Cornelius H. Diary. Virginia State Library, Archives Division, Richmond.

Carroll, John W. Autobiography and Reminiscences Manuscript. Tennessee State Library and Archives, Nashville.

Chadick, Mary Iona. Diary, 1862–65. Alabama Department of Archives and History, Montgomery.

Chambers, William Pitt. Journal. Mississippi Department of Archives and History, Jackson.

Civil War Correspondence: Middle Tennessee, vol. 3, Tennessee State Library and Archives, Nashville

Civil War Memories of Robert C. Carden Company B, 16th Tennessee Infantry. Published as a series by Boone (Iowa) *Independent*, 1912. Clippings in possession of descendant, Robert C. Carden, and available online.

Clark, G. Letter. Appomattox Courthouse National Historic Site, Virginia.

Crenshaw, Edward. Diary. Alabama Department of Archives and History, Montgomery.

Cumming, Kate. Diary. Alabama Department of Archives and History, Montgomery.

Curry, Jabez Lamar Monroe. Papers. Alabama Department of Archives and History, Montgomery.

Davis, Matthew Jack. Manuscript. "War Sketches as Seen and Remembered by the Writer, Matthew Jack Davis of Co. K Mississippi Infantry." Lucas Collection, Sherman, Texas, Public Library.

Downes, Townsend. Diary, 1865. Delaware Public Archives, Hall of Records, Dover.

Edwards, Jesse. Letter. Ronald Leonard Collection, Cana, Virginia.

Evans, Moses F. T. Letters, 1861–65. Virginia State Library, Archives Division, Richmond.

Finley, Jesse Johnson. Letter. Jesse Johnson Finley Family Collection. Museum of the Confederacy, Richmond, Virginia.

Foster, Kate D. Diary. Mississippi Department of Archives and History, Jackson.

Furry, William, ed. *The Civil War Journal of Reverend Francis Springer.* Excerpt published as pamphlet by Sangamon County (Illinois) Historical Society.

Grider, Henry. Letter. Milliken Collection, Kentucky Museum, Bowling Green.

Hall, Violet. "Reconstruction: 1866," WPA Papers from the Louisiana Writers Project. The Louisiana Collection, State Library, Baton Rouge.

Hill, Bettie Pearl Fisher. Manuscript. Carrollton (Georgia) Public Library.

Jones, John. Poem. Ronald Leonard Collection, Cana, Virginia.

Jones, Margaret Mackay, ed. *The Journal of Catherine Devereux Edmonston, 1860–1866.* Manuscript. Kentucky State Historical Society, Frankfort.

Killebrew, J. B. Manuscript. Tennessee State Library and Archives, Nashville.

Lincoln, Abraham. Pamphlets. v. 1, A–L. Kansas State Historical Society, Topeka.

Lloyd, A. E. Manuscript. Museum of the Confederacy, Richmond, Virginia.

Loving, Jesse. Manuscript. Lucas Collection. Sherman, Texas, Public Library.

McBride, William Gillespie. Manuscript. "Blacks and the Race Issue in Tennessee Politics, 1865–1876." Ph.D. dissertation, Vanderbilt University, 1989. Tennessee State Library and Archives, Nashville.

Moody, Mary D. Moody Family Letters. Museum of the Confederacy, Richmond, Virginia.

Owner, William. Diary, 1865, 1866. Library of Congress.

Rhoades, Marcus Morton. Diary. Western Historical Manuscript Collection, Columbia, Missouri.

Rives, Mary Elizabeth Carter. Diary. Special Collections, Louisiana State University, Baton Rouge.

Ryan, Milton Asbury. *Experience of a Confederate Soldier in Camp and Prison in the Civil War, 1861–1865.* Electronic Edition. Carter House, Franklin, Tennessee.

Smith, Janie. Letter. Box 9. Eiseschiml Collection, Illinois State Historical Library, Springfield.

Stevens, Thaddeus. Transcript of Speech, December 18, 1865. Library of Congress.

Vass, Jennie. Memoir. Museum of the Confederacy, Richmond, Virginia.

Tuttle, John W. Diary, 1860–1867. Special Collections, Kentucky Historical Society, Frankfort.

Walker, Rev. Cornelius. Diary, 1865. Museum of the Confederacy, Richmond, Virginia.

Walsh, William. Manuscript. Lucas Collection, Sherman, Texas, Public Library.

Watt, William E. Diary. Museum of the Confederacy, Richmond, Virginia.

Weisiger, O. F. Letter. Virginia Military Institute Archives, Lexington.

PERIODICAL ARTICLES

Adams, Charles. "The Trial of the Century That Never Was." *Southern Partisan,* first quarter, 1998.

"After Appomattox," *Confederate Veteran,* 1923.

Alexander, Roberta Sue. "Hostility and Hope: Black Education in North Carolina During Presidential Reconstruciton." *North Carolina Historical Review,* April 1976.

Ash, Stephen V. "White Virginians under Federal Occupation, 1861–1865." *The Virginia Magazine of History and Biography,* April 1990.

Bowden, J. T. "How a Confederate Got Home in 1865." *Confederate Veteran,* 1909.

Bradwell, I. G. "Making Our Way Home from Appomattox." *Confederate Veteran,* 1921.

Brown, Ann L. B. "Fort Delaware: The Most Dreaded Northern Prison." *Civil War Quarterly.* September 1987, v. 10.

Buni, Andrew, ed. "Reconstruction in Orange County, Virginia: A Letter from Hannah Garlick Rawlings to Her Sister, Clarissa Lawrence Rawlings, August 9, 1865." *The Virginia Magazine of History and Biography,* 1967.

Callaway, W. A. "Reminiscences of War at the Close." *Confederate Veteran,* 1909.

Henriques, Peter R., ed. "The Civil War Diary of Anne Frobel, Part II." *Northern Virginia Heritage: A Journal of Local History,* June 1987.

"How Jefferson Davis Was Shackled." *Confederate Veteran,* 1909.

Lankiewicz, Donald. "Journey to Asylum: A Secretary of State Runs for His Life." *Civil War Times Illustrated,* December 1987.

Lovett, Bobby L. "Memphis Riots: White Reaction to Blacks in Memphis, May 1865–July 1866." *Tennessee Historical Quarterly,* spring 1979.

McClure, Joseph. "Wounded Texan's Trip Home on Crutches." *Confederate Veteran,* 1909.

McNeilly, James H. "Surrender and Homeward Bound." *Confederate Veteran,* 1923.

Mitchell, Charles W. "Maryland and the Fort Sumter Crisis." *Maryland Historical Magazine,* spring 2000.

Murray, Robert B. "The End of the Rebellion." *North Carolina Historical Review,* October 1967.

Richardson, Joe M., ed. "The Memphis Race Riot and Its Aftermath: Report by a Northern Missionary." *Tennessee Historical Quarterly,* 1965.

Robertson, James I., Jr. "Danville under Military Occupation, 1865." *The Virginia Magazine of History and Biography,* 1967.

Sutherland, Daniel E. "Virginia's Expatriate Artists: A Post-Civil War Odyssey." *The Virginia Magazine of History and Biography,* April 1983.

"War Was the Place: A Centennial Collection of the Confederate Soldiers Letters." *Chattahoochee Valley Historical Society Bulletin,* November 1961.

Whitman, James P. "Incidents of Reconstruction." *Confederate Veteran,* 1923.

DOCUMENTS

House Report 101, 39th Congress, 1st Session, "Memphis Riots and Massacres."

House Report 122, 39th Congress, 1st Session, "Riot at Memphis."

NEWSPAPERS

Alton (Illinois) *Telegraph,* 1865.

Alexandria *Louisiana Democrat,* 1865, 1866.

Anderson (South Carolina) *Intelligencer,* 1865.

Augusta (Georgia) *Daily Chronicle,* 1865.

Augusta *Loyal Georgian,* 1866.

Baton Rouge (Louisiana) *Weekly Advocate,* 1865, 1866.

Charleston *South Carolina Leader,* 1865.

Charlotte (North Carolina) *Western Democrat,* 1865.

Chattanooga Daily Rebel, 1865.

Chicago Tribune, 1865.

Council Bluffs (Iowa) *Bugle,* 1865.

Daily Memphis Avalanche, 1866.

Fort Smith (Arkansas) *Herald,* 1866.

Fayetteville (North Carolina) *News,* 1866.

Fort Smith (Arkansas) *New Era,* 1865.
Greensboro (Alabama) *Beacon,* 1865.
Greensboro (North Carolina) *Patriot,* 1865, 1866.
Houston (Texas) *Chronicle,* 1947.
Houston (Texas) *Tri-Weekly Telegraph,* 1865.
Indianapolis Daily Journal, 1865.
Indianapolis *Daily State Sentinel,* 1865.
Jackson *Daily Mississippian,* 1865.
Leavenworth (Kansas) *Daily Conservative,* 1865.
Lexington (Kentucky) *Observer and Reporter,* 1865.
Livingston (Alabama) *Journal,* 1865.
Louisville (Kentucky) *Democrat,* 1865.
Louisville (Kentucky) *True Presbyterian,* 1864.
Macon (Mississippi) *Beacon,* 1865.
Memphis Daily Argus, 1865, 1866.
Meridian (Mississippi) *Daily Clarion,* 1865.
Mobile (Alabama) *Nationalist,* 1866.
Montgomery (Alabama) *Daily Mail,* 1865, 1866.
Mount Sterling (Kentucky) *Sentinel,* 1865.
Nashville *Colored Tennessean,* 1866.
Nashville Daily Press, 1865.
Natchez (Mississippi) *Daily Courier,* 1865.
New Orleans Daily Picayune, 1865.
New Orleans Times, 1865.
New Orleans Tribune, 1865.
New York Times, 1865.
Owensboro (Kentucky) *Monitor,* 1865.
Weekly Panola (Mississippi) *Star,* 1865.
Pekin (Illinois) *Tazewell Register,* 1865.
Petersburg (Virginia) *Index,* 1866.
Raleigh (North Carolina) *Daily Progress,* 1865.
Salem (North Carolina) *People's Press,* 1865.
Selma (Alabama) *Morning Times,* 1865.
Springfield *Daily Illinois State Journal,* 1865.
Springfield (Ohio) *Daily News and Republic,* 1865.
St. Louis Dispatch, 1865.
Statesville (North Carolina) *American,* 1865.
Wadesborough *North Carolina Argus,* 1865, 1866.
Washington, D.C., *Daily Constitutional Union,* 1865.
Washington, D.C., *Evening Star,* 1865.
Washington, D.C., *Daily Morning Chronicle,* 1865.
Wilmington *Delaware Republican,* 1865.

BOOKS

Abel, Annie Heloise. *The American Indian Under Reconstruction.* Cleveland: Arthur H. Clark, 1925.

Alexander, Thomas B. *Political Reconstruction in Tennessee.* Nashville: Vanderbilt University, 1950.

Anderson, John Q., ed. *Brokenburn: The Journal of Kate Stone, 1861–1868.* Baton Rouge: Louisiana State University, 1955.

Andrews, Sidney. *The South since the War.* 1866. Reprint, Boston: Houghton Mifflin, 1971.

Armstrong, Joan Tracy. *History of Smyth County, Virginia: Ante-Bellum Years Through the Civil War.* Vol. 2. Marion, VA: Smyth County Historical and Museum Society, 1986.

Ash, Stephen V. *When the Yankees Came: Conflict and Chaos in the Occupied South, 1861–1865.* Chapel Hill: University of North Carolina, 1995.

Avary, Myrta Lockett. *Dixie After the War.* New York: Doubleday, Page & Company, 1906.

———. *A Virginia Girl during the War.* New York: Appleton, 1903. Electronic edition: docsouth.unc.edu.

Bak, Richard. *The Day Lincoln Was Shot: An Illustrated Chronicle.* Dallas: Taylor, 1998.

Battle, Laura Elizabeth Lee. *Forget-me-nots of the Civil War: A Romance, Containing Reminiscences and Original Letters of Two Confederate Soldiers.* St. Louis, MO: A. R. Fleming, 1909.

Beitzell, Edwin W. *Point Lookout Prison Camp for Confederates.* Abell, MD: n.p., 1972.

Berlin, Ira, Barbara J. Fields, Steven F. Miller, Joseph P. Reidy, and Leslie S. Rowland. *Free at Last: A Documentary History of Slavery, Freedom, and the Civil War.* New York: New Press, 1993.

Bonner, James C., ed. *The Journal of a Milledgeville Girl, 1861–1867.* Athens: University of Georgia, 1964.

Booth, Asia. *The Unlocked Book: A Memoir of John Wilkes Booth by His Sister Asia Booth Clarke.* New York: Benjamin Blom, 1971.

Booth, George Wilson. *Personal Reminiscences of a Maryland Soldier in the War Between the States, 1861–1865.* 1898. Reprint, Gaithersburg, MD: Butternut Press, 1986.

Bryan, George S. *The Great American Myth.* 1940. Reprint, Chicago: Americana House, 1995.

Burlingame, Michael. *Lincoln Observed: Civil War Dispatches of Noah Brooks.* Baltimore: Johns Hopkins University, 1998.

Burr, Virginia Ingrahm, ed. *The Secret Eye: The Journal of Ella Gertrude Clanton Thomas, 1848–1889.* Chapel Hill: University of North Carolina, 1990.

Burton, Orville Vernon. *In My Father's House Are Many Mansions: Family and Community in Edgefield, South Carolina.* Chapel Hill: University of North Carolina, 1985.

Carroll, Gordon, ed. *The Desolate South, 1865–1866: A Picture of the Battlefields and of the Devastated Confederacy.* 1866. Reprint, Boston: Little, Brown, 1956.

Carter, Hodding. *The Angry Scar: The Story of Reconstruction.* Garden City, NY: Doubleday, 1959.

Carter, Samuel III. *The Last Cavaliers: Confederate and Union Cavalry in the Civil War.* New York: St. Martin's, 1979.

Castel, Albert. *The Presidency of Andrew Johnson.* Lawrence: Regents Press of Kansas, 1979.

———. *William Clarke Quantrill: His Life and Times.* Norman: University of Oklahoma, 1999.

Cater, William D., ed. *As It Was.* San Antonio, TX: n.p., 1981.

Cauthen, Charles E., ed. *Family Letters of the Three Wade Hamptons, 1782–1901.* Columbia: University of South Carolina, 1953.

Childs, Arney Robinson, ed. *The Private Journal of Henry William Ravenel, 1859–1887.* Columbia: University of South Carolina, 1947.

Christ, Mark K. *Rugged and Sublime: The Civil War in Arkansas.* Fayetteville: University of Arkansas, 1994.

Clare, Virginia. *Thunder and Stars: The Life of Mildred Rutherford.* Oglethorpe, GA: Oglethorpe University, 1941.

Clift, G. Glenn, ed. *The Private War of Lizzie Hardin: A Kentucky Confederate Girl's Diary of the Civil War in Kentucky, Virginia, Tennessee, Alabama, and Georgia.* Frankfort: Kentucky Historical Society, 1963.

Cockrell, Monroe F., ed. *Gunner with Stonewall: Reminiscences of William Thomas Poague.* Jackson, TN: McCowat-Mercer, 1957

Confederate Reminiscences and Letters, 1861–1865. Atlanta: Georgia Division, United Daughters of the Confederacy, 1996.

Cotton, Gordon A. *The Murder of Minerva Cook.* Vicksburg, MS: author, 1993.

Cutrer, Thomas W. and T. Michael Parrish, eds. *Brothers in Gray: The Civil War Letters of the Pierson Family.* Baton Rouge: Louisiana State University, 1997.

Davis, Burke. *The Long Surrender.* New York: Random House, 1985.

Davis, Jefferson. *The Rise and Fall of the Confederate Government.* 1881. Reprint, New York: Yoseloff, 1958.

Davis, William C. *Jefferson Davis: The Man and His Hour.* New York: Harper-Collins, 1991.

———, ed. *Diary of a Confederate Soldier: John S. Jackman of the Orphan Brigade.* Columbia: University of South Carolina, 1990.

DeLeon, Thomas C. *Four Years in Rebel Capitals.* 1892. Reprint, Spartanburg, SC: Reprint Company, 1975.

Dennett, John Richard. *The South as It Is: 1865–1866.* New York: Viking, 1965.

Durkin, Joseph T. *John Dooley: Confederate Soldier, His War Journal.* South Bend, IN: University of Notre Dame, 1963.

Dyer, Gustavus W., and John Trotwood Moore, eds. *The Tennessee Civil War Veterans Questionnaires.* Greenville, SC: Southern Historical Press, 1985.

East, Charles. *The Civil War Diary of Sarah Morgan.* Athens: University of Georgia, 1991.

Edwards, John N. *Noted Guerrillas: or, the Warfare on the Border.* St. Louis, MO: Bryan, Brand, 1877.

———. *Shelby and His Men; or, The War in the West.* Waverly, MO: General Joseph Shelby Memorial Fund, 1993.

Eggleston, George Cary. *A Rebel's Recollections.* Bloomington: Indiana University, 1959.

Exley, Jo Ella Powell, ed. *Texas Tears and Texas Sunshine: Voices of Frontier Women.* College Station: Texas A & M University, 1985.

Fearn, Frances Hewitt. *Diary of a Refugee.* New York: Moffat, Yard, 1910. Electronic edition: docsouth.unc.edu.

Fletcher, William A. *Rebel Private, Front and Rear: Memoirs of a Confederate Soldier.* New York: Dutton, 1995.

Gallagher, Gary, ed. *Fighting for the Confederacy: The Personal Recollections of General Edward Porter Alexander.* Chapel Hill: University of North Carolina, 1989.

———. *The Confederate War.* Cambridge, MA: Harvard University, 1997.

Golay, Michael. *A Ruined Land.* New York: John Wiley, 1999.

Good, Timothy S. *We Saw Lincoln Shot: One Hundred Eyewitness Accounts.* Jackson: University Press of Mississippi, 1995.

Goodrich, Thomas. *Black Flag: Guerrilla Warfare on the Western Border, 1861–1865.* Bloomington: Indiana University, 1995.

Gordon, John B. *Reminiscences of the Civil War.* New York: Charles Scribner's Sons, 1904.

Grant, Ulysses S. *Memoirs and Selected Letters, Personal Memoirs of U. S. Grant, Selected Letters 1839–1865.* New York: Library of America, 1990.

Griffith, Lucille. *Alabama: A Documentary History to 1900.* Tuscaloosa: University of Alabama, 1968.

Hague, Parthenia Antoinette. *A Blockaded Family: Life in Southern Alabama during the Civil War.* 1888. Reprint, Boston: Houghton Mifflin, 1971.

Hale, Laura Virginia. *Four Valiant Years in the Lower Shenandoah Valley, 1861–1865.* Front Royal, VA: Hathaway, 1986.

Hanchett, William. *The Lincoln Murder Conspiracies.* Urbana: University of Illinois, 1986.

Hamilton, J. G. de Roulhac. *Reconstruction in North Carolina.* Gloucester, MA: Peter Smith, 1964.

Hancock, Harold Bell. *Delaware during the Civil War: A Political History.* Wilmington: Historical Society of Delaware, n.d.

Harrell, Carolyn L. *When the Bells Tolled for Lincoln: Southern Reaction to the Assassination.* Macon, GA: Mercer University, 1997.

Harrison, Mrs. Burton. *Recollections Grave and Gay.* New York: Charles Scribner's Sons, 1916.

Hatcher, Edward N. *The Last Four Weeks of the War.* Columbus, OH: 1891.

Henry, Robert Selph, ed. *As They Saw Forrest: Some Recollections and Comments of Contemporaries.* Jackson, TN: McCowat-Mercer, 1956.

Hesseltine, William Best. *Civil War Prisons: A Study in War Psychology.* New York: Frederick Ungar, 1930.

Hildebrand, John R. *A Mennonite Journal, 1862–1865.* Shippensburg, PA: Burd Street Press, 1996.

Hill, Benjamin H., Jr. *Senator Benjamin H. Hill of Georgia: His Life, Speeches and Writings.* Atlanta: H. C. Hudgins, 1891.

Hurmence, Belinda. *Before Freedom: 48 Oral Histories of Former North and South Carolina Slaves.* New York: Mentor, 1990.

Jones, J. William. *The Davis Memorial Volume; or, Our Dead President, Jefferson Davis, and the World's Tribute to His Memory.* Waco, TX: Yeager, 1890.

Jones, Katherine M. *Heroines of Dixie: Confederate Women Tell Their Story of the War.* Indianapolis: Bobbs-Merrill, 1955.

———. *Ladies of Richmond: Confederate Capital.* New York: Bobbs-Merrill, 1962.

———. *When Sherman Came: Southern Women and the "Great March."* Indianapolis: Bobbs-Merrill, 1964.

King, Spencer Bidwell, Jr. *The War-Time Journal of a Georgia Girl, 1864–1865.* Macon, GA: Ardivan, 1960.

Kunhardt, Dorothy Meserve, and Phillip B. Kunhardt, Jr. *Twenty Days.* New York: Harper & Row, 1965.

LeConte, Emma. *When the World Ended: The Diary of Emma LeConte.* New York: Oxford University, 1957.

Leech, Margaret. *Reveille in Washington, 1860–1865.* New York: Harper and Brothers, 1941.

Leon, Louis. *Diary of a Tarheel Confederate Soldier.* Charlotte, NC: Stone, 1913. Electronic edition.

Marszalek, John F. *Sherman: A Soldier's Passion for Order.* New York: Free Press, 1993.

Massey, Mary Elizabeth. *Dixie: Women in the Civil War.* Lincoln: University of Nebraska, 1966.

McGee, Charles M., Jr., and Ernest M. Lander, Jr., eds. *A Rebel Came Home.* Columbia: University of South Carolina, 1961.

McMillan, Malcolm C. *The Alabama Confederate Reader.* Tuscaloosa: University of Alabama, 1963.

Miers, Earl Schenck, ed. *A Rebel War Clerk's Diary.* New York: Sagamore, 1958.

Millhouse, Barbara Babcock, ed. *Recollections of Major A. D. Reynolds, 1847–1925.* Winston-Salem, NC: Reynolds House, 1978.

Mixson, Frank M. *Reminiscences of a Private.* N.d. Reprint, Camden, SC: J. J. Fox, 1990.

Myers, Robert Manson, ed. *The Children of Pride: A True Story of Georgia and the Civil War.* New Haven, CT: Yale University, 1972.

Nevins, Allan, ed. *The Diary of George Templeton Strong.* New York: MacMillan, 1962.

Nicolay, John G. and John Hay. *Abraham Lincoln: A History.* New York: Century, 1890.

Owen, William Miller. *In Camp and Battle with the Washington Artillery of New Orleans.* Boston: Ticknor, 1885.

Perkins, J. R. *Trails, Rails and War: The Life of General G. M. Dodge.* Indianapolis: Bobbs-Merrill, 1929.

Pringle, Elizabeth W. Allston. *Chronicles of Chicora Wood.* Boston: Christopher, 1940.

Pryor, Sara Agnes Rice. *Reminiscences of Peace and War.* New York: Macmillan, 1906.

Rable, George C. *But There Was No Peace: The Role of Violence in the Politics of Reconstruction.* Athens: University of Georgia, 1984.

Raines, C. W., ed. *Six Decades in Texas; or, Memoirs of Francis Richard Lubbock, Governor of Texas in War Time, 1861–63.* Austin, TX: B. C. Jones, 1900.

Ramsdell, Charles William. *Reconstruction in Texas.* Gloucester, MA: Peter Smith, 1964.

Rawick, George P., ed. *The American Slave—A Composite Autobiography.* Westport, CT: Greenwood, 1972–79. Electronic edition: *American Slave Narratives: An Online Anthology,* xroads.virginia.edu/~hyper.

Recollections and Reminiscences, 1861–1865. South Carolina Division, United Daughters of the Confederacy, 1990.

Reminiscences of the Women of Missouri during the Sixties. N.d. Reprint, Dayton: Morningside House, 1988.

Richter, William L. *The Army in Texas during Reconstruction, 1865–1870.* College Station: Texas A & M University, 1987.

———. *Overreached on All Sides: The Freedmen's Bureau Administrators in Texas, 1865–1868.* College Station: Texas A & M University, 1991.

Robertson, Mary D., ed. *A Confederate Lady Comes of Age: The Journal of Pauline DeCaradeuc Heyward, 1863–1888.* Columbia: University of South Carolina, 1992.

Russell, Traylor. *History of Titus County, Texas.* Waco, TX: W. M. Morrison, 1965.

Ryan, Milton Asbury. *Experience of a Confederate Soldier in Camp and Prison in the Civil War, 1861–1865.* Electronic edition. Copy in possession of Carter House, Franklin, Tennessee.

Sad Earth, Sweet Heaven: The Diary of Lucy Rebecca Buck. Birmingham, AL: Buck, 1992.

Sanders, Mary, ed. *Diary in Gray: The Civil War Letters and Diary of Jared Young Sanders.* Baton Rouge: Louisiana Genealogical and Historical Society, 1994.

Scarborough, William Kauffman. *The Diary of Edmund Ruffin. Vol. 3: A Dream Shattered, June, 1863–June, 1865.* Baton Rouge: Louisiana State University, 1989.

Schwartz, Gerald. *A Woman Doctor's Civil War.* Columbia: University of South Carolina, 1989.

Shelton, James P., ed. *The Reconstruction: A Documentary History of the South After the War, 1865–1877.* New York: G. P. Putnam's Sons, 1963.

Simkins, Francis Butler, and James Welch Patton. *The Women of the Confederacy.* 1936. Reprint, St. Clair Shores, MI: Scholarly, 1976.

Simkins, Francis Butler, and Robert Hilliard Woody. *South Carolina during Reconstruction.* 1932. Reprint, Gloucester, MA: Peter Smith, 1966.

Smith, Daniel E. Huger, Alice R. Huger Smith, and Arney R. Childs, eds. *Mason Smith Family Letters, 1860–1868.* Columbia: University of South Carolina, 1950.

Smith, Paul David. *Frontier Defense in the Civil War: Texas' Rangers and Rebels.* College Station: Texas A & M University, 1992.

Smythe, Mrs. A. T., Miss M. B. Poppenheim, and Mrs. Thomas Taylor. *South Carolina Women in the Confederacy.* Columbia, SC: State, 1903.

Spencer, Cornelia Phillips. *The Last Ninety Days of the War.* 1866. Reprint, Wilmington, NC: Broadfoot, 1993.

Sterling, Dorothy, ed. *The Trouble They Seen: Black People Tell the Story of Reconstruction.* Garden City, NY: Doubleday, 1976.

Stevenson, Mary, ed. *The Diary of Clarissa Adger Bowen, Ashtabula Plantation, 1865 and the Pendleton-Clemson Area, South Carolina, 1776–1889.* Pendleton, SC: Foundation for Historic Restoration, n.d.

Strode, Hudson. *Jefferson Davis: Tragic Hero: 1864–1889, The Last Twenty-five Years.* New York: Harcourt, Brace & World, 1964.

Sutherland, Daniel E., ed. *A Very Violent Rebel: The Civil War Diary of Ellen Renshaw House.* Knoxville: University of Tennessee, 1996.

Sword, Wiley. *Southern Invincibility: A History of the Confederate Heart.* New York: St. Martin's, 1999.

Taylor, Richard. *Destruction and Reconstruction: Personal Experiences of the Late War.* New York: D. Appleton, 1879.

Trindal, Elizabeth Steger. *Mary Surratt: An American Tragedy.* Gretna, LA: Pelican, 1996.

Troutman, Richard L., ed. *The Heavens Are Weeping: The Diaries of George Richard Browder, 1852–1886.* Grand Rapids, MI: Zondervan, 1987.

Trudeau, Noah Andre. *Out of the Storm: The End of the Civil War, April-June 1865.* Baton Rouge: Louisiana State University, 1994.

Turner, Thomas Reed. *Beware the People Weeping: Public Opinion and the Assassination of Abraham Lincoln.* Baton Rouge: Louisiana State University, 1982.

Tyler, Ronnie C., and Lawrence R. Murphy, eds. *The Slave Narratives of Texas.* Austin, TX: Encino, 1974.

Van Noppen, Ina Woestemeyer. *Stoneman's Last Raid.* Boone, NC: n.p., 1961.

The War of the Rebellion: A Compilation of the Official Records of the Union and Confederate Armies. Washington, DC: Government Printing Office, 1880–1901.

Weddle, Robert S. *Plow-Horse Cavalry: The Caney Creek Boys of the Thirty-Fourth Texas.* Austin, TX: Madrona, 1974.

Werner, Emmy E. *Reluctant Witnesses: Children's Voices from the Civil War.* Boulder, CO: Westview, 1998.

Wilbarger, J. W. *Indian Depredations in Texas.* 1888. Reprint, Austin, TX: Eakin, 1985.

Wiley, Bell Irvin, ed. *Fourteen Hundred and 91 Days in the Confederate Army: A Journal Kept by W. W. Heartsill.* Wilmington, NC: Broadfoot, 1987.

———. *"This Infernal War": The Confederate Letters of Sgt. Edwin H. Fay.* Austin, TX: University of Texas, 1958.

Woodward, C. Vann, ed. *Mary Chesnut's Civil War.* New Haven, CT: Yale University, 1981.

Woodward, C. Vann, and Elisabeth Muhlenfeld, eds. *The Private Mary Chesnut: The Unpublished Civil War Diaries.* New York: Oxford University, 1984.

Worsham, John H. *One of Jackson's Foot Cavalry: His Experience and What He Saw During the War, 1861–1865.* New York: Neale, 1912.

Younger, Edward, ed. *Inside the Confederate Government: The Diary of Robert Garlick Hill Kean.* New York: Oxford University, 1957.

INDEX

Italicized page numbers denote photograph of individual